Quality Management in the Nuclear Industry: the Human Factor

Conference Planning Panel

J R A Lakey (Chairman)
John Lakey Associates
Meopham
Kent

P Ball
British Nuclear Fuels Limited
Sellafield

D Clarkson
Rolls Royce and Associates
Caithness

C J Holliday
Nuclear Installations Inspectorate
Bootle

A P Hudson
National Radiological Protection Board
Leeds

K Millard
Gilbert Associates (Europe) Limited
Twickenham

J Molloy
PWR Power Projects
Knutsford

P Myerscough
Consultant
Stroud

P Parkman
Nuclear Electric
Bristol

D W Phillips
AEA Technology
Warrington
Cheshire

Proceedings of the Institution of Mechanical Engineers

International Conference

Quality Management in the Nuclear Industry: the Human Factor

17–18 October 1990
Institution of Mechanical Engineers
Birdcage Walk
London

Sponsored by
Power Industries Division of the Institution of Mechanical Engineers

In association with
Institution of Electrical Engineers
Institution of Civil Engineers
Institution of Nuclear Engineers
British Nuclear Energy Society
Safety and Reliability Society
ESRA
Institute of Quality Assurance

IMechE 1990–11

Published for the Institution of Mechanical Engineers by
Mechanical Engineering Publications Limited

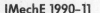

British Library Cataloguing in Publication Data
Quality Management in the Nuclear Industry: the Human Factor.
1. Nuclear power stations. Safety measures
621.3125

Printed by Waveney Print Services Ltd, Beccles, Suffolk

Contents

Quality

Gilbert Associates (Europe) Ltd provide Quality Management services for a wide spectrum of nuclear, industrial, power, commercial, service and engineering clients.

✦ *TOTAL QUALITY MANAGEMENT*

✦ *QUALITY STRATEGY*

✦ *QUALITY IMPROVEMENT*

✦ *QUALITY ASSURANCE*

✦ *QUALITY SYSTEMS*

✦ *QUALITY AUDITING*

✦ *QUALITY TRAINING*

The company's wide range of training programmes includes the IQA recognised Lead Assessor training courses which has been attended by over 2000 delegates.

GA (E) L's consultants working alongside your quality teams will enable you to realise the full potential of your business. The Company's consultancy, training and auditing services can assist you in achieving that leading edge so that your customer's highest expectations are satisfied.

Quality Management Consultants

Gilbert Associates (Europe) Limited
Fraser House, 15 London Road, Twickenham TW1 3ST.
Telephone: 081 891 4383, Facsimile: 081 891 5885

New Titles on Pressure Vessels and Piping!

Finite Element Analysis, Computer Applications, and Data Management (PVP Vol 185)
A topical guide, this book discusses finite element methods and applications, data management in CAE, micro\mini computer and engineering applications, and analysis of bolted joints.
Editor: K H Hsu 124 pages **£29.00 Order Ref: H00604**
ISBN 0 7918 0496 8

Codes and Standards and Applications for Design and Analysis of Pressure Vessel and Piping Components – 1990 (PVP Vol 185)
This important volume addresses such topics as code advancement, nuclear codes and standards, advancement in codes and standards for piping, components and supports, and nondestructive examination.
Editors: R F Sammataro, F Osweiller, O F Hedden, F Seshadri, B Gowda, F E Gregor, C D Cowfer 224 pages
£43.00 Order Ref: H00605 ISBN 0 7918 0497 6

System Interaction with Linear and Nonlinear Characteristics (PVP Vol 187)
The papers in this book cover a broad spectrum of subjects, ranging from linear response spectrum analysis of systems to sophisticated analytical techniques, and test confirmation of parameters for designs with localised nonlinearities.
Editors: C W Lin, W S Tseng 100 pages **£22.000**
Order Ref: H00606 ISBN 0 7918 0498 4

Design and Analysis of Piping and Components - 1990 Including Valve Testing and Applications (PVP Vol 188)
This authoritative work deals with the analysis of elbows (bends), tees and localised stresses.
Editors: Q N Truong, W E Short III, L I Ezekoye 96 pages **£22.00**
Order Ref: H00607 ISBN 0 7918 0499 2

Flow-Induced Vibration (PVP Vol 189)
A comprehensive work, this book addresses flow field and fluid forces, flui\structure coupling, axial-flow-induced vibration, crossflow-induced vibration of tube arrays, and flow-induced vibration of structures with other shapes.
Editors: S S Chen, K Fujta, M K Au-Yang 320 pages **£50.00**
Order Ref: H00608 ISBN 0 7918 0500 X

Transient Thermal Hydraulics and Resulting Loads on Vessel and Piping Systems - 1990 (PVP Vol 190)
Presenting the results of recent research work, this title looks at waterhammer effects, pressure pulse suppression, safety relief valve flows, and resulting load responses from thermal hydraulic phenomena.
Editors: F J Moody, Y W Shin, J Colton 80 pages **£18.00**
Order Ref: H00698 ISBN 0 7918 051 8

Flow-Structure Vibration and Sloshing - 1990 (PVP Vol 191)
The aim of these symposia is to aid future research and to upgrade the current design and analysis of various fluid-structure systems under dynamic loadings. Contents include: advances in seismic design of cylindrical liquid storage tanks; evaluation of fluid effects on the seismic response of an LMR core mock-up.
Editors: D C Ma, J Tani, S S Chen 176 pages **£36.00**
Order Ref: H00610 ISBN 0 7918 0502 6

High Pressure Technology, Fracture Mechanics, and Service Experiences in Operating Power Plants (PVP Vol 192)
This timely work addresses various topics such as, toughness requirements and the effect of pre-stress on high pressure vessels; fracture mechanics applications and service experience in operating power plants.
Editors: S Y Zamrik, E H Perez 108 pages **£22.00**
Order Ref: H00611 ISBN 0 7918 0503 4

Damage Assessment, Reliability, and Life Prediction of Power Plant Components (PVP Vol 193, NDE Vol 8)
Among the topics covered are: materials characterisation and property determination; on-line monitoring and nondestructive evaluation; predictive models for fatigue, creep, erosion, corrosion and wear.
Editors: R N Pangborn, R V Narayanan, K H Means, C B Bond
124 pages **£29.00 Order Ref: H00612** ISBN 0 7918 0504 2

Analysis of Pressure Vessel and Heat Exchanger Components - 1990 (PVP Vol 194)
Current theories and practices in design and analysis of pressure vessels are presented in this volume.
Editors: W E Short III, G N Brooks 120 pages **£29.00**
Order Rerf: H00613 ISBN 0 7918 0505 0

Fatigue, Degradation, and Fracture - 1990 (PVP Vol 195, MPC Vol 30)
Covering a broad range of topics, this excellent work discusses environmental fatigue crack growth; fatigue analysis and fracture assessment; and degradation of ferritic, austenitic and duplex stainless alloys in nuclear service.
Editors: W H Bamford, C Becht IV, S Bhandari, J D Gilman, L A James, M Prager 224 pages **£43.00 Order Ref: H00614** ISBN 0 7918 0509 3

Composite Materials for PVP Applications (PVP Vol 196)
This publication presents the latest research concerning buckling, vibration and NDE aspects of composite structures. '
Editors: D Hui, T J Kozik 96 pages **£22.00 Order Ref: H00615**
ISBN 0 7918 0509 3

Seismic Engineering - 1990 (PVP Vol 197)
An authoritative guide, this book presents recent developments in the areas of seismic damping; seismic design and analysis methods; seismic\dynamic testing and analysis of pressure vessels and piping; and structural dynamics of design and analysis issues.
Editors: T H Liu, M L Aggarwal, E G Berak, L H Geraets, S L McCabe, K Suzuki, Y K Tang, A G Ware 320 pages
£50.00 Order Ref: H00616 ISBN 0 7918 0510 7

Advances in Dynamics of Piping and Structural Components PVP Vol 198)
The papers in this volume concentrate on dynamic analysis, random vibrations, fracture\crack and thermal striping fatigue of pipelines and other structural components.
Editors: H H Chung, E C Goodling Jr, S Mizra, J Sinnappan 92 pages
£18.00 Order Ref: H00617 ISBN 0 7918 0511 5

Regulatory Philosophy and Intent for Radioactive Material Transport - Incuding Transport of Components from Decommissioned Nuclear Facilities (PVP Vol 199)
This important volume focusses on the regulatory philosophy behind the approach to safety that must be present in the design of packages intended to transport radioactive materials.
Editors: R W Carlson, L E Fischer, C K Chou 60 pages **£15.00**
Order Ref: H00618 ISBN 0 7918 0512 3

Seismic, Shock, and Vibration Isolation - 1990 (PVP Vol 200)
The papers presented here are representative of the current R & D activities and design studies in seismic, shock and vibration isolation.
Editor: H H Chung 64 pages **£15.000 Order Ref: H00619**
ISBN 0 7918 0513 1

New Alloys for Pressure Vessels and Piping (PVP Vol 201, MPC Vol 31)
The new alloys discussed in this interesting title include the modified nine chromium materials which are being used today for more demanding electric power applications.
Editors: M Prager, C Cantzier 204 pages **£43.00 Order Ref: H00620**
ISBN 0 7918 0514 X

 The American Society of Mechanical Engineers

Quality management of personnel in the nuclear industry: the human factor

J G TYROR, MSc
AEA Technology, Culcheth, Cheshire

As the Director of Safety for AEA Technology, I have a very immediate interest in, and responsibility for, the safety of operations undertaken by AEA Technology. The range of operations is very wide. On the one hand it includes engineering work which covers not only feasibility studies and design but also design assessment, development of methods and facilities, and scientific and engineering research. On the other hand there are practical activities associated with running workshops, experimental rigs, nuclear reprocessing plant and nuclear reactors and the construction of such facilities.

During my years in AEA Technology, I have had direct practical experience of many of these operations and have a first hand appreciation of the importance of providing management systems to ensure that the operations are correctly planned, controlled and executed. In addition, and particularly whilst I was the Director of the General Nuclear Safety Research Programme within AEA Technology, I came to appreciate the scope and importance of research into understanding how plant operators can affect plant performance and plant safety. I also came to appreciate not only how complicated this 'human factor' aspect could be but how it was a necessary factor in coming to an appreciation of safety and risk.

I would like to enlarge upon the relevance of my particular interests and responsibilities to the theme of this conference in two areas.

The first concerns the relationship between a familiar aspect of quality assurance - the quality audit - and the more specific issue of quality management as addressed by the safety audit. These two types of audit are complementary. The degree of overlap between them is an issue related to the question of the scope and purpose of quality management, as is the need to understand and control the interface between quality audits and safety audits. This is a topic which this conference can address and I would be interested to learn of views which may emerge.

The second area is central to the nuclear industry and is at the top of what could be seen as the 'hidden agenda' of this conference - and that area is safety. The link between safety, quality management and people is plainly shown by any analysis of accidents. Whether the accidents are those in the nuclear industry or industry generally, and whether they are the high consequence accidents which attract immediate media attention or the low consequence 'near misses' of interest primarily to the operators and the safety assessor or regulator, human frailty will usually be found high on the list of contributory causal factors. Examples of the role of the human factor in accidents are unfortunately too easy to find but are highly instructive and I would expect that the lessons available to be learnt from the accident record form an important element in this conference. I personally would like to pose a number of particular questions which you might like to consider during this conference, and which have exercised me in recent months.

The first question concerns the relationship between the safety record of an organisation or industry and its management structure, culture and style. I believe that some studies have addressed this question with semi-quantitative analyses in an attempt to establish how such characteristics as effectiveness of communication, delegation of responsibility, degree of democracy or bureaucracy, etc., can lead to improved performance, as reflected perhaps in safety achievements. These considerations also lead on to questions of how organisational structure can be arranged to allow it to meet both commercial and safety goals and whether a small organisation, such as a US electricity utility, can achieve a better safety record than a larger one, such as a European electricity generating company. In this context it is interesting to consider the safety record of western commercial airlines with their similarities in aircraft types but documented differences in accident statistics.

A final question which interests me and which I would like to draw to the attention of this conference, is the extent to which human failures, again in the context of accidents, are attributable to management systems and procedures rather than individual failings. It is often tempting for the accident investigator to conclude that the primary cause of an accident is the inappropriate response of an individual but it is more revealing to expose underlying factors such as conflicts between safety and other requirements, inadequate procedures, poor supervision or unclear policy.

You can see from this background that I have considerable empathy with the aims of this conference and am impressed by your ambition of covering such a wide field in just two days. Indeed, the breadth of topics is apparent from the titles of the sessions and I am sure that it will be with some difficulty that you will find time to fully explore them all. However, I think it an extremely valuable exercise to discuss openly how the various aspects of quality assurance and the human factor are viewed by the different sectors of the nuclear industry. It is of particular interest to see just how regulatory bodies such as the NII treat these topics, and to obtain an insight into the initiatives currently being developed by the EEC.

As you will appreciate, given my previous understanding of the role of human or operator factors in achieving high safety standards, the session on 'Selection and Training' is of special interest, as it is quite clear that even if you have the 'best' plant in the world, you need the right people with the correct skills, fulfilling the numerous specialist roles, to have the necessary degree of assurance that high standards of safety will be achieved. I expect that some mention will be made in this context of the prospect for the safe operation of fully automated plant which minimises the role of people and so offers the possibility for a degree of freedom from human failings. I feel that this prospect is still some way off.

This topic of personnel selection and training becomes even more relevant if we consider the control of interfaces between organisations and, in particular, between people so that reliable communication and interaction takes place at all times, and the feedback from operational experience is properly used to improve these interfaces, especially where these are important for safety considerations. The session on 'Interfaces and Performance' and 'Feedback' should shed some light on how various organisations have addressed these issues and how reliability factors can be estimated and used in establishing risk. Overall, the value of showing the inter-relationships between these seemingly diverse topics, and how the principles of quality assurance can be used to manage these inter-relationships is considerable, and this conference should be a major step in identifying those links.

I have referred to the term 'quality assurance' and perhaps I should say a few words at this stage regarding it. Whilst I have not been directly involved in the implementation of quality assurance within AEA Technology, as Director of Safety I see quality assurance as a key tool in the management of safety. I have seen the concept of quality evolve over the years, starting with inspection, through quality control to quality assurance, and even now we are hearing of its next metamorphosis, namely 'total quality management'. The central theme to all of these has always been 'getting it right', whatever it is, to ensure that the design is correct, the equipment is made properly, the plant is operated correctly, that emergency procedures are appropriate and are followed correctly, and so forth. The developments that have taken place have always been such that the approach to quality is becoming more pre-emptive, resulting in the introduction of better management disciplines

into an organisation. This can only be beneficial for us all, as the quality assurance disciplines require us to work in a logical and professional manner, with appropriate checks and balances to ensure that relevant factors have been considered during the various phases of a particular job. As one would expect for such an important philosophy, British Standards have had a selection of 'quality' standards in their repertoire for a number of years now. One, of which you are all probably aware, is BS5750 'quality systems' which, after much discussion on the international scene, has been issued as an ISO standard in the ISO9000 series. Furthermore, this standard has now also been issued in the EEC forum as an EN standard in the EN29000 series.

In the nuclear industry it has long been accepted by owners and operators that the processes of design, manufacture, construction and commissioning of nuclear plant must be subject to strict disciplines if high standards of safety and operability are to be maintained. For this reason, some years ago, when BS5750 was being developed to cover manufacturing industries, owner-operators of nuclear plant felt that they needed a standard that addressed the special quality assurance issues such as plant procurement, certification and records, process control, etc. So British Standards responded to these demands by introducing BS5882 'A Total Quality Programme for Nuclear Installations', which is currently compatible with IAEA Standard 50-C-QA 'Quality Assurance for Safety in Nuclear Process Plants'. Furthermore, 50-C-QA, which reflects the IAEA's safety remit, has a number of supporting safety guides which address themselves to factors that are being considered by this conference. In particular they feature such topics as the design of control rooms and the selection and training of operators, where the relationship between task and function specification, management of safety goals and people is vital. I am sure that over the next two days we shall be hearing more about the research and development that has been focused on this important aspect of nuclear plant operational safety and safety assessment.

In conclusion, I am convinced of the value of applying the concepts, principles and practices of quality assurance to the nuclear industry, especially to those areas where it is necessary to achieve and to demonstrate the achievement of the highest possible standards of safety, performance and reliability. I feel that the understanding of how this can best be implemented in those areas where management and people play a central role should be one of the aims of this conference. This has always been important in the nuclear industry and, at a time of growing awareness of safety and environmental issues and a growing understanding of the role which people play in achieving or improving those standards, this conference is particularly welcome.

I wish you success.

Initiatives taken by the Commission of the European Communities in the field of training and information in radiation protection

H ERISKAT
Radiation Protection Division, Nuclear Safety and Civil Protection Commission of the European Communities, Luxembourg

This paper describes the work of the Commission of the European Communities in training and information in radiation protection.

Nowadays nuclear science and technology has many applications ranging for beyond nuclear power and medical X-rays to include interalia conventional industry, agriculture and research.

This means that the need for radiation protection of workers has become correspondingly more widespread, as has concern for the general public and the environment – not only in the case of a nuclear accident – but also, at a more mundane level, ongoing health protection of the public, for example by monitoring radioactive emissions from nuclear installations in routine operation.

While this has led in turn to a major expansion of work in the many facets of radiation protection I will restrict myself today to a review of the Radiation Protection division's activities in training and information. However, it should be remembered that all workers are firstly members of the public and I will therefore include more general aspects and not confine myself to those concerning workers in radiation-related occupation.

The radiation protection has a long European pedigree.

In 1957 the Euratom Treaty established the European Atomic Energy Community, and one of the principal tasks attributed to the Community in the field of radiation protection was the preparation of uniform safety safety standards for protection of the population and of workers, and the monitoring of their application.

Chapter III of the Euratom Treaty lays down the procedures to be followed for this purpose and it was on the strength of its provisions that in 1959 the Council of Ministers of the Community first approved a directive laying down the basic standards for the protection of the health of workers and the general public against the dangers arising from ionizing radiations. Even in this first Directive, provision is made – in Article 24 – for the training and information of workers.

The Directive has been updated and expanded periodically, the most recent comprehensive revision having been in 1980 with amendments in 1984; a further comprehensive review is scheduled for 1991. However, training and information have remained and will continue to remain an integral component of the Standards. This Community precedent has led to radiation protection being taken as a model in other sectors.

It should be noted that it is the responsibility of Member States to implement the requirements of Directives but the Commission nevertheless has a role to play in monitoring their implementation, in seeking to harmonize their practical application and in taking initiatives to assist Member States in coordinating and improving our standards.

Since 1975 the Commission has also organized conferences on training and information, attended by radiation protection specialists, and by representatives of the competent authorities and of the trade unions. The most recent of these was held in Luxembourg in November, 1988, and led to a number of fruitful proposals and exchanges of opinion regarding :

– the introduction of professional training in radiation protection and drawing up a standard guide incorporating the necessary teaching material;

– a critical evaluation of the levels of training in radiation protection attained by qualified experts;

– an evaluation of the situation of individuals working outside the nuclear industry, in particular those working in medicine and transport, to establish whether some rapprochement of training systems should be considered;

– the implications arising from the drawing up of emergency plans, and the need to improve the training of those who might be involved in dealing with such emergencies.

These proposals demonstrated that the Commission's practical approach to information distribution was the right one.

Amongst these practical applications we have the brochure "Radiation and you", which sets out the main facts about radioactivity, its effects, its uses, and the radiation protection measures which accompany those uses. The Commission has also been responsible for various videocassettes, prepared by the University of Sheffield aimed at providing general information and at assisting in radiation protection training.

In practice, the public rarely have any understanding of radiation hazards and protection since the subject is not covered in the primary or secondary education curriculum of any Member State. Workers who are exposed to radiation, for example, first learn the basics of radioactivity and radiation protection only when they begin job training.

This is why in July, 1989, the Commission called a meeting of representatives of Member States concerned with questions of education and health. The Commission proposed that it should initiate the preparation of a handbook on radioactivity and radiation protection for use by primary and secondary school teachers.

Our aim was to offer the teacher the means of preparing a course on the subject, by providing a set of factual scientific information on the subject.

The Commission's action as regards public information is likewise based on the Euratom Treaty and on a legal instrument, responsibility for the matter having been conferred on the Commission by the Council Directive of 27 November 1989. The directive seeks to define common objectives for informing the general public about health protection measures to be applied and steps to be taken in the event of a radiological emergency.

The Directive makes special reference to one particular group of the population: those likely to be involved in the organization of emergency assistance in the event of a nuclear accident. These may be the police, ambulance or fire services – people who are not regularly faced with the problems of radiation protection but who must have prior information on the associated risks and on the precautions needed in such circumstances. To this end the Commission is promoting a guide written for the use of such emergency services crews, setting out the various radiation protection measures and giving advice on nuclear emergency situations.

Equally, the Commission has decided to prepare a manual covering both routine and accident situations for use by those involved in the transport of radioactive material: drivers, warehouse workers and others.

The risks arising from intervention in a radiological emergency are largely hypothetical for the man in the street, and form only one piece in the jigsaw of radiation protection. He is far more likely to have first hand experience of the medical uses of ionizing radiation. Indeed one patient in four in the hospitals of the European Community benefits from the techniques of medical diagnosis or therapy and correspondingly high proportion of medical staff are involved. For this reason the Commission is currently pursuing a number of measures aimed at promoting radiation protection in the medical world, and is considering training programmes for radiation protection specialists.

At the same time, a review of the technical standards of radiodiagnostic equipment should result in European harmonization in the form of a European certificate of type-approval.

With a view to supplementing the training of radiation protection specialists from the nuclear industry, the Commission has noted that the highest radiation doses are received during maintenance operations, particularly during major work while the reactor is shut down. During such operations radiation protection optimization can do much to reduce exposure and accordingly the Commission is financing a course in relevant management techniques. This course was devised jointly by the British National Radiation Protection Board (NRPB) and the French Centre d'Études sur l'Évaluation de la Protection dans le domaine Nucléaire (CEPN); the first course will be held in France from 19 to 23 November 1990. The course will be partly theoretical and partly practical, using the installations and scale models of the Chalon-sur-Saône maintenance and experimental facility. This European training module for those who are the actual practitioners of radiation protection should allow additional impetus to be given to the dissemination of the principles of radiation protection and their practical application.

Moreover, a conference of power station radiation protection specialists held recently in Luxembourg confirmed that in some Member States up to 80% of the collective annual dose is received by individuals employed by outside contractors. This demonstrated that the Commission has been right in its concern with the need for better dosimetry monitoring of such workers. With this in mind the Commission has prepared a Directive on the protection of outside workers working on installations where use is made of ionizing radiation. This Directive also refers to the need for information, or even specialist training, as essential to proper radiation protection.

Whether in the nuclear industry or in the medical world, radiation protection will maintain its advance and its high standards only so long as the radiation protection experts who are responsible for training workers exposed to radiation have themselves a high level of expertise built on unassailable scientific fact.

In this field, the training of radiation protection specialists, the Commission is currently updating a census of available courses in radiation protection in the European Community.

Still with the same aim of high-level expertise, the Commission gives financial support to various research projects, programmes comparing dosimetry equipment, and conferences where information is exchanged.

The result of all this will of course be not only greater knowledge, but a widespread diffusion of uniform information. Sight must not be lost of the fact that radiation protection will have a role in the Single Market after 1992, since differences in national practices must not be allowed to stand as a barrier to the free circulation of goods and more particularly of the individual who is exposed to ionizing radiation.

There was a time when radiation protection measures were perceived by the nuclear industry and the medical world as a constraint: nowadays we can see that the applications of radiation protection principles such as ALARA result not only in a reduction in dose but also in general in an improvement in the efficiency and quality of the work.

Training and information is consequently one of the main lines of the Commission's work in radiation protection, and I trust and expect that this will continue to help maintain the high level of expertise needed in nuclear and other installations.

COMMISSION OF THE EUROPEAN COMMUNITIES

Publications:

- Council Directive of 15 July 1980 amending the Directives laying down the basic safety standards dor the health protection of the general public and workers against the dangers of ionizing radiation (Luxembourg, 1981, EUR 7330 EN)

- Council Directive of 3 September 1984 laying down basic measures for the radiation protection of persons undergoing medical examination or treatment (Luxembourg, 1985, EUR 9728 EN)

- Occupational radiation dose statistics from Light Water power Reactors operating in Western Europe (Luxembourg, 1987, EUR 10971 EN)

- Radiation Protection Training and Information for workers; Proceedings of a seminar held in Luxembourg, 28–30 November 1988 (EUR 12117 EN)

- RADIATION AND YOU, Office for Official Publications of the European Communities (Catalogue number: cc.54.88.053.EN.C)

Video tapes (Sheffield University Television)

- RADIATION: Types and effects (22')
                           Origins and control (27')

- RADIATION PROTECTION (111')
                           Scientific background – Units used in radiation protection – Principal types of Hazard – Protection from the external radiation Hazard – Measuring the external Hazard

An overview of human factor principles for the development and support of nuclear power station personnel and their tasks

D WHITFIELD, MA, MSc
HM Nuclear Installations Inspectorate, Health and Safety Executive, Bootle, Merseyside

SYNOPSIS This paper provides a survey of current human factors knowledge and practice which provides the technical input to promoting human performance in nuclear power stations. The areas covered are: personnel and system design, task analysis and design, operator-plant interface, documentation and procedures, operating environment, selection and training, organisation and management, and probabilistic safety analysis.

1   INTRODUCTION

There is little need to rehearse the importance of human performance and human reliability in the safe operation of nuclear power stations: the analyses of many incidents provide examples of the effects of personnel errors, and of the positive contributions made to recovering hazardous situations. Both the Sizewell 'B' and Hinkley 'C' public inquiries placed considerable emphasis on the influence of human factors - Sir Frank Layfield regarded human factors "... as of outstanding significance in assessing the safety of Sizewell B, since they impinge on all stages from design to manufacture, construction, operation, and maintenance." In addition, wider than the nuclear industry, there has been a sharp increase in the recognition of the human components in the causation of major accidents.

The purpose of this paper is to set out a brief review of the major loci of personnel involvement with nuclear power stations, with some indications of accumulated human factors (HF) knowledge and practice in these areas. If a succint definition of HF is required, I would suggest that the aim is to define the capabilities and limitations of personnel, and to ensure that the design and operation of plant exploits the capabilities and compensates for the limitations.

2   PERSONNEL AND SYSTEM DESIGN

The starting point for any systematic approach to HF in nuclear plant must be an appraisal of the functions of the station personnel. Our emphasis in this review is on safety functions, and so an outline of the essential personnel roles would cover the following:

Operations staff:

A schedule of operators' safety tasks, including:

(a)   Operator actions to monitor plant and to maintain plant within limits of operation.

(b)   Any operator action claimed against any postulated fault or hazard.

(c.)   Operator monitoring and diagnosis post-trip.

(d)   Operator actions post-trip.

(e)   Operator actions in response to alarms under unanticipated fault conditions, including monitoring and control of beyond-design-basis events.

Maintenance staff (including test and calibration):

Requirements for planned and reactive maintenance.

Management and supervision:

Definitions of management structure for safety and authority/responsibility of each managerial and supervisory post.

These functional specifications for station personnel provide the basis for more detailed task analysis, as detailed below. They allow some assessment also of the allocation of safety functions between personnel and automatic equipment. Of direct relevance to this is Principle 124 in the NII Safety Assessment Principles for power reactors [1]. This requires automatic initiation of the protection system, no dependence on operator action within 30 minutes of such initiation, and facility for the operator to intervene positively but not negatively. Generally, the operating personnel must supervise and monitor the automatic systems, and their understanding of systems operations and states must be supported by the information which is provided by instrumentation, documentation, and training. The question of diversity in personnel safety functions is important also: one of the post-TMI recommendations was for the novel post of the 'Shift Technical Advisor', to provide independent technical advice to an operating team dealing with plant abnormalities. The French development of this concept [2] is of particular interest: the 'safety engineer' is a post external to the shift team, and he takes charge of post-incident supervision, giving directions to the shift team and monitoring their performance from an independent viewpoint.

Note also that any analysis of personnel safety functions must extend beyond the control room personnel, who have been the focus of much HF work, to maintenance, supervisory, and management jobs. It is more difficult to achieve detailed analysis of personnel requirements in these areas, but a systematic approach is obviously necessary.

3   TASK ANALYSIS AND DESIGN

The previous stage has defined the functions of personnel with respect to safety. The next stage is to evaluate the demands placed on personnel, and this is done by task analysis (TA). There is a variety of different methods for analysing task demands. but the common theme is to delineate the stages of 'human information processing' in responding to the needs of the job. Thus, the human operator has to detect a particular indication from the plant, identify the state of the plant, diagnose its relevance to the system objectives of safety and production, select the appropriate course of actions, implement those actions, and check the subsequent behaviour of the plant.

Specific TA techniques vary in the way in which they interpret these information processing stages, and in the level of detail which is appropriate for a particular set of tasks, and in their development as paper-based analyses or walk/talk throughs on mock-up or actual equipment. However, the essential aim is to produce human 'performance specifications' which will provide the basis for designing and evaluating:

- procedures,
- operator-plant interfaces,
- training schemes,
- organisation of teams,
- assessment of work load,
- communications systems.

4   OPERATOR-PLANT INTERFACE

This is the most immediately obvious facet of the relationship of operators with the plant. The displays and controls provided in the central control room (CCR) and at other locations are the vehicles of information and action for the personnel. There has been considerable research into all aspects of interface design which bear on compatibility with the characteristics of human operators, and much guidance is available to the designer; for example [3] is a design guide prepared specifically for nuclear power station CCRs, and [4] is a concise introduction to control room design in general.

It is important to consider the design of the interface at various levels of detail. At the 'device' level, the design of an individual display or control item will influence the effectiveness of information transmission between operator and plant. At the 'panel' level, the spatial and dynamic relationships between functionally associated displays and controls can influence effectiveness. At the general level, the way in which display/control panels are configured in the CCR contributes to the operators' understanding of plant design and function. The overall objective, as outlined in sec.3 above, is to promote the operators' functions of detection /identification/diagnosis/ selection/implementation/checking.

For 'conventional' or 'hard-wired' instrumentation, device design recommendations are available in the various handbooks and design guides, as above. At the panel level, related displays and controls can be associated in a variety of ways. For the general understanding of the plant, the overall organisation and layout of intrumentation panels is particularly important, including the clear separation and demarcation of different functional areas, and arrangements which permit the operator to take a 'hierarchical' approach - scanning plant state at a high level before examining individual areas in more detail.

There is increasing use of computer-based display systems, and once again design guides, e.g. [5], [6], provide recommendations for the detailed elements of individual VDU screen pages and the preferred screen layouts. Computer-based displays are essentially 'serial' (only a limited portion of the plant variables can be presented on one screen at a time), as compared with hard-wired displays where all of the information is available in 'parallel'. This has the disadvantage that the operator has to select screen contents as required, but this is balanced by the capability for combining separate items of plant information into a screen designed for a particular task, including perhaps analogue, digital, trend, and alarm indications. Moreover, the hierarchical organisation of information referred to above can be realised effectively with a computer-based system, as long as the network is designed to help the operator find his way around it.

Alarm information is an area with several complexities. The basic requirement of an alarm is that it indicates to the operator that part of the plant is in an undesirable state: thus, alarms should not be used to indicate merely a change of state which is acceptable, nor should alarms be allowed to persist when the operating mode of the plant renders them non-significant, for example in shut-down conditions. In nuclear plant alarms are numerous and inter-related: the operator is likely to be overloaded by alarm information in a transient. To mitigate these effects, hierarchical organisation of alarm displays will help, and alarms can be integrated into computer-generated display formats; other more advanced approaches, which manipulate sets of alarm signals for efficient understanding by the operator, are exemplified by the HALO concept developed by the OECD Halden Project [7]. It is generally found that a large proportion of human errors occur in maintenance and testing tasks. Seminara and Parsons [8] list common causes of maintenance errors from a survey of US nuclear power plants, including: faulty procedures, problems in tagging equipment, inadequate equipment identification, facility design problems, deficient work practices, and adverse environments. 'Slips' may typify many errors: Persinko and Ramey-Smith [9] survey examples of actions performed on the wrong train in a redundant set, or on the wrong unit in a multi-unit set. The implications for clear identification of plant items and areas are obvious. Badalamente et al. [10] and Pack [11] set out human factors guidelines for the design of maintenance tasks and equipment.

5   DOCUMENTATION AND PROCEDURES

The previous section covered the dynamic plant information provided for the operator. A complementary source of information is operating instructions and procedures, and here there is the same imperative to make the information relevant to the task and compatible with the operator's capabilities. The requirements of the plant must be analysed, and the resulting tasks assessed for feasibility of human operation.

Then, the presentation of the information must be designed for efficient use. For the typical text presentation, logical organisation, clear layout, and concise wording promote communication to operators. Recommendations for procedure design arising from USNRC research after TMI-2 are summarised in [12], and a useful general

account of the recommended approaches to the whole process of assembling the basic information for procedures and then arranging and presenting it for efficient use by the 'target' operators is given by Zimmerman and Campbell [13]. Their guidance covers the areas of:

-    Planning (determining purpose, collecting, analysing, and organising information);

-    Drafting (format, design, guidelines for text and graphics);

-    Review (independent verification and validation).

Note, once again, the initial emphasis on task analysis.

Some of the particular aspects emphasised in the design of procedural information are:

-    The need for a general overview of the procedure, to put the various elements into perspective. This may be achieved best by a flow diagram, and, indeed, the use of such alternatives to text may be useful in other parts of procedures.

-    Ensuring that adequate supporting or explanatory

    information is available in the procedure, or is referenced properly.

-    Pruning the procedure to the minimum length and number of words, consistent with its usability.

-    Consistent use of specific words and terminology.

-    Clarity through the use of short direct sentences, and the avoidance of difficult constructions such as negatives and the passive voice.

-    Providing aids to the operator keeping his place in a sequence of operations, such as 'tick sheets' or signing off points.

-    Ensuring that the general organisation and presentation, and updating arrangements, assist the user's understanding of the instructions and execution of the tasks.

A significant development in the general philosophy of procedures is the distinction between 'event-based' and 'symptom-based' modes, particularly for faults and emergencies. Conventional formulation of procedures requires that the operator has diagnosed the plant state or event, and thus can select the appropriate procedure. The symptom-based type works more or less directly from plant indications, in an attempt to guard against operators' misdiagnoses and to cater for unexpected events which might not be covered by a pre-classified set of procedures. The concept of symptom-based procedures originated from the analyses of the TMI-2 accident, and the approach is being applied particularly to emergency operating procedures.

Of course, all of the above comments, apart from the last, apply equally to maintenance procedures. Maintenance errors frequently involve omission of particular steps, and careful design of procedures can alleviate such failures.

Another important aspect of working documentation which has been identified in some incidents is the plant logs and other records which provide communications between different shifts and different departments. The communication of information on plant state and modifications is promoted by systematic procedures and design of logs which ensure systematic, comprehensive, and clear coverage of the required information.

6   OPERATING ENVIRONMENT

Human performance is affected by a variety of environmental parameters, and there is considerable guidance on optimum conditions in the human factors literature. e.g. [14]. The achievement of good working conditions may not be difficult in the relatively well controlled setting of the central control room, but the plant context is more of a challenge to the designer.

The most immediate aspect is the general design of the workplace. Data on ranges of body measurements, and on requirements for seeing displays and for operating on controls, form the input to design, e.g. [15]. For control room design and layout, the requirements for the wide range of activities are complex, but good designs are achievable. For tasks out on the plant, there are many more problems to be overcome, as illustrated in the previously cited survey by Seminara and Parsons [8].

The aspects of lighting, noise, and heating/ventilation are, again, easily specified and fairly easily attained for the control room. Lighting is the most difficult, particularly with VDU displays, where there is often a conflict between the constraints imposed by VDU operation and the more general illumination needs across the rest of the working area. Guidance on

the workspace and environmental requirements for VDUs is available, e.g. [16], [17].

On the plant, environmental conditions obviously are more difficult to control within recommended limits. A specific, more extreme, environment is that created inside protective clothing, and special measures are required for maintaining human performance: an example is given by [18].

Yet another aspect of working conditions on nuclear plant is shift work arrangements. Human factors principles relating to the design of shift schedules are based on our knowledge of the circadian (roughly 24 hr.) rhythms which affect physiological and psychological processes. Social and family effects are important also. Precise recommendations should be tailored to particular tasks and jobs, but Tepas and Monk [19] suggest some features which are likely to cause problems:

- Too many night shifts without a break;

- Morning shift start time before 0700;

- Weekly rotation schedules;

- Limited off-time;

- Backward rotation (morning > night > evening);

- Excessive regular overtime or weekend working.

A recent USNRC investigation [20] put forward recommendations for limits on hours of work over periods from one day to one year, and for the organisation of 8 hr./day and 12 hr./day shift schedules.

7   SELECTION AND TRAINING

For selecting and training personnel, as for the design of tasks, interfaces and procedures, the essential starting point is comprehensive specifications of tasks and jobs.

Selection procedures can incorporate the following techniques:

- Psychological tests and assessments;

- Interviews;

- Requirements for qualifications and experience;

- Medical tests, including colour vision.

In the UK nuclear industry there is general use of all of these methods, except for psychological tests and assessments.

Licensees report that they have no information to endorse the use of specific methods of this type; this view seems to be supported by a recent survey of the literature. However, there could be safety benefits for the utility in being able to identify good candidates at an early stage, and so more research is desirable in this area.

The organisational arrangements and liaison between operational management and the training function are important. It is essential that the ultimate responsibility for training should rest with the manager, but there must be specific advice for him, often supplied by a specialist department. The utility should carry out regular reviews of training arrangements at each station, and it is essential that adequate records of individuals' training are maintained on each nuclear site.

The current "systems approach" to training [21] emphasises the crucial importance of defining objectives for the justification and control of each segment of the training programme. These detailed objectives are derived from the job requirements identified in task analysis, and it is necessary to consider both initial and refresher training.

There is a variety of training techniques. Classroom teaching is suitable for introductory and detailed knowledge and information. Full-scope control room simulation allows the rehearsal of actual skills under controlled conditions, and is essential for the complex performance required of plant operators. Part simulation allows cost-effective concentration on specific elements of knowledge or skills. Zanobetti [22] has provided a general survey of the present state of the art in training simulators, and Madden and Tompsett [23] describe current CEGB facilities. On-job training methods have the advantage of incorporating the real context for tasks: however, the potential conflicts between training requirements and production requirements have to be anticipated.

It is essential that each trainee's enhanced knowledge, skills, and performance should be assessed at the end of each part of the training programme. Such assessment should be against the training objectives, and various subjective and objective procedures are available. The assessments of individuals must be transmitted to station management, as part of their responsibilities for the competence of station staff.

The evaluation of training is distinct from assessment of an individual: the concern here is with the contribution of each part of a training programme to the safety of nuclear operations. Obviously, a cumulative record of individual assessments

will provide some indication, but there must be other feedback, for example from supervisors and from operational experience.

Some of the above aspects of training are covered in recent papers in [24] and [25].

8   ORGANISATION AND MANAGEMENT

The concept of the 'safety culture' arose from the analyses of the Chernobyl accident. It is a concept which still has to be developed into a fully comprehensive model of the organisational and personal influences on the safe operation of a system as complex as a nuclear power station, but it is clear that management has the fundamental responsibility for generating and maintaining that culture. This is to be achieved by setting out safety policy, creating an organisational structure to implement it, and designing procedures to promote and control that implementation.

Nuclear safety policy has to be formulated explicitly at the level of the station manager, and has to be promulgated and put into action at all levels of the station personnel. The commercial objectives of the organisation have to be recognised, and possible conflicts between production goals and safety goals have to be anticipated and resolved in advance of their occurrence. Such planning must cover all of the likely states of normal and abnormal operation, and also other less predictable states: extended maintenance, outages, system tests and experiments. It is extremely important that any possibility of organisational or departmental pressure degrading safety is covered.

The organisational structure, and the definitions of job descriptions within it, must cover exhaustively and clearly the patterns of responsibility for safety. Overlapping of responsibility, gaps in responsibility, and ill-defined sharing of responsibility, all betray a structure which is inadequate. The organisational structure should also set out an appropriate and reliable pattern of communications between departments and individuals. One special requirement for nuclear stations is independent checking of plans and decisions, as for example in the nuclear safety committee which advises the station manager, and in the mechanisms of QA systems.

Management procedures will be designed for normal, abnormal, and emergency modes of operation. However, where feasible for safety requirements, reliance should be placed on engineered systems rather than on purely administrative controls. An important class of procedures is that which gives feedback on safety performance. The achievement of the production goals mentioned above is measured relatively easily, but analogues for safety are somewhat more intractable. Obviously, all transgressions of safety rules must be investigated and the results communicated to those who have potential future involvement in similar situations. The amount of information must be expanded by collecting information on near-errors and near-incidents: there are useful developments in confidential reporting schemes for operations personnel to draw management attention to specific unsafe operating practices and habits (e.g. the INPO Human Performance Evaluation System [26]). Further extension to a full third party, no penalty scheme similar to that already operating in civil aviation has been the subject of a feasibility study in the US [27].

The basic mechanism supporting the safety culture is the attitudes of the people involved. No amount of structures and procedures will generate high standards of safety without the active commitment of the personnel who have to make them work. This will be promoted by the safety policy emanating from top management, by informed approaches to management and supervision at all levels, by the appropriate design of tasks and facilities, and by the pattern of training and re-training.

9   PROBABILISTIC SAFETY ANALYSIS

Probabilistic Safety Analysis (PSA) must take account of human activities and operations which influence safety. It has to be accepted, at present, that many of the significant influences, including the factors covered in the two previous sections, cannot be included explicitly in any PSA. As Rasmussen [28] has argued, these form the basic assumptions which support the PSA analysis: thus, the structures and procedures outlined have to be put in place and monitored for maintenance of the required standards.

For the human operations which have a more direct input into safety procedures, a broad classification has been proposed:

(a)   Activities which affect the availability of safety systems;

(b)   Activities which can contribute to initiating events;

(c)   Activities which are part of post-fault management and recovery procedures.

To take proper account of the human input to fault and event trees for these classifications, these are the major stages of analysis:

(i)   Define the human actions required by the safety case;

(ii)   Model the associated human tasks, to represent the detection/identification/diagnosis/ selection/implementation/ feedback components of the behaviour involved;

(iii) Model the possible errors and recovery routes;

(iv)   Assess the influences of dependencies and other factors;

(v)   Assign probabilities for human error to the various components defined in (ii) and (iii) above.

(i) is derived from plant and systems analysis. (ii) and (iii) are certainly difficult to perform exhaustively, but they follow from the task analysis requirements which have been emphasised above. (iv) acknowledges the pervasiveness of dependency or 'common mode' effects in many human operations. (v) requires some kind of data-base of human error probabilities.

There certainly are problems in gathering substantial quantitative data on human errors, for stage (v), and various techniques have been developed. Objective data is available from experimental and operational studies, and a complementary source, as in other areas of PSA, is systematic expert judgement. A recent UK study [29] compared the major techniques currently available.

Nevertheless, stages (i) to (iv) are important, in ensuring that the human components are represented properly in the PSA. It is probably true that, in the past, too much attention has been paid to the processes of quantification, and too little to these fundamental stages of establishing the models of the operators' contributions.

10   CONCLUSION

This survey has presented an outline of the human factors approach to the design and operation of nuclear power stations. The major areas of interaction between personnel and the systems have been defined, and basic principles have been described. The final point is that all of the areas outlined have important bearings on safety: effective quality management of the 'human factor' in nuclear safety requires attention to all of them.

This paper sets out the personal views of the author (in some cases benefitting from the influence of his NII colleagues), and does not necessarily represent the views of the Health and Safety Executive.

11 REFERENCES

[1] Nuclear Safety: HM Nuclear Installations Inspectorate Safety Assessment Principles for Nuclear Power Reactors. Health and Safety Executive, July 1982. (London: HMSO).

[2] BERTRON L., MECLOT B. and CHEVALLON J.C. Operator organisation for the management of a nuclear accident in a power plant. Nuclear Safety, 1988, 29, 115-124.

[3] KINKADE R.G. and ANDERSON J. Human factors guide for nuclear power plant control room development. Electric Power Research Institute, Report NP 3659, August 1984.

[4] IVERGARD T. Handbook of Control Room Design and Ergonomics, 1989, (London: Taylor and Francis).

[5] GILMORE W.E. Human engineering guidelines for the evaluation and assessment of video display units. U.S. Nuclear Regulatory Commission, Report NUREG/CR-4227, July 1985

[6] FREY P.R. et al. Computer-generated display system guidelines. Vol.1: Display design. Electric Power Research Institute, Report NP 3701, vol.1, September 1984.

[7] OWRE F. and MARSHALL E.C. HALO: Handling alarms using logic: background, status, and further plans. ANS/ENS International Topical Meeting on Advances in Human Factors in Nuclear Power Systems, Knoxville TN, April 1986, pp.71-74.

[8] SEMINARA J.L. and PARSONS S.O. Human factors engineering and power plant maintenance. Maintenance Management International, 1985, 6, 33-71.

[9] PERSINKO D. and RAMEY-SMITH A. Investigation of the contributors to wrong unit or wrong train events. U.S. Nuclear Regulatory Commission, Report NUREG-1192, April 1986.

[10] BADALEMENTE R.V. et al. Recommendations to the NRC on human engineering guidelines for nuclear power plant maintainability. U.S. Nuclear Regulatory Commission, Report NUREG/CR-3517, 1985.

[11] PACK R. W. et al. Human engineering design guidelines for maintainability. Electric Power Research Institute, Report NP 4350, 1985.

[12] NUREG-0899 Guidelines for the preparation of emergency operating procedures. U.S. Nuclear Regulatory Commission, August 1982.

[13] ZIMMERMAN C.M. and CAMPBELL J.J. Fundamentals of Procedure Writing, 1988, (London: Kogan Page).

[14] SALVENDY G. (ed.) Handbook of Human Factors, Part 6: Environmental Design, 1987, (New York: Wiley).

[15] PHEASANT S.T. Ergonomics - Standards and Guidelines for Designers, 1987, (Milton Keynes: British Standards Institution).

[16] BS 7179:1989 British Standard Recommendations for Ergonomics Requirements for Design and Use of Visual Display Terminals (VDTs) in Offices.

[17] GILMORE W.E. Human engineering guidelines for the evaluation and assessment of video display units. U.S. Nuclear Regulatory Commission, Report NUREG/CR-4227, July 1985

[18] FEATHERSTONE G. Development and use of an air-cooled suit for work in nuclear reactors. Ergonomics, 1988, 31, 1025-1029.

[19] TEPAS D.I. and MONK T.H. Work schedules. In: SALVENDY G. (ed.) Handbook of Human Factors, 1987, (New York: Wiley).

[20] LEWIS P.M. Recommendations for NRC policy on shift scheduling and overtime at nuclear power plants. U.S. Nuclear Regulatory Commission, Report NUREG/CR-4248, July 1985.

[21] ROMISZOWSKI A.J. Designing Instructional Systems, 1981, (London: Kogan Page).

[22] ZANOBETTI D. Power Station Simulators, 1989, (Amsterdam: Elsevier).

[23] MADDEN V. J. and TOMPSETT P. A. The use of plant specific simulators at the CEGB's Nuclear Power Training Centre. IEE Second International Conference on Simulators.

[24] Institution of Mechanical Engineers. Symposium: Training of Technical Staff for Nuclear Power Stations, 1986.

[25] Special issue on operations and training. Nuclear Energy, vol.27, no.4, 1988.

[26]   INSTITUTE OF NUCLEAR POWER
        OPERATIONS. Tracing the causes of
        human error: the Human Performance
        Evaluation System. INPO Review,
        1988, 8 (2), 16-23.

[27]   FINLAYSON F.C. and NEWTON R.D.
        Nuclear power safety reporting
        system - final evaluation results.
        U.S. Nuclear Regulatory Commission,
        Report NUREG/CR-4132, February
        1986.

[28]   RASMUSSEN J. Approaches to the
        control of the effects of human
        error on chemical plant safety.
        Professional Safety, December 1988,
        23-29.

[29]   SAFETY AND RELIABILITY DIRECTORATE.
        Human reliability assessor's guide.
        UKAEA Report RTS 88/95, August
        1988.

C409/021

The application by the Nuclear Installations Inspectorate of quality assurance licence conditions to operating nuclear installations

C J HOLLIDAY, BSc, CEng, MIMechE
Nuclear Installations Inspectorate, Health and Safety Executive, Bootle, Merseyside

SYNOPSIS

The paper provides an overview of the Nuclear Installations Inspectorate's quality assurance licensing requirements and its assessment and auditing of the resultant arrangements being introduced at operating nuclear installations. It concludes with reference to some of the observed benefits from applying QA at these installations and identifies future developments receiving attention within the NII.

1.   INTRODUCTION

Within the United Kingdom, the regulatory body having responsibility for the licensing of nuclear installations is the Health & Safety Executive (HSE). The Nuclear Installations Inspectorate (NII) is that part of HSE which administers this function.

The conditions contained within a nuclear site licence define areas where the HSE require special attention to be paid in the interests of safety. However, they are not prescriptive. The quality assurance licence condition (Appendix 1) is one of several that are linked with the theme of "quality management in the nuclear industry: the human factor". This paper discusses the QA licence condition of an operating nuclear installation, the resultant documentation structure and the NII's assessment and auditing of these arrangements. In addition it will consider the benefits that result from introducing formal QA arrangements at operating nuclear installations and provide some indication of possible future developments.

2.   HISTORICAL BACKGROUND TO INTRODUCING AN OPERATIONS QA LICENCE CONDITION.

In the mid-1970s the NII reviewed existing national and international QA practices. The review concluded that site licences for future UK nuclear plants should include a QA condition. This requirement commenced with the licensing of the Heysham 2 and Torness nuclear power station projects in 1979. It was also decided by the review that a guide covering the preparation of QA programmes for

nuclear power plants should be prepared and in 1978 the NII published "A Guide to the QA Programme for Nuclear Power Plants" which took into account current national and international codes and standards and UK experience. Although the guide was intended primarily for use by NII staff, it also

indicated to licensees and their contractors the range of requirements considered necessary. The guide consists of QA principles which are applicable at all phases throughout the life of a nuclear plant and requirements for specific stages in the building and operation of the plant.

In 1982 the CEGB and SSEB formally adopted QA for all their activities, including non-nuclear. BNFL were also known to be following a broadly similar course in the introduction of QA to its reactor and chemical reprocessing plants. The NII's interest in these developments was to ensure the progressive introduction of formal QA arrangements to the operating nuclear installations and to the organisations that serviced them. In support of these developments the NII decided to introduce a uniform QA condition for all licensed sites. This condition was modelled on the one that was used successfully at Heysham 2 and Torness and was attached to all licences during 1987.

3.   POTENTIAL BENEFITS FROM THE INTRODUCTION OF AN OPERATIONS QA LICENCE CONDITION.

Both the licensees and the Inspectorate anticipated that there would be safety benefits from applying QA to the activities needed to operate a nuclear installation. From a regulatory viewpoint the most significant potential benefit would be that the formal, coherent documented arrangements would define responsibilities and working procedures within an ordered management structure suitable for audit and review. This would facilitate self-regulation by the licensee supplemented by the NII carrying out its own audits and inspections. The adoption of formal QA arrangements was also expected to contribute towards improved working standards and to assist in the training process by helping to identify training requirements.

4. DOCUMENTATION STRUCTURE INTRODUCED AT OPERATING NUCLEAR INSTALLATIONS.

When the QA licence condition was imposed on operating nuclear installations in 1987 the licensees were already operating to written procedures. The task was to organise these into a coherent system and to adapt existing arrangements to ensure the absence of overlaps or gaps and that all documentation was to a consistent standard.

The documentation structure implemented by most of the licensees can be divided into three tiers. This hierarchy of documentation does not signify the contribution each element makes towards safety but provides a logical way to cohesively link all the arrangements. The top tier contains management policy and commitments, typified by an operational quality assurance programme. The second tier provides general explanation of how the commitments made in the top tier document will be achieved. An example of a second tier document would be a Departmental Manual which defines responsibilities and describes the procedures and practices adopted by the Department to meet the requirements of the top tier document. Below this are the third tier detailed working arrangements which nonetheless include operating rules and instructions, maintenance instructions, station standing orders, the emergency plan and records. This structure needs to be sufficiently flexible to cater for those arrangements that relate to more than one department.

The QA licence condition enables the NII to specify the status it wishes to attach to any of the documented arrangements. These can be approved, furnished or available. Approved documents are those which require NII approval and cannot be amended without the Inspectorate's agreement. A furnished document is issued to the NII on a controlled circulation. Changes to a furnished document can be implemented prior to it being issued to the NII. An available document is supplied to the NII, if requested. It is current NII policy to approve only the licensee's top tier document. Approval is dependent upon a satisfactory outcome to the assessment process.

5. ASSESSMENT OF QA ARRANGEMENTS AT AN OPERATING NUCLEAR INSTALLATION.

Prior to a top tier document being submitted for approval, the NII will have informed the licensee of the assessment criteria that it will use and will also have provided the licensee with an opportunity to discuss any points of ambiguity.

The criteria against which the top tier document are assessed are the site licence conditions, NII safety assessment principles (Ref 1 & 2) IAEA 50-C-QA Safety Series (Ref 3), BS5882 (Ref 4) and the NII Guide to QA Arrangements for Nuclear Installations (Ref 5). These provide the framework for the type of information that needs to be included but does not prescribe the phraseology or format that has to be used. The criteria not only incorporate all the significant activities to operate, maintain and modify the plant but also the management systems that will promote good working practice.

Because the top tier document will be subject to NII approval the assessment will check that it contains sufficient detail to impose adequate control on the licensee's safety arrangements and yet not require frequent revision due to minor changes within the QA system. Typically, this means that it will describe the management structure, state the resultant responsibilities of senior management posts down to departmental head or equivalent and provide links to second and third tier documentation.

Although the top tier document is reasonably detailed, it is still mainly geared towards making a commitment and allocating responsibilities. Consequently the NII has decided as a matter of policy that it needs to assess the second tier documentation before approving the top tier. This assessment is intended to confirm that these documents are consistent with each other and adequately reflect the requirements of the top tier document. They are also checked to ensure that adequate links are made with third tier arrangements.

The assessment process will normally involve visits to the installation to discuss assessment comments with the licensee and agree any revisions. It does not involve any implementation checks or assessment of the adequacy of third tier documents. Inspections carried out by NII site inspectors and NII audits address these aspects.

6. AUDITING OF QA ARRANGEMENTS AT AN OPERATING NUCLEAR INSTALLATION.

The NII have found that the most effective way to check for compliance with the QA licence condition is to audit the arrangements of the licensee. These audits are complementary to those carried out by the licensee or on their behalf by manufacturers and contractors.

The NII carries out about 8 audits per year. This means that each operating installation receives an audit visit once every 2-2½ years. The Inspectorate makes its audit programme known to the licensee at an early date so that the licensee can take it into account in arranging his own programme of audits.

The topics included in the NII audit programme are derived from requests received from its Assessment and Inspection Branches along with those which the QA Section consider it to be worthwhile investigating. When producing the programme, weighting is also given to those licensees either in the early stages of implementing QA arrangements or where particular problems worthy of auditing have been identified. An annual audit programme is typified in Appendix 2.

The NII's audits are intended to review the adequacy of the arrangements and to confirm that they are being effectively implemented. They generally provide an in-depth check of a specific topic such as training, operating instructions or health physics, and are carried out in accordance with the NII's audit procedure which is explained below. Once the installation to be audited and the audit topic have been decided, this procedure requires the lead auditor and site inspector to form an audit team and agree the scope of activities to be audited during the 1½ days that is usually required for carrying out the site check.

The audit team is normally limited to 4 people of a multi-discipline background. Its lead auditor is a QA specialist who is able to assess whether the documented arrangements represent a coherent system and adequately reflect the requirements of the QA licence condition. The NII Site Inspector is included because of his site knowledge derived from his own programme of inspection and surveillance. It is normal practice to include a technical assessor in the team who provides the specialist knowledge needed to assess the technical content of the documented arrangements and the adequacy of the work carried out in implementing them. The fourth member of the team will either be an additional specialist or another representative from the Inspection Branch.

The scope of NII audits at operational installations can be categorised into two types. The first is called a vertical audit whereby the team checks a narrow but detailed sample of a topic or a system. For example, it may consider the activities and arrangements that relate to implementation of operating rules. This could include looking at actions taken by operators, the systems for writing operating instructions, assessing the adequacy of instructions, assessing the process for reviewing the documented arrangements and training arrangements for staff who have to use the instructions. The second type of audit can be categorised as a horizontal audit. It is used to check how different departments carry out an equivalent activity. A suitable example would be the training arrangements organised by department managers. Audits of this type provide the opportunity to check whether consistently high standards are achieved throughout an organisation.

Once an outline scope has been agreed, the Site Inspector in conjunction with the licensee, then identifies the relevant documentation needed by the audit team to prepare for the site check. Assessment of this documentation is used by the team to define the audit scope and to identify the specific activities it will investigate, produce an initial set of questions that can be asked at the commencement of the site visit and identify (by position) the staff with whom it may wish to hold discussions.

The team will agree how it will carry out its investigations and will draw up a programme for the site visit. This programme will include time for the team to review its progress during the audit visit and to decide whether changes are required. A broad outline of the programme is then issued to the licensee about two weeks before the audit. This enables the licensee to make arrangements so that the appropriate personnel are available during the period of the audit visit.

At the completion of the one-and-a-half days of investigation the team will collate its initial thoughts about both the positive and negative features observed during the audit visit. A brief closing meeting is held at the end of the site visit at which the team's initial observations are presented verbally. A written report of the audit is subsequently issued to the management of the NII. A copy is also sent to the licensee with a request for any follow-up action that may be required.

The audit report includes an appendix which contains a detailed account of the site check, a section of observations and conclusions and a section which details any required follow-up actions. The observations and conclusions represent the significant aspects of the site check that either confirm satisfactory implementation of the QA arrangements or call for improvements. They are not intended to address minor non-compliances but are aimed at identifying activities which need to be improved in order to satisfy the QA licence condition. These observations and conclusions are then carried over into the audit report section on follow-up actions and are invariably not prescriptive. It usually takes from several months to more than a year to close out any follow-up actions and usually involves a dialogue between the licensee, the NII Site Inspector and the audit team leader. Where an audit finding is found to be of a more significant nature and which requires immediate action, there are mechanisms for short-circuiting the normal process for closing out the audit report.

7.   OBSERVATIONS ON THE BENEFITS FROM
     INTRODUCING QUALITY ASSURANCE AT
     OPERATING NUCLEAR INSTALLATIONS.

This paper has already alluded to some of the benefits that were anticipated when licensees undertook to introduce QA arrangements at their operating nuclear installations. Whilst the process of introducing a coherent structure throughout the three tiers of documentation is not yet complete, the progress to date and the NII's assessment and auditing carried out during the last three years provides the basis for the following observations.

The NII QA assessment process of the licensee's top tier document is not only used to confirm that the topics of BS5882 are addressed but also checks that explanations are provided as to how all the other site licence conditions are satisfied by the hierarchy of documentation. In carrying out this task the NII have taken into account the more wide-ranging requirements of the IAEA's 50-C-QA Safety Series Code. Thus the QA arrangements reflect not only the UK standard but also that of the IAEA.

The licensee's corporate commitment to implementing QA principles and the Inspectorate's assessment of the arrangements have led the licensee at some nuclear installations to review his management objectives, specification and allocation of responsibilities, working practices and management systems. The decision to fully assess and approve the top tier documents and to generally assess but not approve the second tier documents enables the NII to have confidence in the licensee's management arrangements and to verify that an adequate documented system is in place.

The existence of a management system incorporating clearly defined objectives, responsibilities and task delegation can familiarise site staff where they fit into an organisation, what their duties are and how these should be performed. Equally, management can relate these requirements to a person's experience and qualifications in deciding whether any training is required prior to a person being allocated a particular task.

The existence of documented arrangements at operating installations contributes to safety case assessment by providing the NII with the means not only to examine in detail the drawings and description of the plant, but also its method of operation.

The documented arrangements comprise procedures which have been assessed and are known to be safe, and which are in accordance with the general policies set down by plant management. Reviews and audits can then be used by both the licensee and the Inspectorate to confirm compliance with these procedures.

There is a safety benefit for the NII and licensees to have complementary audit programmes. This spreads the activity of review and audit over as wide a field as possible. In addition, although the licensees may not be scheduled to audit and review a particular set of arrangements, there can be a concentrating of the mind when an installation is made aware that these arrangements may be investigated during an NII audit.

Experience has confirmed that the effectiveness of QA audits is enhanced by having a multi-discipline team, which is able not only to confirm that documented arrangements exist and are being implemented but also to assess their technical adequacy and effectiveness. This should indicate to the licensee that it is not sufficient for their own audit and review system to be limited to document compliance checks but that they should also confirm whether the arrangements adequately cater for the engineering requirements of the activity being considered.

QA audit activity has been of benefit to NII Site Inspectors and technical assessors alike. The NII Site Inspector has been able to use his involvement with QA audit to carry out planned inspection of management systems and working arrangements or to carry out detailed investigation of activities that are giving some cause for concern at site. The NII technical specialist has been able to contrast plant design safety assessment with what subsequently happens in practice at the nuclear installation.

Benefits also accrue from issuing a detailed report of each audit. Collectively the reports provide a clear statement of the work of nuclear safety regulation and a useful source of reference.

8. FUTURE DEVELOPMENTS.

After reflecting upon some of the benefits that have accrued from the introduction of QA at nuclear installations, it is considered worthwhile to highlight two aspects currently receiving attention within the NII. During the construction of Heysham 2, Torness and currently Sizewell B it has been well established that the decision as to how much QA is required should be derived from a procedure which provides guidance on how to apply QA in a graded manner. It has been recognised that an equivalent approach is required at operating nuclear installations which links the extent of management control, procedures and records, to safety implications, technical sophistication and novelty. The implementation of this particular application of a graded approach is in its infancy and hence its adequacy will have to be monitored by both the licensee and Inspectorate.

Team inspections of nuclear installations are being introduced by the NII's Inspection Branches. These will be additional to the programme of QA audits that have been described in this paper. It is likely that a QA specialist will be a member of some of these teams with a remit to consider whether a coherent management system exists and is being implemented.

In the light of experience the NII believe that QA makes an important contribution to the safety of nuclear installations and should continue to form part of the regulatory framework.

9. ACKNOWLEDGEMENTS

This paper is published with the approval of Mr E A Ryder, Chief Inspector, Nuclear Installations, but the views expressed are those of the author and do not necessarily represent the views of the NII or the Health & Safety Executive.

The author wishes to thank Mr J C Lynn and Mr J A Carver for their helpful guidance in the preparation of this paper.

REFERENCES

1   H M Nuclear Installations Inspectorate
    Safety Assessment Principles for Nuclear
    Power Reactors, Health and Safety
    Executive, HMSO 1979, 0 11 883235 2.

2   H M Nuclear Installations Inspectorate
    Safety Assessment Principles for Nuclear
    Chemical Plant, Health and Safety
    Executive, HMSO 1983, 0 7176 01536

3   International Atomic Energy Agency,
    Quality Assurance for Safety in Nuclear
    Power Plants: A Code of Practice (Safety
    Series
    50-C-QA), Vienna (1978)

4   British Standards Institution, BS5882: A
    Total Quality Assurance Programme for
    Nuclear Installations

5   Health & Safety Executive, Nuclear
    Installations Inspectorate, A Guide to
    the Quality Assurance Programme for
    Nuclear Power Plants, Issue 2,
    (NII/R/38/78), London (1978)

APPENDIX 1

THE QA LICENCE CONDITION

1. Without prejudice to any other
    requirement of the conditions attached
    to this licence, the Licensee shall make
    and implement adequate quality assurance
    arrangements in respect of all matters
    which may affect safety.

2. The Licensee shall submit to the
    Executive for approval such part or
    parts of the aforesaid arrangements as
    the Executive may specify.

3. The Licensee shall ensure that once
    approved no alteration or amendment is
    made to the approved arrangements unless
    the Executive has approved such
    alteration or amendment.

4. The Licensee shall furnish to the
    Executive such copies of records or
    documents made in connection with the
    aforesaid arrangements as the Executive
    may specify.

APPENDIX 2

A TYPICAL ANNUAL NII AUDIT PROGRAMME

LICENSEE	SUBJECT	DATE
A	Training	January
B	Health Physics	February
B	Maintenance Schedule	March
A	Civil Construction	April
C	Control System Software	May
D	Commissioning Instructions	June
E	Operating Instructions	August
B	Fuel Route	September
A	Mechanical Design	September
D	Independent Examination	October
C	Mechanical Construction	November
B	Operating QA Arrangements	December

Quality assurance in research and development

G F LASLETT, CBE, CEng, MIMechE
Vital Technologies (UK) Limited, Cheltenham
C H WAKER, BSc(Eng), CEng, MIMechE
Nuclear Installations Inspectorate, Health and Safety Executive, Bootle, Merseyside

SYNOPSIS

It is propounded that, a given high status for the Research and Development (R&D) activity of the company or site, "freeing" the scientists and engineers involved at the innovative decision-taking point helps quality. Effort and money to raise the latter may be best spent in ensuring better calibre, background and training of them, making more meaningful the teamwork across the supplier/customer interfaces, and avoiding risk of misunderstanding of the use to be made of the outcome of the R&D endeavour. But the staff's conscience towards quality, hand in hand with safety, must be constantly stimulated, - without gloves of course!

A respected researcher on quality practices at the US Department of Defence, NASA, and the US Nuclear Regulatory Commission, Frank J.Muller, wrote of the research and development (R&D) community:-

"There is a singularly important asset to those who wish to expand QA and QC: people want to do a good job. If expansion ever does occur, it will happen because scientists and engineers are convinced that QA and QC will actually help them do a better job and not be an impediment to their efforts." (1)

1 INTRODUCTION

Most people setting out on any job want to make a success of it. The fundamental factor which distinguishes the R&D community is their belief that the most important commodity in the research process is the ability of their trained brainpower to be innovative. This, coupled with the normal end-product being derived data, make application of quality assurance (QA) or quality control (QC) measures, as we generally think of them, particularly difficult.

The work control procedures may also be very different between areas of activity. What is appropriate for an analytical chemistry group may be completely inhibiting for a group undertaking more speculative research. The quality-assessing must therefore be a flexible approach. We also believe it must be a dynamic process as will become clear.

In what follows, we make no attempt to propose a QA system for the management of R&D. That must be for management to define, and each application is likely to be different. Rather, we hope to provoke and stimulate a fresh approach which, by discussing the essential quality management issues and strategies for addressing them, will lead to a QA system which those to whom it applies will identify with and will want to own.

Clearly therefore, the position and status of the R&D department within the unit, has a great influence. Is it the pool of excellence of technical knowledge relating to the principal present and envisaged future functions of the unit. Is it afforded opportunity to develop expertise based on distillation of experience with generations of previous products of the unit, combined with opportunities for acquaintance with outside activity in similar or related fields. Too often we find the above expectation of the department is there without senior management of the unit appreciating the requirements to achieve it, not least in career development and selection of personnel to staff the department.

2 PRELIMINARY CONSIDERATIONS

2.1 The Role of R&D

For most nuclear units, be they companies or sites, R&D activity carries the expectation that on its end-product depends the future profitability of the unit of which it is a part, indeed, maybe even the unit's continued existence. In discussing strategy for the quality management of R&D personnel, we have assumed the vital importance of their activities is recognised by management.

2.2 The Nature of R&D

R&D can conveniently be broken down into four chronological areas of activity:-

(A) Fundamental research, - leading to a concept on which design work can be justified.

(B) Development, - work to support the design process to committal to construction of more than just the prototype.

(C) Evaluation testing, - testing of designed or brought-in components, equipment, instrumentation, and systems, frequently in simulation of anticipated usage in service. Includes assistance to commissioning.

(D) In-service support, - including analytical and laboratory services, which may also be tapped by the above.

The ideal might be when the activity of the department contains a blend of the above aspects, and is at the frontiers of new break-through in some respect. The latter need not be on the fringe of widening scientific knowledge; high motivation can come from endeavour in other directions, such as to be more cost-effective in the production process, or from making the product more consumer- or environment-friendly. The work does not necessarily have to be all done in-house, but there remains a need for the department's scientists and engineers to be available and knowledgeable to appraise and interpret such work, besides manage the contracts for its procurement.

We suggest that the R&D department should be a Business Centre, with strong customer/supplier interfaces, both with the rest of the unit, and with the outside for bought-in work. As the significance of the department reduces below this model we have outlined, so will the potential difficulty of achieving quality increase, not least because of risk of de-motivation of staff. So often we find people unsure whether transfer into the R&D department is not relegation. Worst is where the only valued part of the department is its laboratories for conducting routine sample testing, because that is identified with today's problems with current production. Gone will be the freedom of mind to be intuitive; it so easily will be a stifling plethora of paper and procedures in the name of quality. Then perhaps the best staffing approach is to make it a new entrant pathway to better things, quickest passage for the brightest.

2.3 Quality Management Style

Imposed introduction of any discipline, even for safety, needs for success to be accompanied by general acceptance amongst the staff of "it not being unreasonable". There will be a greater need of "hearts and minds winning" effort to achieve this minimum for quality measures, than for health and safety reasons. On quality measures, it is perhaps necessary to go even further and gain the consensus "this could really help us do a better job". There must be no question of whatever is introduced being set aside when the pressure is on, unless there is high confidence its lessons have become inherent in the way people work. For inevitably in R&D there will be such occasions, for example when called in on a production plant breakdown, or when a design deadline suddenly hinges on the justification for extrapolation outside the near-certainty of the derived data. The golden rule in any critical commercial or safety related situation, must be that where there is any doubt over the supporting data, a hold must be placed on the decision to proceed.

There is a well documented history in US literature of the foundering of early attempts there to impose QA and QC on R&D organisations as a planned and systematic pattern to cover all actions necessary to provide enhanced confidence in its end-product. The introduction to the Muller paper (1), from which we quoted at the start, is an example, noting that it is where the QA is inappropriate that foundering is most often the end result.

2.4 Selective Application

Another hazard is the poorly thought-through unit-wide introduction of QA and QC initiatives. The Head of the R&D department must be influential enough to argue resistance against adoption where he or she believes the measures will inhibit the staff. Resentment is only natural at imposition; it is much better in such a department to steer seemingly self-generated ideas for quality improvement. It is also much better to start addressing quality at the outset of a project, and keep a conscience going about it, rather than introduce it at a later stage.

A universal approach may not be appropriate throughout a department, by reason that the R&D projects can be very different in nature and timescale, requiring, as George W.Roberts in his book on QA in R&D put it, - 'some degree of individualised planning to accommodate their uniqueness.'(2)

After the apt reminders above, Roberts offers the following on what quality systems need to be implemented: 'Hardware may be produced for an individual project, but the end result of most R&D effort is data. The quality programme must establish systems that are pertinent to assuring the quality and validity of the data or results. Sections of a production QC programme may be quite specific as to how specific pieces are to be inspected, tested, packaged, and shipped; but in a R&D QA Manual, the question is always whether these activities have a real effect on the validity of the research'.

In summary so far therefore, we consider that since the success of R&D is largely dependent on the intellect, knowledge, and innovative initiative of most of its scientific and engineering staff, we feel it is particularly important to avoid any pressure being brought to bear which they would regard as stifling and de-motivating. This is not to say that the R&D department should not be required to make use of such centralised quality controlled facilities as have been set up within the unit, for example, for material and equipment procurement, or calibration services.

2.5 Quality Management and Safety

Muller gives a cautionary note from experience in the USA. After the failures mentioned above, QA began to achieve some success in the 1970's, but the enhanced confidence in technological performance was at a cost to safety, notably with on-going activities. He writes - 'Unfortunately though, there is evidence that many organisations (some with excellent quality/safety programs) tended to abdicate their responsibility for nuclear power safety. They found themselves unable to do the things they thought provided safety because what they wanted to do contradicted regulations or because the regulations diverted staff attention in other directions'. He mentions some recent safety problems as evidence of this problem. Thus, if not actually grafted on to safety, any QA system must dovetail with it closely.

3 A STRATEGY FOR QUALITY MANAGEMENT IN R&D

3.1 Factors for QA Application

With these virtual pre-requisites out of the way, and bearing in mind the pitfalls highlighted, what is it that the R&D department should be looking for in furtherance of quality? We believe it should be the aspects of the work that the vast majority of scientific and engineering staff would see as reasonable areas in which to apply discipline relating to quality.

Rather as BS 5882 in para.1.1.4 looks for factors on which to base methods and levels of QA, we have selected the following for further consideration:

(A) That the calibre and training of staff needs to be of the highest order possible in order to help guarantee the end-product of their R&D.

(B) That the dynamic situation and balance between technical progress, cost and timetable need to be carefully controlled, because they are inextricably intertwined.

(C) That control is best achieved by making maximum use of the key customer/supplier relationship in the work.

(D) That frequently, on the validity of the findings of the R&D hangs the success or failure of present, but more probably future, unit profit-earning production or processes. These latter usually involve infinitely greater real and potential cost significance compared to the cost of the R&D, and have other implications, for example on public health and safety. Thus recording the basis of those findings needs exacting control.

If the above were agreed as the basic starting point for furthering quality in R&D, then this philosophy could with benefit be set down in a very simple statement of quality strategy. This should make clear that application of QA is a dynamic process, and the above is only a start point, allowing that aspects may expand, be abandoned, or become accepted practice not needing such future emphasis as continued inclusion in the strategy.

Quality consideration would thus be kept a live probing concept. We would encourage seeing it as a discipline of looking sideways at what is done, So far, we have been talking of common initiatives across the department. Nothing

should make these exclusive areas for endeavour towards improving quality, because many self-generated ideas for particular activities amongst smaller groups within the department may prove as or more worthwhile. However it is fair to require that priority of effort goes towards the major common departmental quality initiatives, and that all should be involved to see they can live with what emerges.

3.2 Levels of QA

In applying these departmental initiatives, section or project managers, or in some cases individuals, should be clear to relate the overall approach to their own work, thinking of the key attributes and criteria involved. For example the latter might include:

a. The severity of the safety implications of getting it wrong.

b. The degree of dependence of future profitability of the unit on the findings of their piece of R&D.

There must be a forum or means by which disquiet can be made known, and consensus gained.

One would thus be recognising, and perhaps should make the point in the strategy statement, that different levels of QA can be justified as applicable in different areas of R&D, within the same QA objective for the whole of the department. Effectively one is thus recognising the possibility of different levels of quality-driven methods of working in various parts of the department. Roberts draws attention to an interesting approach towards quality levels in the Canadian Standards Association CAN3/Z 286 and 299 series of standards.

3.3 The Quality Manager

In any sizeable department, we do not favour the Head of the department feeling he could fulfil this sideways-looking quality-seeking role. Nor do we like the idea of doubling this role up with that of the departmental safety officer. Preferred is a suitably trained scientist or engineer within the department, answerable direct to Head of department, but preferably not at immediate deputy level. Ideally acting independent of all other functions, the person should engender a feeling of being approachable for all. The responsibilities of this quality manager should include keeping under review all QA interest in the department's activity, refining and expanding its scope, assessing cost of quality, sensing weakness and staff response, and suggesting incentive of 'carrot and stick' to achieve better staff reaction to improvement initiatives. The person should be the focal point of outside contact with the department on quality matters, and should, along with the safety officer, monitor self-audit and be on the look-out for needs of, and opportunities for, external audit. It has been proved time and time again, that, if there is not such a person charged with taking the pulse of the quality system, then it tends to fade to the point of being totally ignored.

That we have specified the background for this quality manager is deliberate. Muller attributes failure of past QA initiatives towards R&D, partly on QA practitioners having been outsiders with lack of ability to understand the nature of R&D.

3.4 Documentation

There is nothing in the fore-going which conflicts with even that most stringent of the British Standards towards quality assurance, BS 5882, applicable in the nuclear installations field. Indeed, we find it significant that BS 5882 does not stipulate the form of documentation, or the method of audit. It does not even include mention of a Quality Manual!

It will be for the Head of the R&D department to decide what should be written down by way of directive in the interests of quality. Certainly, we would expect a committal to satisfying one appropriate British Standard, with regard to the whole R&D activity being taken as one programme. For this there should be, as para.0.4.16 of BS 5882 puts it:- 'A description should be of the overall management and procedures covering the quality assurance actions for the execution' of the work. This must include an organisational chart of the management of the department, which we believe should be aimed at strengthening the customer/supplier interfaces for each project and contract, rather than being predominantly a hierarchical structure. More on this later. The directive on standards should make clear that having an overall standard applicable may not exclude the necessity to conduct individual parts of the programme to different standards, as discussed above.

The bottom line with regard to a statement on procedures, is, in our view, that everyone in the department should be left in no doubt as to the documentation and way of working which are applicable to all in the department; not just quality related matters, but covering health and safety, procurement procedures, etc. This does not mean the quality manual, in whatever form it takes, should be inclusive of full text; rather, a listing giving advice where staff can have access to a copy of each plan or procedure. The latter should be handy; staff should feel confident any copy they pick up is in date, and has a sponsor with whom they can raise any questions.

With the latter in mind, care should be taken to avoid inclusion of details which may rapidly change. Not only is the amendment task made so much simpler, but finding incumbents' names are wrong, or example contracts are things of the forgotten past, at once brings all documentation into disrepute for loss of credibility.

Another point we would make, with which the QA professional might not agree, is that once an adjustment has been made in the name of quality, there is no need to necessarily perpetuate the link. Let the changed regime become the norm, without enshrining it in QA tablets of stone and identification. There is a grave danger in making QA documentation too all embracing. To make it a 'bible' in which the text of every conceivable aspect of activity in the department is contained is to do it a disservice. Quality interest should be provoking amendment within, rather than then plucking out and supplanting.

4 IMPLEMENTING THE QUALITY MANAGEMENT STRATEGY

Clearly, if the strategy elements in 3.1 (A)-(D) selected above were accepted, it would be for the Head of the department to act on the consensus view of how they should be implemented. In what follows, we seek to indicate some of the considerations to which each might lead, more in illustration of the strategy than any attempt to recommend firmly the following of this particular course. They are made having in mind a department, at least fifty strong on scientific and engineering professional staff, sub-divided into groups basically customer project orientated, except for a laboratory based, say Analytical Chemistry and Metallurgy, group.

4.1 (A) - Calibre and Training of Staff

The current Staff Organisational Chart should form the basis for the compilation of a listing of the numbers of categories of personnel in the department. We might call this the Complement Schedule - the ideal staffing for the department to tackle its present and perceived future workload. Senior management of the unit might recognise this as the ideal, but not be prepared to man the department to that level. They would fix a Staff Budget which would relate to the Complement Schedule, but most probably differ from it for policy reasons, for example, accepting long-term overtime working, or increasing the dilution of numbers of graduates straight from college because recruiting happens to look easier now than in the future. To change the Staff Budget would involve demonstration that the Complement Schedule needed to be changed, or that other policy measures explaining differences no longer applied. Each slot for a category of person on the Complement Schedule, in order to be filled ideally, would correspond with a target qualification, skill level and/or experience level. These would be annotated against the listing, as might any training needed immediately before a person filled a position within the category. The actual manpower at any particular time would almost certainly differ from both the Complement Schedule and the Staff Budget, due to the difficulties of the Personnel department in recruiting, training and transferring the right people. By grade marking actual level above and below these targets, management would be able to measure the degree of actual incumbent match to the target, individually, by special area, say analytical chemist, by group, etc.

Head of the R&D department would be free to juggle his Staff Organisational Chart to suit changing workload, or manage job rotation, at the same time seeing the effect he was having on dilution against targets. Poor performance in an area might indicate need to raise the targets. Training whilst with the department might be relatable to achieved improvement of the match with targets, and so on. But whenever Head of department could no longer meet his obligations with the extant Complement Schedule, then negotiations with Personnel for an adjustment to it, would be facilitated by the existence of this performance indicator on calibre of staff. Equally, effects of changing the Staff Budget would be more readily apparent to those responsible for doing so.

The methodology for Staff Assessment should be defined, with consideration given to having some scientists or engineers having at least two mentors eg. separately for managerial competence and for professional ability. In some cases, we sense the former might be better done by project leader, even across the supplier/customer divide, than using line management. Take an expert engineer in charge of two others almost always out on operating plant, say inspecting pipework and pressure vessels. Might not the works manager of their major customer be better placed to assess that engineer's managerial skill, than the nominal line manager in the hierarchy of the department? And vice versa, a physicist working with and under engineers, could probably more fairly have his professional competence judged by a more remotely placed senior physicist, particularly if some of our proposals later on verification of work were implemented. A listing of reporting superiors should exist for all to see. A system of audit to judge accuracy of staff assessment, and its utilisation in personnel advancement and remuneration might be considered.

The department's influence on policy and actual moves in recruitment and in staff transfers needs definition. This may not just be with transfers in and out of the department, but with the selection and grooming of potential people to become the experts the department will need. Their career development may necessitate earmarking of certain experience-gathering positions elsewhere in the unit on the basis of long term planning for anticipated future R&D.

One of the issues frequently arising is the financial remuneration situation within the R&D department. The dilemma frequently stems from the hierarchical organisation affording insufficient genuine management positions for equality of seeming responsibility, compared with other areas in the unit. For those who have to stay for long periods in the department (not that we advocate this for more than the minimum) financial incentives based on periodic increments, or for growth in professional competence, without advancement managerially, may be necessary. Generous bonuses for contribution towards the future profitability of the unit are another avenue for attracting the brighter staff trained outside the department on the unit's normal pay structure. Thus they can be recompensed for a relatively lowly place in the team of experts in the R&D department, once they join it. These are matters the Head of department must be prepared to argue through; matters which have even been known to influence the senior management of the unit to despair and taken the easy, but probably less satisfactory and more costly, solution of contracting out the work.

A factor which can help, is to make it abundantly clear that the 'flyers' in the unit can all expect at least one appointment in the R&D department. For this to be effective, the reputation needs to be that duration of appointments in the department are normally not excessive. Perfectly satisfactory would be recognition throughout the unit that an appointment to that department would normally be for no more than a factor of 1.5 times the length of appointment elsewhere. This carries implications of acceptance that elsewhere in the unit there is generally an expectation of changing jobs on a regular basis, and not just on promotion.

Without some special financial remuneration situation, the departmental hierarchy, we find, tends to become tall and thin, striving to maximise the number of managerial levels and positions at each in order to have pay differentials, and yet keep in line with elsewhere in the unit. The penalties of one over one over one are elaborated on later.

Frequently we find the R&D department is the first appointment for the new graduate intake into the unit. In this situation, the training of staff requires the recognition of the wider professional and managerial needs of the scientist and engineer, as well as those related to the R&D function.

Senior management must recognise the need for generosity in providing opportunities for the staff in R&D to have contact outside the unit, and expect to allow them self-elevation by contributing papers, attending seminars, etc. This may need delicate financing through, nominally, training budgets, but is a necessary overhead which will benefit the department's end-product. Certainly a margin in Staff Budget needs to be built in over Complement Schedule for training and motivation related activities, if, as we believe it should, the Complement Schedule has been strictly drawn on the manhours for the work principle.

4.2 (B) - Status of Technical Progress against Cost and Time

We find that spend against budget by work package very often seems to be divorced from assessment and redirection for technical progress. This frequently arises because there exists a series of purely technical committees meeting across the customer/supplier divide, where spend against time is barely mentioned. On examination, it is commonly because up to date statistics on the latter are not available to that committee. Many Heads of R&D departments will argue the view that the purely technical aspects at working level should not be cluttered with such mundane details; the Head and a separate set of managers should relieve them of such concern. We do not altogether agree. But certainly somehow the Head of department, at least, must have some indicator of the state of all three, if he is to manage effectively, and utilise his resources to best advantage.

As a starting point, consideration might be given to compilation of subjective views, from whoever is best qualified to judge, on the three aspects, say monthly on the basis of classifications such as:- critical, major weakness,widespread minor weakness, satisfactory with some minor weakness, in good shape. Tabled at Head of department's say monthly management meetings, these could highlight problems and trends, on which focus might be needed. This simple guide could be related to other performance indicators, in reviewing priorities and resources. That responsible people at the supplier/customer interface were thus effectively responsible for direct reports to top management, would enhance their standing and make possible a reduction in reporting significance up the line hierarchy. This latter we shall comment on further. This subjective impression of project status would be easily kept up to date, and not too much for the technical committee to take on board. When alarm bells rang from that status, then they should seek greater detail of actual cost and timescale concerns.

Methodology for collection of spend information, and other finance related information needs visibility. The cost of its compilation can so often be out of proportion to its value, eg. if some element of its make-up, like overheads, is too inaccurate or arbitrary. But on the other hand, if R&D department is to be a Business Centre, it must be able to predict costs fairly accurately, and keep to them or show reason why not. This is why a detailed specification of what is important, for only against this can the department note change in requirements of them to justify the cost and timescale implications outside their control. Many of these specification changes stand a high risk of slipping through in technical committee deliberations, unless there is the cost and timescale conscience present which we advocate.

4.3 (C) - Management Structure and Customer/ Supplier Relationship

Almost all the scientists and engineers in the R&D department will be making a unique contribution to a process either leading to the design of, or continued operation of, something which is furthered outside the department. This is the cause of our objection to the departmental organisational chart which shows only a very steep sided conventional pyramid of 'bosses' generally organised up common professional discipline vertical links. Another US author on Quality in R&D, Myron Tribus (3) writes:- 'The first thing that happens when you have an organisation in which people are trying to place their bosses is that whenever people make a report upwards, they put the best possible face on it. When you finally get to the top, the picture that the person at the top sees has nothing to do with what is actually going on at the bottom. So what happens when you organise for people to please their superiors is that there is deceit. You institutionalise deceit. The big difference in managing by quality is that you no longer have trouble getting at the truth.' This management by quality is customer related.

There has to be a hierarchical departmental organisation, but we would recommend it be designed to minimise distraction to people identifying with their place in their process in the above sense. We recommend broader

spans of control for everyone in that hierarchy, positions filled on managerial merit, and with greater scope for workload to dramatically change without that being mirrored in organisation. A reduction in the tiers of management might bring the Head of department closer to where the work is done. Seemingly greater delegation of quality responsibility would be inherent and beneficial, enhancing the all important quality accountability to the customer.

This hierarchical departmental organisation should concern itself more with policy and resource control, than detailed review of technical achievement, setting up the optimum climate in which people can work. It is sufficient to know there is a technical problem, and then discuss resource factors that might relieve it. The hierarchy should allow Head of department to hold meetings with functions represented similar to those a company board chairman might have, eg. personnel and training, accountancy, quality and safety audit, marketing and support services, along with the senior coordinators of the 'work force'. Terms of Reference for the posts in this hierarchy should be written, stressing managerial accountability without cutting across the all important supplier/customer relationship. Indeed the number of senior work coordinators should be kept to a minimum, and, as a guide, never form the majority on the above committee. Their span of control should be tailored to closely match division by customer interests rather than by professional specialisations. Clearly one senior coordinator would need to remain service laboratories orientated, if these are a part of the department.

4.4 (D) - Audit and Recording

This perhaps appropriately comes last, as it is the most difficult. But one thing is easy to recommend. We wholeheartedly endorse the application of self-audit. Where we have encountered it, it seems popular, and that is a great start. This even extends to the scoring of achievement. This is helped by having the assessing managers self-auditing their ambits, being people with a wide span of control, something advocated under strategy concept (C). Internal audit of the department must, of course, also include Head of department not just sitting in his office, or liaising outside the department!

External audit can take many forms. It is incredible how frequently unit senior management shrink from actually going themselves to see R&D work being undertaken. Preoccupation with today's problems should be no excuse. Head of R&D department should pester them to come, instead of being thankful they do not. Where the unit has a QA department, there is positive benefit in keeping in close touch, and carrying them along with the department's initiatives. They will be that much better briefed to conduct their own external audits of the department, and when the unit is subject to some outside licensing authority, etc. to brief that QA inspectorate. Over and above this, nothing but benefit can come from inviting external audit of specialist scientist and engineer activity areas. Finding appropriate people is not easy.

Certainly one person should not be sought, because it will be impossible to find someone who combines being an outside expert in the technical field, in QA in R&D, and with some background knowledge of the unit. Each facet should not be audited separately. A small team with representation of each facet, all without dependence on the unit's products, must be the aim. Some call this extrinsic audit.

Great reliance is clearly placed in the end-product of much done in the R&D department. Whilst the doing of a good job is of paramount importance, it is also vital to know the trust that can be put in the results as written up. The proof of the pudding may not happen for a very long time. Mishap will demand traceability. The application of stringent QA controls in this authorship field will be appreciated, and do more to raise confidence in end-product than anything else. Check lists to authors of aspects in which their work may be utilised, eg. as input to statistical probability studies for reliability, failure modes and effects analysis, fault tree analysis, risk analysis or 'most critical accident' studies, can cause a complete change of viewpoint in writing. The knowledge that the check list may call one to account later, generally leads to some rehearsal of the aspects earlier, with thought to cater for eventually having to give percentage confidence levels, or define proximity to limits of detection. It may even help ensure researchers press for the original specification to be kept up-dated as realisation dawns of potential dependence going to be placed on it. In turn, it may lead to the necessary refining of the experiment, built in at an appropriate time, rather than as a repeat afterthought.

Check lists for report vetting, validation and verification can be invaluable, and appreciated by those facing authorship. Report authorisation solely by line superior perhaps places over-emphasis on the function that that superior should hold in the light of our strategy (C) leanings. A better system might arise from further thought along the lines of the multi-mentor concept we introduced earlier.

Insistence that the design team will also have to disclose their logic in reaching decisions, can also be beneficial. Detailed design disclosure from the earliest stage of specification writing for the innovative work, means the design team acquire a conscience about justification of design decisions. They rapidly become willing vettors of the written output of the R&D fraternity, and should be used as such.

5 CONCLUSIONS

We shrink from drawing conclusions on the foregoing, despite our having sounded at times emphatic on practices for achieving quality in R&D. To do so would be guilty of the very thing we advocate against; it would be drawing a tight glove over the hand that needs dexterity to do the card trick. Look sideways at the hands from all angles, to make sure of the quality of the act. Long may it keep turning up trumps for your company or site. We recognise no two departments are the same; it may need to be trumps of a particular suit!

The best we hope for is that these thoughts will have been provocative. We close with questions focusing attention on the individual person in your unit involved in R&D. Does your unit do enough to make he or she really feel they are a key figure? Has your unit done enough to insure its future through ensuring that right people will be working tomorrow in it's R&D for years to come? Can you really be as sure as you think you are of the quality of each person's work? Do they still want to do a good job as keenly as when they first joined the department?

References

1. Muller, F.C.   A s s u r i n g   Q u a l i t y in Development and Design: An Antithetical Approach; Quality Progress, Vol 17, No.9, September 1984, pp 18-21.

2. Roberts, G.W.   Quality Assurance in Research and Development; Industrial Engineering/8.

3. Tribus, M.   Quality i n R & D; Applying Quality Management Principles; Research Management, Vol 30, No.6 December 1987, pp 11-21.

C409/034

Engineering qualifications for competence

J C LEVY, OBE, BSc(Eng), PhD, CEng, FIMechE
Former Director—Engineering Profession, The Engineering Council, London

INTRODUCTION

The Engineering Council has a responsibility across all fields of engineering to set standards for those who are registered as Chartered Engineers, Incorporated Engineers* or Engineering Technicians. These standards amount to a basic specification of professional competence to which must be added the features needed in each different branch of engineering, such as nuclear, and each particular occupation, such as quality assurance.

This article describes The Engineering Council's general standards and includes a guide to the roles and responsibilities which should lie within the domain of those who are registered with the Council.

The concluding section describes the title of European Engineer and its relationship to the European Community directive governing the movement of professionals across community frontiers.

THE REGISTRATION OF ENGINEERS

A Government committee of enquiry resulted in The Engineering Council being established in 1981 by Royal Charter "to advance education in, and to promote the science and practice of, engineering (including relevant technology) for the public benefit and thereby to promote industry and commerce."

A central duty of The Engineering Council is to maintain the official register of

> Chartered Engineers (CEng)
> Incorporated Engineers (IEng)
> Engineering Technicians (EngTech)

Brief definitions of the qualities represented by these titles are given in Appendix 1.

---

*The title Incorporated Engineer was previously Technician Engineer.

The standards required for registration are published in The Council's policy statement "Standards and Routes to Registration" (1) known by the acronym SARTOR.

THE SECTIONS AND STAGES OF THE REGISTER

Each of the three sections of the Register (CEng, IEng and EngTech) has three stages. Stage 1 indicates the attainment of a recognised academic qualification, Stage 2 the completion of appropriate training and Stage 3 the acquisition of suitable experience, including some of a responsible nature. In the case of Chartered Engineers this normally totals a 7-year package of education, training and experience and the minimum age for a Chartered Engineer is 25 years. It is only upon reaching Stage 3 of a section of the Register that an individual is entitled to use the designatory letters CEng, IEng or EngTech after his or her name (see the Routes to Registration diagram, Fig 1). SARTOR is supported by a comprehensive Code of Practice which defines procedures for registration and for the accreditation of academic courses, training programmes and arrangements for experience. At present there are about 300,000 names on the Register, of which 190,000 are Chartered Engineers.

NOMINATED BODIES

Qualified engineers of tomorrow must be technically competent, market conscious, commercially adept, environmentally sensitive and responsive to human needs.

The Engineering Council's effort to ensure that student engineers acquire these qualities during their education and training is based upon its system of Nominated Bodies as defined in the Council's Charter. Nominated Bodies are engineering institutions judged by The Council as fitted to certify the attainment of individuals seeking admission to the Council's Register as Chartered Engineers, Incorporated Engineers or Engineering Technicians.

AUTHORISED BODIES

An underlying principle of Engineering Council policy for the three stages of the Register is that, as far as possible, arrangements for academic courses, training programmes and experience should be approved in advance to ensure that the 'formation' of young engineers is carefully prepared to develop competence and high professional standards.

With this in mind, some Nominated Bodies may also be 'authorised' to accredit academic courses, training programmes and arrangements for experience.

Students who successfully complete such an accredited route are automatically entitled to be registered in the appropriate section and Stage of the Register.

The advantages for the students are that, besides being assured of fulfilling the requirements for registration, they are spending their time at an important point in their lives on courses and programmes which have been thoroughly vetted to high standards and therefore give the best prospect of later advancement in the profession and practice of engineering.

Candidates for registration who do not possess an accredited qualification are considered by an 'individual case procedure' to judge whether their attainment is at least equal to those completing an accredited route.

EDUCATION - STAGE 1 OF THE REGISTER

SARTOR emphasises that accredited academic courses for CEng, IEng or EngTech must be geared to the real needs of practicing engineers and to the integration of theory and practice. The Engineering Council's view is that each course should embody and integrate theoretical and practical elements commensurate with the level of study being pursued so enabling the student to expand his or her engineering knowledge in a logical broad manner. For those aspiring to become Chartered Engineers the exemplifying level is an enhanced engineering degree of honours standard called Bachelor of Engineering (BEng).

For those on the route to qualifying as Incorporated Engineers or Engineering Technicians the levels are exemplified by a BTEC*/SCOTVEC+ Higher National Certificate or National Certificate respectively.

---

*   BTEC is the Business and Technician Education Council, a national body.
+   SCOTVEC is the Scottish Vocational Education Council.

Each accredited course must contain certain features, listed in SARTOR. The Authorised Body carefully assesses the course subject matter, the facilities available, the calibre of academic staff, the involvement of industry in planning and running the course and a host of other features which are indicators of the quality of what is being offered to students. Particular stress is placed upon the exclusion of obsolete material and ensuring that methods of examining are appropriate and do not inhibit course development. There is also a requirement that studies are included which are related to the social and professional role of the engineer.

If there is a prima facie case for accreditation, a visit to the educational institution by experienced engineers will be organised by the Authorised Body and a decision whether or not to accredit the course and for what period will be made. The whole procedure is monitored by Entineering Council representatives.

TRAINING - STAGE 2 OF THE REGISTER

Accredited training programmes and schemes are no less important than accredited academic courses. Bodies authorised for Stage 2 of the Register enlist the co-operation of industry in providing properly planned and structured training for those aiming at Chartered Engineer, Incorporated Engineer or Engineering Technician status.

Authorised Bodies maintain registers of the trainees whose progress is recorded in log books and by means of periodic reports. Supervision is by qualified engineers at the place of training supported in many instances by academic staff responsible for sandwich and block release courses which The Engineering Council wishes to encourage and which should assume even more prominence in the future.

Sandwich courses, both of the 'thick' and 'thin' variety, in which periods of education alternate with periods of training, tangibly express the integration of education and training.

The satisfaction of the training requirements of accredited programmes may include activities more properly categorised as experience rather than training. A combination of training and experience is fully permissible provided it is part of a planned programme or scheme.

EXPERIENCE - STAGE 3 OF THE REGISTER

When the academic requirements for Stage 1 and the training requirements for Stage 2 have been satisfied, each candidate needs more experience including occupation of a post carrying some responsibility. This involves exposure to the reality of making decisions and bearing personally the outcome, whether good or bad, in manufacture, construction, health and safety or in business negotiations.

That phase is the final pre-qualification tempering of the engineer and is concluded by a Professional Review, including an interview, for those applying for Stage 3 registration as a CEng or IEng.

This is not, however, the end of the story for, as in previous generations, new registrants then carry a personal responsibility to maintain their knowledge by continuing education and training in professional activities which may be expected to change as rapidly in the next generation as in the last.

GUIDE TO THE ROLES AND RESPONSIBILITIES OF REGISTRANTS

The original 1984 edition of SARTOR was silent on the kind of posts which CEngs, IEngs and EngTechs should occupy.

The Engineering Council is occasionally approached by individual registrants who propose that full statutory licensing of engineers should be introduced and this is also frequently suggested in the correspondence columns of journals. It is not Engineering Council policy to support such a general extension of licensing, but the 1990 edition of SARTOR includes the guidelines reproduced in Appendix 2 as a practical step forward.

The implementation of these guidelines will be strongly pressed. They were reached in consultation with the engineering institutions, via the Council's Board for Engineers' Registration, and have also received the approval of the elected Engineering Assembly, so they should now enjoy widespread support.

The guide is organised under nine headings :-

   i)   Design
  ii)   Research and Development
 iii)   Engineering Practice
  iv)   Manufacture, Installation, Construction
   v)   Operation and Maintenance
  vi)   Health, Safety, Reliability
 vii)   Management and Planning
viii)   Engineering Aspects of Marketing
  ix)   Teaching, Training, Career Development

Basically, the guide is intended to underline that engineering matters are best dealt with by those who are recognised nationally as engineers and who have been so judged, against rigorous published standards. This makes for all-round efficiency and instills confidence where matters of safety are concerned - an increasing consideration today, particularly in areas publicly perceived as high-risk, such as the nuclear industry.

As an example, take the question of the use of engineering codes of practice in design. Such codes are carefully developed by qualified engineers for use by other engineers who have an appropriate knowledge of fundamental principles, coupled with the training and experience to use those principles to solve practical problems. It may be dangerous for codes to be used by unqualified persons.

Again, on the business scene it is becoming more important in securing contracts, particularly overseas, that sufficient properly qualified people are seen to be engaged in the work. The best available 'labels', increasingly recognised internationally, are CEng and IEng. Also, in cases of accident, failure or product liability it is important that a demonstration can be made that suitably qualified persons were employed by the manufacturer, contractor or other responsible body.

It is recognised that there is an overlap between the roles of Chartered Engineers and Incorporated Engineers and, to a lesser extent, between Incorporated Engineers and Engineering Technicians. Moreover, engineering activity often requires a balanced team to provide the required range of expertise and management capability. Such a team may embrace all three categories of registered Engineer, as well as multi-skilled craftsmen and also some staff without formal engineering qualifications.

The lists given in the guide (Appendix 2) are not intended to be exhaustive, but to assist individual engineers and employers. It has to be recognised that in the immediate future not all the posts described will in fact be occupied by registrants, nor will all registrants necessarily occupy such posts. Equally, the education and training of engineers fits them to occupy a wide variety of posts, up to the very highest levels, outside engineering.

THE EUROPEAN ENGINEER (EUR ING)

On October 28th, 1987, an historic and impressive ceremony took place in the Luxembourg Palace in Paris, when the first 60 European Engineers received the title from Alain Poher, President of the French Senate, and himself an engineer and recipient of European Engineer certificate No 1. The largest national contingent was from the UK, ten Chartered Engineers representing all sections of the profession and symbolic of the very many Institution members who will now wish to use the title.

The Paris ceremony was the culmination of four years of intensive negotiation and international collaboration within the European Federation of National Engineering Associations (FEANI), in which the UK delegates played a prominent role. It is important that all UK professional engineers understand the background and the significance of the new FEANI Register and of the European Engineer title.

FEANI has 20 member countries, including all those in the European Community. The UK representative body is the British National Committee for International Engineering Affairs (BNCIEA) which is a consortium of representatives from our Engineering Institutions, The Fellowship of Engineering and The Engineering Council, which also provides the administration.

FEANI's main aims are :

- To secure the recognition of European engineering titles and to protect those titles, in order to facilitate the freedom of engineers to move and practise within and outside Europe;

- To safeguard and promote the professional interests of engineers.

The minimum standard set for Eur Ing is a seven-year formation package of education, training and professional experience, similar to the current requirements for Chartered Engineer. This may be considered a vindication of the UK formation system, since all the FEANI members now recognise that a professional qualification in engineering needs, in addition to education, elements of training and experience in a planned and monitored package. All Chartered Engineers, whether they have a degree or an equivalent qualification, are eligible to apply, through their Institutions, for the European Engineer title.

Of about 200,000 CEngs, some 3,000 have already applied for registration, and we know that many more intend to do so. European Engineers receive a registration card and a certificate. Incidentally, the BNCIEA has determined that the designatory letters Eur Ing should be used as a prefix to the name, so conforming to Continental practice.

The FEANI agreement and the EurIng title are the product of negotiation between the professional bodies in the 20 FEANI countries. They are not governmental measures. But, in parallel, the 12 European Community countries have now agreed on a Directive, due to be implemented in 1991, covering the movement of professionals. This Directive on higher education diplomas unfortunately represents a standard lower than that for Chartered Engineer, so there is a danger that immigrants from other EC countries could come here and be able to use the CEng title, without fulfilling our own training and experience requirements or taking the professional review.

Fortunately, however, the European Commission has requested FEANI to produce a draft of a separate engineers' directive and at the time of writing there is an expectation that this will emerge on 'EurIng' lines. If then accepted by the Commission, the EurIng standard, with its minimum formation period of 7 years, will avert the possibility of any lowering of standards.

Should the attempt to secure a separate engineers' directive fail, then in my opinion Europe will be saddled with a general directive which is unsatisfactory for the top echelon of engineering. In such circumstances I am quite sure that the EurIng title will be retained by FEANI and will rapidly become established as the 'quality' title for the European profession. Enquiry among a few employers has revealed a welcome and a willingness to accept such a pan-European title, which provides a basis of comparison of qualifications and could be used in advertisements for staff. At present, some employers are evidently inhibited from asking for CEng because, for example, it would exclude most potential applicants from other European countries.

Assuming that FEANI's effort succeeds, we can look forward to a positive effect on European industry on the basis of a pan-European approach to qualifications and titles assisting our competitive efforts with the USA and Japan. There could also be a consequential enhancement of the status of the engineering profession in this country, on the basis of the EurIng title.

J C Levy
February 1990

REFERENCE

(1) Standards and Routes to Registration (SARTOR) 2nd Edition - January 1990, The Engineering Council, 10 Maltravers Street, London WC2R 3ER. Price £12.00

APPENDIX 1

Definitions

An **Engineer** is one who acquires and uses scientific, technical and other pertinent knowledge and skills to create, operate and maintain safe, efficient systems, structures, machines, plant, processes and devices of practical and economic value.

Chartered Engineers are concerned with the progress of technology through innovation, creativity and change and should be able to develop and apply new technologies, promote advanced designs, introduce new and more efficient production techniques, marketing and construction concepts and pioneer new engineering services and management methods. They need the ability to supervise others and in due time the maturity to assume responsibility for the direction of important tasks.

Incorporated Engineers perform technical duties of an established or novel nature in posts demanding a detailed understanding of a particular technology. They are concerned with maintaining and managing existing technology efficiently. They need communication skills and an awareness beyond the limits of their specific responsibility.

Engineering Technicians are competent to apply proven techniques and procedures with an element of personal responsibility. They should have an understanding of general engineering principles applicable to their role rather than relying solely on established practices of accumulated skills.

APPENDIX 2

THE GUIDE

RECOMMENDED ROLES AND RESPONSIBILITIES FOR CHARTERED ENGINEERS, INCORPORATED ENGINEERS AND ENGINEERING TECHNICIANS

CHARTERED ENGINEERS AND INCORPORATED ENGINEERS

The Engineering Council recommends that posts involving one or more of the duties and responsibilities listed below should be occupied by those registered as Chartered Engineers or Incorporated Engineers.

Chartered and Incorporated Engineers are expected to apply their respective codes of professional conduct, to undertake work within their expertise and to exercise a responsible attitude to society with regard to the ethical, economic and environmental impact of technical need and change.

Each list is arranged in an approximately descending order of responsibility level, though clearly the relative importance of the items may vary somewhat from one situation to another.

There is inevitably an overlap in duties between Chartered and Incorporated Engineers. <u>As indicated by the graphic against the Design heading, it is expected that Chartered Engineers would mainly be concerned with topics in the first part of each list, while Incorporated Engineers would mainly be concerned with those in the second part of each list.</u> Also, it is expected that Chartered Engineers would normally be concerned with a broader range of these activities than Incorporated Engineers.

Activities in various lists may overlap. Quality assurance is a case in point.

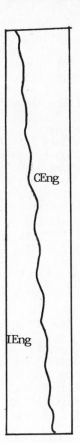

i)   Design

-   Managerial responsibility for an engineering design function or group.
-   Supervising preparation of designs.
-   Engineering design outside the scope of established procedures, standards and codes of practice to a competitive level of cost, safety, quality and reliability.

-   Promotion of advanced designs and design methods. Continual development of standards and codes internationally.
-   Failure analysis and value engineering.
-   Design work involving established procedures and the use of Engineering Standards and Codes of Practice to a competitive level of cost, safety, quality, reliability and appearance.

ii)   Research and Development

-   Leading research and development effort in engineering resulting in the design, development and manufacture of pro- ducts, equipment and processes to a competitive level of cost, safety, quality, reliability and appearance.
-   Managing engineering research and development groups, planning and execution of research and development programmes, carrying out research and development assignments.
-   Evaluation of test results and interpretation of data. Preparing reports and recommendations.

iii) Engineering Practice

- The exercise of independent technical judgment and the application of engineering principles.
- Application of theoretical knowledge to the marketing, operation and maintenance of products and services.
- Development and application of new technologies.
- Monitoring progress on a world-wide basis, assimilation of such information and independent contributions to the development of engineering science and its applications.
- Work involving the need to understand and apply analytical and technical skills and judgement and the use of a range of equipment, techniques and methods for measurement, control, operation, fault diagnosis, maintenance and for protection of the environment.

iv) Manufacture, Installation, Construction

- Managerial responsibility for a production, installation, construction or dismantling function.
- Organisation of cost effective manufacturing functions.
- The introduction of new and more efficient production techniques and of installation and construction concepts.
- Organisation of quality-driven manufacture, installation and construction functions.
- Day-to-day organisation and supervision of manufacturing, installation, and construction functions from raw material input to finished product.

v) Operation and Maintenance

- Managerial responsibility for an operation or maintenance function or group.
- Providing specifications of operational maintainability standards to be achieved in design and production.
- Determining operational maintenance requirements in terms of tasks to be performed and time intervals between tasks.
- Managing the quality of the output of operational maintenance activities.
- Developing and specifying diagnostic techniques and procedures.
- Developing and specifying repair and rectification methods.
- Assessing the actual and expected effect on performance of deterioration in service.

vi) Health, Safety, Reliability

- Making appropriate provision in engineering projects to ensure safety and the required standards of reliability, not only with employees and customers in mind but in the general public interest.

- Responsibility for health, safety, reliability in situations involving engineering plant, systems, processes or activities.
- Accident investigation.
- Supervision of inspection and test procedures.
  (NB: It should be noted that there do exist a few statutory or quasi-statutory provisions under this heading. For example the Quality Assessment Schedule to BS5750 Part 1 relating to civil and/or structural engineering led multi-disciplinary engineering project design states: "For each project the control of the design and design related activities shall be the responsibility of a Project Director who shall be a Chartered Engineer qualified in the relevant discipline").

vii) Management and Planning

- Overall company/commercial responsibility as a director with engineering knowledge.
- Longer range and strategic planning of engineering activities and functions.
- Management of the development and implementation of new technologies with estimation of the cost/benefit of the financial, social and political decisions taken.
- Pioneering of new engineering services and management methods.
- Effective direction of advanced existing technology involving high risk and capital intensive projects.
- Direct responsibility for the management or guidance of technical staff and other resources.
- Supervision of engineering staff and resources and the associated legal, financial and economic practice at a level commensurate with the scale of the activity and size of organisation within the constraints of the relevant environment.
- Short-range planning of engineering activities and functions.

viii) Engineering Aspects of Marketing

- Management responsibility for a technical marketing function.
- Top-level customer and contract negotiations.
- Setting marketing objectives and policies.
- Territorial or market planning forecasts and targets.
- Management responsibility for the dissemination of accurate technical information.
- Customer technical advisory service.
- Market analysis, contract negotiations.
- Non-standard customer requirements.
- Sales operations, efficient market coverage.
- Preparing cost estimates and proposals.

ix) <u>Teaching, Training, Career Development</u>

- Academic (teaching) responsibility for engineering courses and activities at first degree and postgraduate level.
- Career development for Chartered Engineers and Incorporated Engineers.
- Responsibility for training and the supervision of experience for those intending to become Chartered Engineers.

- Academic (teaching) responsibility for courses and activities up to BTEC/SCOTVEC Higher National level in engineering.
- Career development for Engineering Technicians.
- Responsibility for training and the supervision of experience for those intending to become Incorporated Engineers or Engineering Technicians.

ENGINEERING TECHNICIANS

The Engineering Council recommends that posts involving one or more of the following duties and responsibilities should be occupied by those registered as Engineering Technicians. Normally these duties will be undertaken under the general supervision of a Chartered or Incorporated Engineer. It is recognised that there will be some overlap with duties towards the end of the previous lists for Chartered and Incorporated Engineers.

Unlike the previous lists, there is no order of responsibility level of the items under each heading.

i) <u>Design</u>

- Preparation of plans and designs of limited scope and complexity.
- Costs estimates and checking designs and products against specifications.
- Use of standard codes and specifications within established practice.

ii) <u>Research and Development</u>

- Developing and constructing test equipment, conducting and assisting with experiments and investigations.
- Recording and calculating results as scheduled.

iii) <u>Engineering Practice</u>

- Detailed knowledge of appropriate established technology.
- Assistance in manufacturing schedules and production control.
- Fault investigation and correction.

iv) <u>Manufacture, Installation, Construction</u>

- Installation, commissioning and dismantling of specified plant and processes.
- Operational responsibility for manufacturing and construction systems.

- Inspection and fault correction. Work study.
- Assessing processes for production.
- Improving existing plant and processes.

v) <u>Operation and Maintenance</u>

- Preparing programmes to implement operation and maintenance requirements.
- Planning the provision of resources to support the maintenance programme.
- Implementing and controlling the execution of operation and maintenance programmes.
- Ensuring continuity of supply and services as scheduled.

vi) <u>Health, Safety, Quality</u>

- Ensuring efficient day-to-day cleanliness and safety of equipment and services.
- Responsibility for detailed compliance with health and safety requirements.
- Operation and development of detailed procedures for quality assurance and control.

vii) <u>Management and Planning</u>

- Planning manufacturing lay outs, installation and maintenance schedules and procedures.
- Supervision of shop floor and similar activities.
- Technical guidance and organisation of routine tasks.
- Troubleshooting of technical activities.

viii) <u>Marketing</u>

- Cost estimates and proposals to suit customers' requirements for standard engineering plant and products.
- Efficient processing of enquiries, orders and arrangements for delivery.
- After-sales service and technical advice to customers.

ix) <u>Teaching, Training and Career Development</u>

- Technical support functions in laboratory, design office and project work.
- General assistance to academic staff and students in teaching establishments.
- Training of those engaged in craft, maintenance and associated functions.

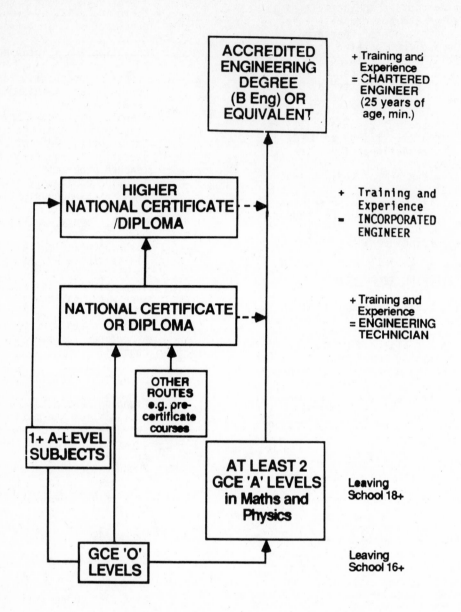

ACCREDITED ENGINEERING DEGREE (B Eng) OR EQUIVALENT

+ Training and Experience
= CHARTERED ENGINEER (25 years of age, min.)

HIGHER NATIONAL CERTIFICATE /DIPLOMA

+ Training and Experience
= INCORPORATED ENGINEER

NATIONAL CERTIFICATE OR DIPLOMA

+ Training and Experience
= ENGINEERING TECHNICIAN

OTHER ROUTES e.g. pre-certificate courses

1+ A-LEVEL SUBJECTS

AT LEAST 2 GCE 'A' LEVELS in Maths and Physics

Leaving School 18+

GCE 'O' LEVELS

Leaving School 16+

Fig 1   Routes to registration

C409/005

Managing for nuclear operational effectiveness

P A NEVINS and **D C KASPERSKI**, PhD
Cresap, Chicago, Illinois, USA

The nuclear energy industry worldwide is changing, with significant implications for nuclear utility managers. While the U.K. and U.S. nuclear industries have many differences, a number of the lessons learned in the U.S. have direct applicability to the U.K. Just as the physics behind nuclear power transcend political boundaries, so do many of the management techniques that are necessary to run an efficient and sound operation.

The U.S. nuclear industry is no longer a construction-based industry, as it has been for years. As nuclear construction slows or stops in many parts of the world and nuclear power comes under increased scrutiny everywhere, the industry is shifting away from a construction emphasis and toward an operations and maintenance emphasis.

In fact, a recent Cresap survey of senior nuclear utility managers in North America highlighted the fact that today, more than one-half of nuclear executives believe that plant operating and maintenance costs, and not construction-related problems, are their number one concern.

Furthermore, when asked what actions they would expect to take as a result of this concern, the majority indicated that the actions would be management-related for the most part, and included items such as:

- Emphasize operating improvements

- Emphasize management improvements

- Upgrade outage management and maintenance management programs

- Increase senior management involvement

- Set management performance criteria.

CHANGING FOCUS

With this shift in focus from a construction-based to an operating and maintenance-based industry comes a natural change in management orientation. Once important issues such as capital expenditures and reviews of management prudence in the construction of major capital additions now take a back seat to those of the more mundane, but no less important, issues of operating and maintenance costs, rate and fuel cost pressures, and staffing efficiencies and effectiveness.

This shift in focus has also been noted by the industry regulators; in the U.S. both the Nuclear Regulatory Commission (NRC) and many state public utility commissions have been turning to operating issues more frequently. Whereas state commissions spent much of the recent past being concerned with the management prudence of nuclear construction costs and practices, today they more frequently look at current operating and maintenance practices of those same plants.

The NRC has also started waving the banner of operational excellence, increasing its vigilance of transgressions in O&M areas in the last few years. It has been especially critical of items such as inattention of detail on the part of operators and maintainers, procedural noncompliance, and management's lack of responsiveness to ongoing problems and lack of commitment to take forceful action to resolve them.

For example, a few years ago, the NRC shut down all of the Tennessee Valley Authority's nuclear plants because of "management's lack of attention to detail" in the plant's operation and maintenance function. Similarly, Philadelphia Electric Company's two-unit Peach Bottom station was shut down because of operator inattentiveness, as well as ongoing maintenance-related discrepancies that were not corrected in a timely manner. Other nuclear stations as well have felt the NRC's wrath because of O&M related difficulties.

OPERATIONAL EFFICIENCY AND EFFECTIVENESS

In addition, U.S. utilities - and especially nuclear utilities - now face a much more competitive marketplace. Competition is more pervasive and competitors are more skilled. And competition comes not only from the traditional competitors such as the local and regional gas and oil companies, but from a whole host of new energy producers such as cogenerators. In addition, all companies, including utilities, are operating in an increasingly global market. Utilities, now more than ever, need to improve the efficiency and effectiveness of their operations.

Currently, this is not the case. One major measure of nuclear plant efficiency and productivity is the Capacity Factor, which compares the amount of energy actually produced in a year to the maximum amount of energy that a plant could produce if it were on-line essentially 100 per cent of the time. Over the past nine years, the overall industry capacity factor (averaged over all licensed U.S. plants) has averaged 59.7 per cent. Furthermore, there has been no significant trend toward improvement on an industrywide basis over this nine-year time period. (Figure 1).

Another major measure of nuclear plant productivity is the Forced Outage Rate, which measures the amount of time a plant is shut down and unable to produce energy because of plant difficulties, which are often operational or maintenance-related. Over the past nine years, the American nuclear industry's forced outage rate has averaged 14.4 per cent, and shows no sign of improvement. (Figure 2).

It is natural, of course, to look toward changes in resource levels as a source of operational improvements. The connection seems logical - after all, more people should mean more and better work. There is evidence, however, that suggests that operational improvements cannot be made through resource adjustments alone. In fact, there tends to be no correlation between nuclear plant productivity - as measured by capacity factor - and various resource inputs such as total manpower (Figure 3), or manpower by unit of plant output (Figure 4), or total plant O&M expenditures (less fuel costs) (Figure 5).
These figures indicate that some utilities are clearly able to obtain better performance/results than others and at lower cost. Increasingly, what differentiates the more efficient nuclear plants and utilities from the also-rans is management...management of operations and management of maintenance.

In today's environment, then, mangagement matters are the key drivers of plant performance and cost, and the management of operations and maintenance costs is an increasingly important part of this complex equation. It is almost deja vu when one remembers new U.S. nuclear plant construction in the early 1980s. At that time, utilities recognized that improved management was the key to resolving issues surounding engineering and construction of new nuclear plants. Now, they are learning that lesson on operating plants as well. If management were not so critical a factor then we wouldn't be finding such a discrepancy between plant operating and cost performance and the resource applied.

MANAGING FOR OPERATIONAL EFFECTIVENESS

In light of this fact, what can be done to improve management effectiveness, especially O&M management effectiveness? Management needs to look at operations using a four-step process we call Managing for Operational Effectiveness. This process provides a framework for evaluating and improving the operations of a plant.

By managing for operational effectiveness, utilities can address questions regarding nuclear power plant operations and maintenance that are important to senior management. These questions include issues involving program safety, reliability, and cost effectiveness. Through this process, responsibility

for these vital issues is moved up in the organization, yet all functional areas of the organization are kept involved in the decision-making process.

In this four-step process, no one step is sufficient in itself; each is necessary for the satisfactory completion of the others. Each step builds on the others. Simply put, it involves the implementation of management policies through suitable processes involving people and appropriate corporate and plant programs. (Figure 6).

Policies

Policies for the nuclear organization need to be in line with the overall corporate goals and objectives. Too often, in the heat of regulatory involvement, nuclear organizations lose sight of this all-important concept.

Responsibility for developing and achieving these goals must also be pushed further up in the organization, and must involve senior management. Moreover, meaningful performance monitoring systems should be developed to ensure that progress towards achieving corporate goals and objectives is tracked, and deviations should be identified so that adjustments can be made early enough to affect the outcome. What we often see is a very detailed and seemingly comprehensive system of performance tracking in place, but all too often, it is merely a paperwork exercise. Because of the amount of detail and supporting information presented to senior and executive management, the use of performance tracking as a true aid to decision-making is diluted to one of explaining variances instead of reducing them.

In addition, a realistic system of prioritizing necessary tasks over the budget cycle should be in place and modified as circumstances change throughout the year. What we often do not find is a true prioritization scheme - one that tracks each required task and allocates limited funds to each in accordance with its priority. Instead, we find a system that lists NRC and other commitments made, and each of these is automatically assigned the highest priority. What usually results is that no monies are left for other needed projects, and what suffers most are those maintenance jobs that get postponed year after year.

This is not to say that regulatory commitments are not very important...of course they are. However, in the real world, all necessary tasks compete for limited dollars, and a realistic and workable scheme must be developed that addresses these competing needs for limited funds. Our experience indicates that management all too often takes the easy way out and doesn't collect the necessary information to help make the tough allocation decisions.

People

The nuclear organization should be structured to facilitate singular accountability for key business and operational functions. People must be treated with respect and professionalism, yet must be held accountable for their performance and that of their organizational units. Results, not activities, must be stressed. Overlapping accountability should be discouraged, as should duplication and fragmentation of responsibility within organizational units.

A company's culture must be well understood in order to get the most out of any organization. Corporate culture has a major effect on how work gets done, and on the quality and timeliness of that work.

Corporate culture includes such often intangible items as:

- Work-related values

- Company history

- Communications, both internal and external

- Policies and procedures, especially those involving human resource issues

- Employee rewards, recognition, and development

Management approaches to decision-making

In addition, knowing a company's culture can help immeasurably in formulating other recommendations for improvement that can be more easily and effectively implemented.

Alternately, changes to corporate culture must be attempted when that culture prevents the company from addressing needed changes.

A instrument for evaluating a company's culture should be developed to assess factors such as:

- The degree to which management communications and reinforces organizational goals

- The extent to which employees accept and work toward these goals

- The extent to which key success factors are understood in the work force

- The values senior management wants employees to support

- Management systems that influence employee behaviour

- The communication processes used

- Levels of employee satisfaction and acceptance of current programs and policies.

One technique for evaluating a company's culture that we have used successfully in several corporate environments, including utilities, which captures this type of data, is a Communications, Values, and Rewards review, which I will describe later.

Programs

Major O&M functional areas and procedures that implement corporate policies must be consistent with those policies, yet go a step beyond and describe how those policies are to be implemented. Examples of major programs include maintenance management, outage management, human resources management, training, fuels management, capital budgeting, and regulatory affairs.

Programs should identify what is to be accomplished and what are the guiding factors in attaining those goals. Needless detail should be discouraged, and needless proscription should be eliminated, yet programs should be specific enough to minimize confusion. For example, there should be a clear linkage between the maintenance work decision process and the manpower resource requirements necessary to complete the work.

There needs to be ongoing monitoring of work effectiveness as well as efficiency. Furthermore, there should be a periodic assessment of the contribution that programs such as the maintenance program amke to the furtherance of higher level corporate goals.

Where appropriate, room for reasonable and informed decision-making should be maintained. What we often find, especially in the nuclear area, is complicated set of procedures written by one group for use by a different group within the organization. All too often, the writers of the procedures are contracted by the organization and emphasize form over substance.

All procedures must be readable enough so that those expected to use them understand what is meant, and can infact use them. And, maintenance personnel must receive sufficient training so that those procedures that are available are, in fact, used. Having procedures that are not used is worse than not having any procedures in the first place.

Processes

Finally, appropriate managment processes, consistent with the desired corporate culture, should be maintained to serve as the glue to hold together management policies, people, and various programs. Management by objectives, management by walking around, and management by exception all have their place. But only by managing from the top down while being sensitive to bottom-up concerns will operational effectiveness be maintained and improved.

Each executive, manager, and supervisor has his/her own management style that he/she brings to the table in leading the organization.

While no one style is particularly better than another for all applications, it is important to be sensitive to the systems in use within a particular organization to ensure that they are, in fact, complementary, and not at odds with one another.

When a utility strives to manage for operational effectiveness, there are several fundamental considerations to keep in mind. First of all, the goals and objectives set up to support the nuclear program must be consistent with higher level corporate goals and objectives. Too often focused programs can lose sight of the forest for the trees and actually end up working against corporate goals.

Because operations is an ongoing process, whatever system for managing operational effectiveness must be disciplined and systematic. A one-shot, quickie improvement program is like cramming for an exam. It helps you pass the exam, or a regulatory evaluation, but it doesn't result in real, long-term, sustainable improvements. One-time improvements also do little to improve a plant's contribution to the utility's competitive postioning. Only decisions based on sound detailed analyses will last.

No nuclear program operates in isolation. It is supported by many functional areas not formally tied to the nuclear program. It also competes with these functions for scarce company resources such as money, people, and time. A review process of nuclear operations needs to include these functions to at least the extent to which they interact with the nuclear program. It also need to be senstive to the overall resource constraints that the company faces.

Nuclear operations draws more than its share of attention from interested outsiders. Whatever programs are implemented must give careful consideration to the reaction, and influence of regulators, environmental groups, and the public in general.

Perhaps the most important group to keep in mind when initiating a nuclear management effectiveness program are employees. ALmost every improvement program will require some reorganization in the initial stages. This can be very disruptive and disturbing to employees and should be dealt with by providing timely, straightforward, and honest communications about the purpose for and expected results from the program.

RIGHTSIZING

If you the make the decision to work toward improving nuclear operational effectiveness, then you must pay attention to your staff. Policies, people, programs, and processes are of little value unless you have the right people with the right skills doing the right things.

Management's challenge when seeking to improve or justify the current staffing situation in the nuclear or any other organization ensure that staff size fits business requirements and that any changes made are sustainable. Arbitrary staff adjustments do not match staff changes to business requirements. Staff adjustments identified by "rightsizing" do.

"Rightsizing" balances staffing changes with work requirement chanhes. It eliminates activities and work before eliminating associated positions, and identifies needed changes in the staffing mix. All departments do not grow at the same rate. That is why it is important to look at the staffing mix and make additions or reductions in a careful, studied manner. What's more, "rightsizing" identifies opportunities to redeploy staff and resources from one area in the company to another.

As a function such as nuclear oprations matures, it naturally takes on more and more nonessential or noncore activities. The "rightsizing" process evaluates all activities of a particular job or function and reassigns or eliminates those that do not support the function's main mission. Resources are thus allocated only to performing those activities to the company and the division. "Rightsizing" also helps redesign individual jobs to make them more rewarding to the employee while they become more productive for the organization.

Also, and very importantly, "rightsizing" helps adjust staff function and the associated philosophy of management. Because "rightsizing" reduces levels of control and pushes accountability further down the organization chart, the staff function is no longer needed as a watchdog to control and coordinate disparate functions. Instead, the staff role becomes that of a counselor, providing service and advice to subordinates without a heavy, controlling hand. Furthermore, a change in management philosophy is initiated, making it more oriented to market needs. Without these important changes to company or division management, the productivity gains acheived through "rightsizing" will not be maintained.

After a utility or division has gone through "rightsizing", the resulting organization structure needs to be placed on a rational basis. "Rightsizing" recommendations help make organizations more responsive to their markets and able to respond more quickly to changes in the external environment. This is acheived by clearing up lines of communications, strengthing accountability of actions and decisions at all levels of the organization, and eliminating extraneous levels of hierarchy.

This increased flexiblity and responsiveness also makes many strategic plans more viable. A sleek, lean operation is more likely to have success with aggresive strategies, such as developing new markets. The lack of bureaucracy allows the company to manoeuvre within the competitive environment.

"Rightsizing" involves six analyses: activity analysis; functional analysis; structural analysis; communications, values, and rewards analysis; and issue analysis; all performed against a backdrop of risk/benefit analysis. The degree to which each of these functions is used varies according to the objectives of the individual rightsizing project.

Two other ingredients are also necessary: a judiciously pragmatic attitude and a good dose of common sense.

Issue Analysis

Early in the "rightsizing" effort, the utility and consultant teams should perform an issue analysis. Issue analysis identifies and assesses the internal and external issues relevant to organizatonal effectiveness. This includes competitive, business, regulatory, and cultural issues. All of these factors will alter, to varying degrees, how you interpret and act upon the results of various "rightsizing" analyses.

Issue analysis is important because every utility operates in a different environment and therefore has very different needs. A large utility with multiple nuclear plants will face different issues than a small, regional utility that only burns coal.

Internal issues need to be looked at. The study team should identify internal variables such as management styles and processes, corporate culture, staff concerns and attitudes, and communications effectiveness. These issues will shed some light on why inefficiencies may exist, how and where changes should be made, and how the recommended changes will be received.

Activity Analysis

Activity Analysis is the cornerstone of most "rightsizing" studies. Cresap's Activity Analysis system allows a ompany to determine the current state of affairs within its organization in a rigorous, comprehensive manner. Activities Analysis can be used to look at an entire company or a specific section, such as nuclear operations. Results can be broken down along almost any predetrmined organizational level. It helps provide a quantifiable database of information that tell the participating company what activities are performed across an organization, how much time is devoted to each activity, what the associated human resource costs are, and how employees value their work.

One thing that makes the Activity Analysis system unique is the level of detail able to be captured. Surveys are administered to all of the employees to identify, from a comprehensive, tailored list of utility activities, those which they perform, then to break down their time across the specific tasks which they perform. This information is coupled with employee compensation data to develop reports of function costs and unit activities at all levels of the organization.

The reports indicate duplication of activities, overlapping functions and roles, fragmented activities and functions, overqualification of some employees for the activities they perform, the underresourcing of strategically important functions, and the variability in costs of performing similar activities across the organization.

The Activity Analysis survey process can also be used to solicit employee suggestions and ideas. This is an important feature because it allows the employees to become part of the eventual solution. Suggestions for cost containment or cost reduction, efficiency improvements, and process enhancements often result in significant improvements.

The same method can be use to evaluate internal service levels. Survey participants are questioned about the current levels of internal

staff support they receive and how the levels should be adjusted.

Functional Analysis

Once a utility determines what activities are performed at various levels of the organization and at what cost, it needs to look at how functions are being performed. Functional analysis addresses what specific units do and why they do it. The analysis determines how well the unit performs the functions and whether or not another unit could perform them more efficiently. Finally, Functional Analysis evaluates the unit's contribution to overall goals and objectives, and whether these can be better met in another way.

Functional analysis looks at a unit's work drivers, or what causes the unit to perform the tasks it does, and how valid these drivers are. Sometimes drivers change or disappear, but associated tasks do not move accordingly. Functional analysis also looks at processes and service standards or levels at which the task is performed. Often a less precise or less frequent product (such as a monthly report vs. a weekly report) will satisfy users. While reducing considerably the work load of the provider. Finally, if the work driver and service standard analysis fails to yield potential work reductions, functional analysis examines the processes by which work is done, to identify opportunities for simplifying or streamlining.

Structural Analysis

Structural analysis examines the company's organization and how it is configured. The object of structural analysis is to identify opportunities to change the company's organization that will improve the efficiency and effectiveness of the activities performed. These opportunities include consolidation of functions and positions, improved spans of control, reduced supervisory levels, improved communications within and between functions and units, and increased flexibility.

Structural analysis addresses questions regarding organizational arrangements, such as:

- What are the strengths and weaknesses of the current organizations?

- How well do these organizations support corporate objectives?

- What management philosophies have driven the development of the current management hierarchy structure?

- Are spans of control and management levels appropriate?

- Are activities and functions grouped in the most logical and effective way?

- What consolidation or other reorganiation options should be considered?

- Is consolidation or decentralization of functions desirable?

- What are the formal and informal relationships and communications channels

among the functional units and managers
within the organization?

- What criteria should be used to select
  the optimal organizational alignment?

- Are accountabilities consistent with
  organizaional reporting relationships?

Although structural analysis can result in
significant organizational change, it need
not always do so. This type of analysis seeks
to maximize the "doers" in relation to the
"guiders and coordinators".

Communications, Values, And Rewards Analysis

Communications, Values, and Rewards analysis
(CVR) seeks to identify the corporate culture
of the organization being reviewed. Culture
has a major effect on how work gets done, and
on the quality and timeliness of that work.
It's the pot in which people issues boil.
Knowing the culture of a company or a group
within a company helps in developing recommendations that are more easily implemented and
in identifying situations in which the existing
culture is preventing the needed changes and
needs to be changed itself.

CVR Analysis is a survey-based system which is
used to assess the following:

- The extent to which mangement communi-
  cates and reinforces organizational
  goals

- The extent to which employees accept and
  work toward these goals.

- The extent to which key success factors
  are understood in the workforce

- The values that senior management wants
  employees to support

- Management systems that influence employee
  behaviour

- The communications processes used

- Levels of employee satisfaction and
  acceptance of current programs and
  policies.

Risk/Benefit Analysis

We realize that almost no change comes without
some risk. And, as circumstances shift, so do
organizations' willingness to accept risk. In
"rightsizing", all recommendations are evaluated on a risk/benefit basis. Risk/benefit
analysis assesses the operational effectiveness
opportunities identified and evaluates the risk
to the organization associated with implementing them. These opportunities are rated on a
scale of risks so that opportunities can be evaluated equally according to the company's
specific needs. For example, a utility in a
reasonably strong position may determine that
it can make relatively modest changes to its
staff makeup and organization without noticeable loss of service and therefore little risk.
On the other hand, the same company in a more
serious situation may need to make more substantial changes to its staff makeup and organization, and contract out for support in peak
periods, but at a greater risk.

SUMMARY

Performance is not a direct function of the
amount of resources available. Good nuclear
plant performance is the result of a complex
set of variables, many of which are responsive
to management iniatives. The four-step framework for Managing For Operational Effectiveness
can help management identify opportunities for
improvemant within their organizations, and
could help improve operational effectiveness
and performance. By identifying and measuring
O&M performance in the areas of effectiveness
and efficiency, and comparing these to planned
values, both efficiency and effectiveness can
be improved.

What all of this boils down to is that effectiveness in nuclear operations is not a technical issue. It is not a resource issue. It is
a management issue. Management must learn to
take responsiblity for maintaining or improving the quality level of nuclear O&M within
its utility just as it has had to take responsibility for construction projects.

MANAGEMENT IS THE KEY VARIABLE AFFECTING
PLANT PREFORMANCE.

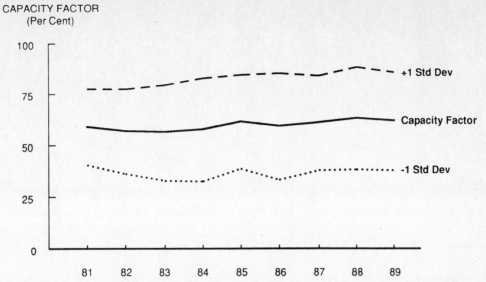

Fig 1   There is no marked increase in nuclear plant performance and manpower the past nine years

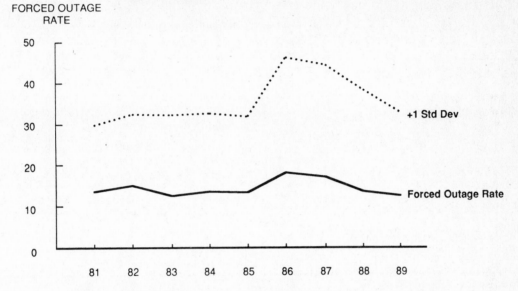

Fig 2   Nuclear plant forced outage rates have not improved in the past nine years

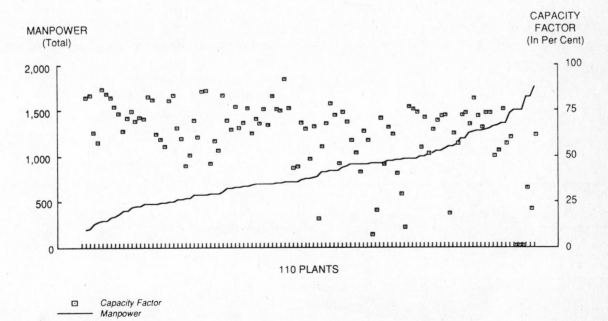

Fig 3   There is no correlation between plant performance and manpower (1987—1989)

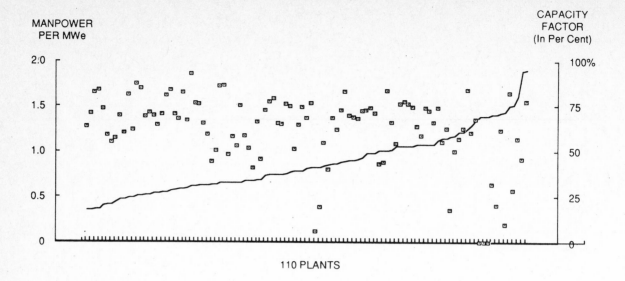

Fig 4   There is no correlation between plant performance and manpower
per MWe (1987–1989)

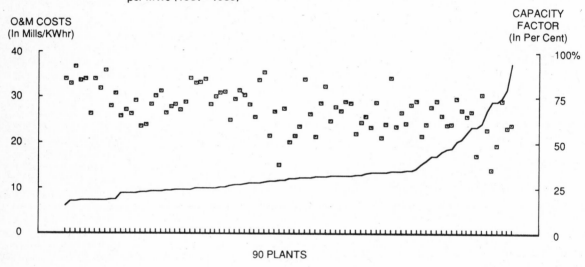

Fig 5   Spending more money on operation and management does not
always mean better performance (1987–1989)

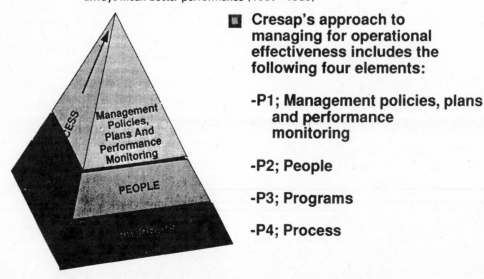

■ **Cresap's approach to managing for operational effectiveness includes the following four elements:**

-P1; Management policies, plans and performance monitoring

-P2; People

-P3; Programs

-P4; Process

Fig 6   Four-step approach to managing for operational effectiveness

C409/035

Total quality at source

A C CHIANDONE
Westinghouse Energy Systems Incorporated, Knutsford, Cheshire

SYNOPSIS The Total Quality at Source philosophy is based on optimizing the effectiveness of people in achieving ZERO-DEFECT results.

By way of introduction, what I am trying to do in this paper is to share a philosophy of what, I have grown to perceive, it takes to get people to perform to the very best of their abilities and thereby achieve the best results they can.

In the examples I shall describe I have played an instrumental role since it has become my belief that any job can always be done better provided that the people doing it can themselves become convinced that they can do better. Clearly there are many ideas on how to do this. The philosophy that I am presenting in this paper is based on my own experience, where I have both participated and observed it being applied; its effectiveness may be judged by the results.

During the greater part of my professional life I always dedicated my attention to the technical aspect without taking into serious consideration the human engineering aspect. After 35 years of industrial activities, with more than half spent in nuclear, I have come to the conclusion that to address the human aspect, communication, motivation and teamwork are the essential ingredients to achieve quality and consequently productivity, because quality means productivity. In nuclear, without quality there is no acceptable production.

Quality means meeting all requirements. The best Quality means doing it right the first time. Quality goes in at source; neither repeated inspections nor voluminous records can add to the quality of a product. Getting it right the first time gives you the highest quality product, minimises inspection time, avoids (costly) repair cycles and maximises the possibility to meet the schedule. The best quality assurance system in the world, endorsed by the best management, implemented by the best QA organisation, will not produce the best results unless the workers actually doing the job are inspired and dedicated to do the best job they can, striving in conjunction with their fellow workers, as a team, in pursuit of the common goal.

What do I mean by TQS (Total Quality at Source)? Very simply it is the motivation of the individual, through good communication, leading to the collective development of a teamwork approach in pursuit of the best job that can be performed by everybody working together. The best job of course means completing the operation, a weld for example, fully meeting all requirements without the need for any repair.

Over a considerable period of time, I developed the practice of listening, trying to understand what the speaker is saying, what he means, but most of all what he thinks. That starts the real communication process.

We have to communicate in order to motivate ourselves and others as well as to build and keep alive the required teamwork; we must perceive what is going on in order to improve our knowledge and to develop sound professional experience.

Once good communication has been established, the means to motivate others are at hand. What motivates people? Well, reward; that means money. With money, the individual can fulfil his basic needs. What else? Self esteem, peer recognition, the satisfaction of doing a good job. Is motivation of the individual enough by itself to ensure a good job is done? No, of course it's not. What is needed is for all the people involved with the job to be similarly motivated, and further, for them all to recognise that in order to do the best job it is necessary to understand and recognise the need to work closely together as a team - that way they have the best chance to do the best job they can.

The psychology of teamwork is widely written about and understood - look into any really successful company and you will almost certainly find a very dominant element of good teamwork.

To demonstrate how effective the TQS philosophy can be, I am going to talk about the fabrication of the Reactor Pressure Vessel for the Sizewell B Nuclear Plant.

In 1985 I was appointed by Westinghouse to follow the fabrication of the Sizewell B RPV - this vessel having been ordered directly by the CEGB. Strictly speaking my responsibility was to monitor that the specification requirements were met during fabrication, however, I made it my objective to work closely with the fabricator to try to help to achieve a quality of welding such that no repairs would be required, i.e. ZERO-DEFECT welding.

In order to pursue the TQS objective on the Sizewell B RPV it was necessary for me to achieve integration with the shop personnel and develop good communication at all levels in order to try to encourage motivation and teamwork philosophy. A specific team for the Sizewell B RPV welding was formed. Individualized responsibilities were assigned and everybody became convinced that with a common participative effort it was possible to achieve the ambitious objective of ZERO-DEFECT welding.

One of the operations in the fabrication of RPV is the manual buttering of a safe-end which must be performed by two qualified welders, one on one side and one on the other side of a dividing plate (see Figure 1). They were to weld half a portion each according to a qualified procedure, with the specified equipment and welding material and in compliance with the applicable QA System. Before starting the welding operation I carefully checked the qualification of the welders, the calibration of the equipment, and the material. I spoke with the two welders and I noticed that one of them was emotionally affected, he was stressed and unable to relax which made me somewhat preoccupied, but there were no official reason not to allow him to start welding. Also, I was new at the factory, I did not yet know the people as I would have liked to. The welding operation was performed, and afterwards we found that the fusion line of the half portion performed by the stressed welder had some flaws and had to be repaired. The other welder performed a perfect job. I made an investigation and found out that the subject welder had some personal problems that day and was therefore stressed and emotionally affected and consequently unable to fully concentrate on his job.

I should add that in accordance with the requirements of the Sizewell B Contract, all such operations had been fully validated, procedures, equipment, operators and all. However, this case demonstrates that the attitude of mind of the welder, when he actually does the job, is of fundamental importance in determining the actual result that is achieved.

The QA Systems were implemented but the welder was not in the psychological condition to perform his job to the best of his capabilities. Emotions can be impacted according to how we react with the boss, with a colleague, a friend or anybody else. We are human and should try to have a better understanding of the people that we are working with and improve our communication in order to minimize the impact of these adverse situations. This was the only one of the eight safe-end nozzles which required repair.

When I started to work in the nuclear industry in the late 1960's, obviously the RPVs were not built as today; the capacity of the material suppliers was not developed to produce the required big parts of a RPV as they are today, for example a bottom head was made in six pieces, a spherical part and five petals welded together (See Figure 2).

Today the technology allows us to have one single part. I remember the very wide angle design of the welds. Well, that design was against quality because we have to consider that the shrinkage of a wide weld is detrimental to the weld joint. I have always been convinced that adequate investment should be made in order to develop welding heads capable of producing very narrow gap welds. Today most of the welds are narrow gap and are performed with an automated welding head. One way of achieving quality is, of course, to invest money for automated and sophisticated equipment and very skilled personnel and expert supervision. But I am convinced that with the most sophisticated equipment and the best skilled personnel but without communication, motivation and teamwork the desired quality cannot be achieved. We have to consider the import-

ance of motivation, the importance of human engineering. We are all human and consequently affected by various circumstances during our professional as well as our private lives.

The TQS philosophy is to prevent any deficiencies and is focused on the psychological as well as the professional and technical preparation and particularly the high motivation of all involved personnel. An analytical preparation must be made of the required machines, welding sets, tools and control instruments, which should be primarily used for an integrated in-process control system. In order to maintain the motivating effort and stimulate the participation, the individual quality performance as well as the quality oriented ideas should be quantified and rewarded.

Having strived to produce TQS, i.e. ZERO-DEFECT welding, we must then perform the NDE (Nondestructive Examination) in order to demonstrate and record the absence of defects and confirm that compliance with the applicable Codes and Requirements has been achieved.

Another significant example - I have many examples but I am trying to present the ones that may have future applicability - was the last weld of the two subassemblies, the upper subassembly and the lower subassembly which are joined by the weld B/C (See Figure 3).

The longer portion of the weld is performed from the outside surface. To perform this weld the fabricator developed a very reliable piece of equipment. It is performed with a welding head equipped of electronic sensors. The sensors control the position of the welding electrode from the sides of the weld chamfer and from the bottom. In order to have this reference accurate, the weld chamfer must be machined and it is strongly recommended never to have the sensors controling on uneven ground surfaces. Operators must constantly check if the electrode is in the required position. For that purpose there is a spotlight projected to the edge of the chamfer and gives the information for any eventual required manual correction and any possible uncontrolled movement. When the welding from the OD is completed the required gouging and grinding on the ID weld chamfer is performed with a mechanized stone. A similar welding head is set, all the required controls are carried out and the weld is completed.

It is to be considered that these big parts weigh about 300 metric tons, 600,000 pounds, and there are many handling and alignment difficulties. During welding some manual corrections are required. The method is very reliable because the electronic sensors position the welding head and the spotlight demonstrates to the operator the welding head real position. Problems may arise after gouging and grinding, as irregularities may be generated and the spotlight reference may no longer be reliable. When I inspected the ID weld chamfer I realized that the objective of quality at source was jeopardized. With the irregularities of the weld chamfer the sensors would not have worked as required and we would have faced exposure to defects. An urgent meeting was called with the shop manager, welding experts and affected personnel and an adequate programme was established in order to compensate for the weld chamfer irregularities. First of all we eliminated the sensor, secondly we established that, instead of working three shifts of 8 hours, 24 hours per day, we would work only two shifts of 8 hours. The welding supervisor was assigned full time to advise the operator and all the required corrections were done manually, and the weld was completed. All welding activities were checked and when the weld was finished, before the NDE, I was fully confident that it would be another successful ZERO-DEFECT weld - it was.

Suffice to say, during the last two and a half years of vessel fabrication, no defects were detected in any welds for the Sizewell B RPV. In other words, no repair was necessary. That is TQS.

Of course technology moves on. However, even with the further optimisation of the welding technology, it will still be necessary to apply the TQS process in order to arrive at the desired results - ZERO-DEFECT welding.

Here I would like to add a word of caution regarding what we might term lack of control over communication', or failure to adequately control the operator environment.

When I used to qualify a welder I developed the technique of observing him discreetly from afar. Once I was convinced he understood what he had to do, I walked away from him, out of his sight and, as far as he was concerned, left him to do the job by himself. Of course I was never really out of sight, I was in fact watching how he went about the job without him being aware that I was watching.

This is very important. The worst thing you can do when a weld is in process is to distract the operator. We have all seen the all too frequent groups of visitors, VIPs making their shop tours, some of you have probably been amongst them. What do they do, they all stop and try to observe whatever operations are in progress, which is not easy, since usually without actually sitting in the operator's place, there is very little if anything to see!

What is the impact on the operator? Potentially very bad. Just think if you yourself were performing a difficult operation in your home, like replacing a light fitting, and you were continually distracted by groups of neighbours coming in to watch you, would you do your best job? I think it very unlikely.

The solution, either keep out all 'visitors', VIP or not, or totally enclose the operator and his process such that he is shielded from well meaning onlookers.

I have another example. 100 percent surveillance during inspection - say a UT examination - ie an inspector is always looking over the shoulder of the operator who is reading the signals on the screen; how motivated in terms of doing his best job according to his skills and qualification do you think the operator would be? After all, the onus is not fully on him, there is somebody else looking over his shoulder - wouldn't there be a tendency for the operator to start to rely on the other person.

TQS requires that you provide the best environment for the man doing the job and you charge him with, and he accepts, the responsibility to do his job

in the best way he knows how. Then you let him do his job, with minimal interference.

In the nuclear industry we work with some of the most sophisticated technologies known to man, however; I can't help but remember when, as a small boy, helping my father to do a job at home, where there was a problem to solve, my father said "we shall succeed". Of course there was already good communication between us, like between most fathers and sons. That 'we', when I was just a small boy, and my father appeared almost 'god-like', so stimulated my motivation because 'we' were going to do this job together, that I gave him my best attention and 'we', with optimum teamwork, succeeded in doing a good job. I actually remember, to my surprise - and my father's too, that I anticipated his needs and put into his hands the required tool at the right moment.

That is motivation, and in the good memory of my father I would like to suggest that we think of using the pronoun 'I' in order to motivate ourselves and 'we' in order to respect, embrace and motivate others.

That all happened of course many more years ago than I care to remember. It was a very powerful lesson in the 'people' aspect of what it takes to get a job done well.

During my subsequent career, I am ashamed to say that I did not always remember that lesson as I should have. Caught up in the challenge of the technology, I had for a long time a tendency to instruct a welder in what he had to do, to check that he was qualified and had the right paper work and equipment. Now I think differently. Technology alone cannot achieve the best result - it is the combination of people and technology that matters, and at the end of the day, when the technology is proven, it is the people, or to use the modern term 'human engineering' factor which can only ensure the best result. This is being increasingly recognised throughout the Nuclear Industry, where man-machine, man-man and man-himself interfaces are receiving their rightful consideration and attention.

People remain the key application of

- COMMUNICATION
- MOTIVATION
- TEAMWORK

which, when all blended together, can give you the TQS result.

In conclusion, I would hope that after sharing with you today these ideas and thoughts, you will agree that not only is TQS achievable, but that for the nuclear industry, if we are to meet the requirements, stay within estimated costs and work to programme, it is the only way ahead.

Although in themselves Communication, Motivation and Teamwork are relatively simple concepts, they are the building blocks which when put together can provide us with a really powerful tool with which we can all achieve TOTAL QUALITY AT SOURCE.

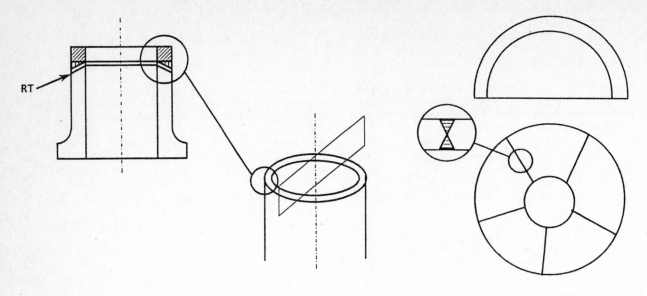

RT

Fig 1   Safe end

Fig 2   Bottom head

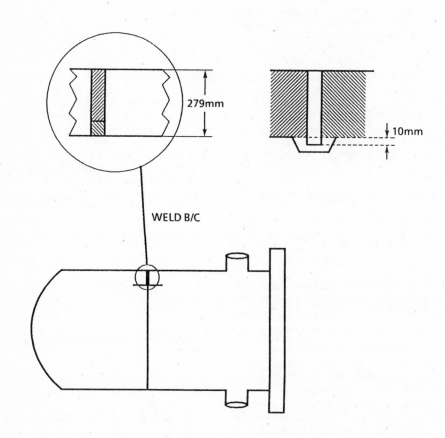

279mm

10mm

WELD B/C

Fig 3   Lower and upper sub-assemblies

C409/001

Taking account of human factors for interface assessment and design in monitoring automated systems

J-F MUSSO, Y SICARD and **M MARTIN**
CORYS SA, Grenoble, France

SYNOPSIS Optimum adequation between control means and the operator capacities is sought for to achieve computerization of Man-Machine interfaces. Observation of the diagnosis activity of populations of operators in situation on simulators enables design criteria to be defined which are well-suited to the characteristics of the tasks with which they are confronted. This observation provides an assessment of the interfaces from the standpoint of the graphic layer, of the Human behaviour induced by the Machine and of the nature of the interaction between these two systems. This requires an original approach dialectically involving cognitive psychology, dynamic management of the knowledge bases (artificial intelligence) in a critical industrial control and monitoring application.

1 INTRODUCTION

In all industrial processes, the present trend in control room design is towards ever-increasing computerization. In the nuclear field, switching from desks to graphic imagery enables the interface design to be rethought, with respect to the operators' task. In spite of the high degree of automation of the installations, the operators still occupy a decider's position in many situations. Interface ergonomics design has therefore not only to take account of the dynamic aspects inherent in continuous processes, but also to define the operator's requirements and take them into account in order to give him improved help in terms of efficiency of performance and prevention of human error. To this end, a series of interface comparisons has been undertaken. These studies have made it possible to qualify operator requirements with regard to the envisaged situations and have enabled the associated design criteria to be defined.

2 PURPOSE - METHODOLOGY

2.1 PRESENTATION

A series of interface comparisons was undertaken in collaboration with Electricité De France on the Chemical and Volume Control System of a 900 MW PWR Reactor.

This trend tends to take into account the dynamic aspects of information acquisition and processing by the users, i.e. not only training cost and user convenience criteria, but also operator performance efficiency and human error prevention criteria. However the Human Factors study in Man-Machine interfaces must go further than simple performances analysis and look into the question of the internal representation that the operators have of the system's physical reality.

According to these different aspects of interfaces assesment three studies have been developped:
They provide an assessment of the interfaces from the standpoint of the graphic layer, of the Human performance induced by the Machine and of the nature of the interaction between these two systems.
Study one and two proved the necessity of adapting the interface to suit the activity of the operator. With the third one we are devoting our efforts to a systematic approach to decision aids specifications based on operators solving activities analysis.
For this three studies an iterative comparison method was implemented.

2.2 - SIMULATED SYSTEM

System

The use of a simulator enables the problems inherent in studies on actual processes to be overcome (blocking the process...). The interfaces are connected to a numerical simulator of the Chemical and Volume Control System (CVCS) of a 900 MW PWR reactor. The function of this system is to perform control of the primary system volume. The associated Reactor Boron and Water Make-up System (RBWMS) controls the reactivity by boration or dilution.

The numerical model is run on a SUN type 4-110 computer. A desk-type interface is connected to the model via an RS-232 line. The graphic interfaces designed with a graphic editor providing great flexibility of definition, are fitted on a very high resolution (1150*900) 19" colour monitor.

Description of the incidents

The incidents were chosen by EDF on actual cases which caused problems in previous years. It deals with situations which sollicit the "strategic" level of the incident recovery activity and on the other hand present a potential risk for the system as a whole.

1) Break on the letdown line inside the reactor containment downstream from the letdown orifices.

The letdown pressure control closes the valve to keep the pressure constant. The valve controlling the cooling flowrate follows the temperature change so as to keep T = 46°C. The letdown flowrate drops, the sump level rises slowly, whereas the CVCS level will decrease.

2) Break on the charging line between the on-off valve and the check valve.

The charging valve control will compensate for the leak. The flowrate will however increase slowly whereas the pressuriser level drops. The sump level rises slowly.

3) Letdown filter fouling.

In order to maintain the letdown pressure at its nominal value, the control will open the pression valve, until saturation if this occurs. No other parameter is modified.

4) Break on CCS upstream from the non-regenerative heat exchanger

A rapid peak is observed on the cold letdown temperature compensated by the control of valve which opens to reduce the temperature.

2 - 3 EXPERIMENTAL DEVICE

These studies required an interface generation software to be created providing, in addition to the creation of reliable interfaces, the possibility of high-speed specification and modification of the graphic layer which is indispensable to an interface analysis approach. An analysis of interface impact on human actions requires iteratively:

1 - Choice of two opposite mode of information presentation :

choice based on lit erature, empirical observations, or prior analysis (aim of the third study)

2 - population choice, familiarization
3 - process simulation, and graphic definition,
4 - experimental protocol development
5 - prototype operating interface testing,

Observables :

test log : a chronological account setting out he operator's actions, his images choice, the evolution of important parameters of the simulation, the alarms and automatic actions, process caracteristics after actions video recordings (verbal and non verbal protocols) symptom detection, variables monitoring, hypothesis expressing, verification action, incident location...), visual strategy.

6 - comparison of performances for each prototype
Depending on the study qualitative, modeling or stastistic analysis are developped.

7 - definition of subsequent interface design criteria.

3 RESULTS

3.1 - STUDY ONE

We deal first of all with the question of the impact of the

information symbolism and with the breakdown of image. From the information presentation standpoint, one of the imagery is conventional (animated mechanical layout diagram) whereas the second one makes use of the functional symbols introduced by Lind.

Furthermore, the information is organized in the first case page by page, considering the material limits of the circuit, whereas in the second case it meets functional criteria with the possibility of windowing within each image.

In order to have a conventional yardstick, we then produced a desk connected to the same simulation model.

Assesment

Compararison of "topological and "functional" imagery system : 72 incidentals tests (24 for each interfaces, 6 test for each incident) was analysed. As the imagery systems are concerned, the choice of two design approaches (purposely very different) leads us to determine by comparison the criteria inducing a disturbance in the diagnosis activity. The overall performance is assessed by the enumaration of events-unsatisfactory performances. When a test is the object of a major unsatisfactory performance, the diagnostic is wrong or inexistant ; one or more minor unsatisfactory performances delay diagnosis without changing its conclusion.

Unsatisfactory performance	"topological" imagery	"functional" imagery	Desk
Major	25 %	50 %	50 %
Minor	42 %	42 %	25 %
None	33 %	17 %	25 %

In terms of events-unsatisfactory results the performances on the desk are not as good as those observed on the topological graphic interface. They are comparable to those observed for an experimental interface of the "functional" type.

The analysis, notably by an occulo-graphic study enables us to outline the succession of three different phases in the diagnosis. These phases are necessarily looped at different levels. It is however possible to discern three types of pseudo-chronological activity : detection, interpretation, and incident location.

The interfaces tested reflect specific diagnostics qualities of the phases of activity. We extract from this experiment

design criteria for new interfaces. The effective image need to be different for each stage notably by their abstraction level and the presence of aids. Three classes of images were therefore designed and tested.

Design criteria : Task presentation and nature abstraction level

Quick, complete detection will be favoured by a synthesis of all the sensors associated with a function. Our orientation is therefore towards a synthesized presentation with a high abstraction level enabling abnormal drifts to be identified quickly. The system alignment display enables the drift observed on the sensor involved to be identified quickly.

Decision aid image : at this level the requirements are mixed : the abstraction level required to formulate hypotheses is high, whereas the system has to be presented in more concrete form. For the control image all the components must be presented in detail.

Windowing techniques avoid overloading the screen and judiciously meet the operator's requirements. The optimum number of items of information accessible in an image cannot be defined as such, for the information density depends on the nature of the task associated with the image.

On this basis a new interface comprised of three images (detection, interpretation, action) which the subject can call up according to his needs has been created.

3.2 - STUDY 2

The second study is an extension of the first one. The previous performances on the desk are compared with those on the new interface.

Overall analysis

Looking for factors influencing the behaviourist variables led us to proceed with different variance analyses and to look for correlations between the different variables. The following factors are studied :

- type of imagery (desk, three-image interface)
- type of incident
- detection value (full or not)
- interpretation value (correct or not).

The dependent variables on which the influence of these factors can be exerted are :

- time required to identify the problem
- time required to solve the problem fully
- time devoted to each image (monitoring, decision-making, action)
- detection value (full or not)
- interpretation value (correct or not).

The following hypotheses are tested :

1 - Impact of the type of imagery

This study deals basically with the possible impact of the type of imagery on performance. We chose to study its effect on the total problem-solving time, which we expect to see decrease for the new imagery.

- A variance analysis involving the influence of the type of imagery on the time required for the operators to accurately identify and locate the incident shows the real favorable impact of the imagery systems on the operator's performances ($p < .0001$).

2 - Impact of the type of incidents

Does the use of different types of incidents enable this global result to be modified, the impact of the imagery varying according to the type of incident ?

- The study of the interaction between the type of imagery and the type of incident is negative : the impact of the imagery does not vary significantly according to the type of incident.

In addition, the total time is statistically not a function of the type of incident, and yet the number of symptoms differs greatly from one incident to another.

In incidents where numerous symptoms are present, an extensive automatic control takes place the logic of which has to be understood by the operator for him to be able to discern the causal relations of the problems connected with the incident. Incidents with few symptoms on the other hand require hypotheses to be made in a broader context. This could explain why the total time required to solve the problem is the same.

We were thus able to ascertain that, despite their essential differences, the incidents were all demanding from the cognitive problem-solving standpoint and met the choice criteria for experimentation well.

3 - Impacts of the quality and duration of the different phases

The largest sources of variability now have to be looked for. Seeking to achieve impact of the imageries does not only involve increasing performance but also stabilizing it.

- The total solving time is not a function of the quality of detection.

This shows that the new imagery has considerably improved detection from the qualitative standpoint. The value of the detection is therefore for this imagery no longer a critical factor determining performance.

- The total problem-solving time depends massively on the quality of interpretation ($p < .0001$).

Interpretation thus remains an extremely variable critical factor at the outcome of this study and one which is therefore not enhanced stability-wise by the new imagery, the impact of the value of interpretation on performance being moreover very great as this variance analysis also shows.

From the quantitative standpoint however, the imagery cancelled out the effect of the duration of this phase on performance. It should therefore be envisaged that this work be continued taking the operator's needs into account to a greater extent in order to help them in their interpretation and maybe lead them to make a more systematic investigation of the hypotheses.

- The total problem-solving time is correlated at .003 to the time taken in the action phase.

From the quantitative standpoint, only the duration of the action phase is linked to the total duration. We therefore note for this phase a variability problem as far as time is concerned which significantly influences the total problem-solving time. The impact of the imagery on the duration of the action phase is not significant. A specific study on this imagery therefore needs to be set up. Unlike the previous point, the problem here seems to be linked not with the ability to use knowledge but directly with the availability of knowledge. This problem therefore seems to hinge more on training requirements than on software aid requirements.

This study proved the necessity of adapting the interface to suit the activity of the operator. This requires a systematic approach to decision aid, the aim being to provide the operator not with a diagnosis but with all the elements he needs to make the right diagnosis.

Analysis by phase of activity

On the basis of the verbal protocol we designate each phase as :

Detection : Complete (every symptoms detected)
Incomplete (main symptoms detected)
Late (some main symptoms are detected during the interpretation phase)
Guided (help must be given in order to continue)

Decision : Complete (find the problem and identify the componants)
Incomplete (find the problem)
Incorrect (Doesn't find the problem)

Location : Accurate (Locate precisely the problem)
Inaccurate (Locate the problem zone)
Partial (Locate part of the problem)
Non-existent (no location)

Taking all the incidents together, the performances of each phase of activity are improved.

- For monitoring, all the detections are complete and fast.
- The interpretations of symptoms made on the decision aid image are more seldom incorrect.The range of hypotheses envisaged is considerably reduced when the operators use this image. No hypotheses are formulated in contradiction with what has been detected and identified.
The number of accurate locations is high.

3.3 STUDY 3

This study is designed to test the impact of different aid systems on the quality and modalities of the interpretation phase. A preliminary study presented here aims to determine operator decision aid system requirements.

We took the data provided by study n° 2 but with a different methodological approach based on the study of cases and of interpretation and explanation techniques. The object of this preliminary study is on the one hand to study the procedure according to which the information provided by the interface is used, and on the other hand to establish the resulting aid requirements, and finally to set up the experiment which will enable the impact of these aid systems on the solving processes to be analyzed.

Phases of activity		Desk %	Imagery %
Detection	Complete	66	92
	Incomplete	10	0
	Late	8	8
	Guided	16	0
Decision	Complete	25	83
	Incomplete	25	12
	Incorrect	50	5
Location	Accurate	50	87
	Inaccurate	25	0
	Partial	25	13
	Non-existent	0	0

Fig 1   Qualitative analysis of performance for the different tasks

The strategy adopted by the operators is determined by studying the order in which the symptoms are taken into account, and the connections the operators note between these symptoms. This naturally only constitutes an approximation proper to a preliminary study, and the subsequent stages of this work will require objective criteria to be drawn up enabling the strategies used to be determined in finer detail.

This detailed study of the order in which the symptoms are taken into account enabled us to construct operator strategy modellings which are presented here in simplified and schematic form, processing being parallel in reality.

Characteristics of the different models

Model n° 1 : first formulation of a hypothesis

Schematic description

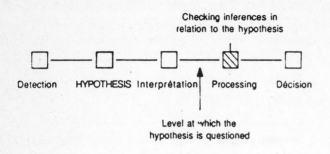

Checking inferences in
relation to the hypothesis

Detection — HYPOTHESIS — Interprétation — Processing — Décision

Level at which the
hypothesis is questioned

Characteristics :

This model transcribes an intuitive type of problem-solving, based on deep knowledge (experience, training, analog processing). The hypotheses formulated belong to a predefined register and can only be questioned very late in the course of this type of problem-solving process. This model covers a rigid procedure.

The operator very quickly follows a line of interpretation : the detection phase merely serves the purpose of giving a global impression which he ties in with deep knowledge (recently encountered incident, current incident...).

The operator very quickly follows to the decision-making image. He details portions of the inference diagram, but tie all the events in with his initial idea.

Two points should be underlined for this type of activity

- the initial idea may be right or wrong. If it is right, the time-saving is considerable. If it is wrong, a hypothesis has to be reformulated and the symptoms read under the light of a new hypothesis. This method may be either very favourable or detrimental.

In addition it is difficult to determine what motivates the hypotheses.

- The deep knowledge may be relevant or not. This type of model is used by very experienced, very intuitive operators, and also by operators who are not.
It nevertheless remains that this type of activity is random. It is difficult to explain it from a general standpoint as it is based on deep knowledge, the individual's experience. Its frequency in the tests is far from negligible.

Model n° 2 : construction of a complete inference graf

Schematic description

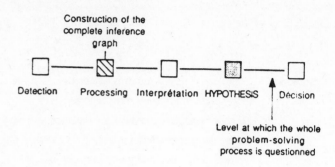

Construction of the
complete inference
graph

Detection — Processing — Interprétation — HYPOTHESIS — Décision

Level at which the whole
problem-solving
process is questionned

Characteristics :

This model transcribes a very rational problem-solving mode, based on exhaustive knowledge of the process. Unlike the previous model, the behaviour described here is very adaptative.

The construction of the inference graph seems to be performed in stages. These stages have a chronological reason but also seem to have a unity of meaning : at the end of each stage the operator specifies the incident progressively, and constructs an interpretation. These stages lead to summaries which enable the memory load to be decreased, but which at the same time reduce the amount of information. If the operator asks himself a question outside the scope of the interpretation which he has progressively established, he then no longer possesses the elements he needs to give the answer. His inability to answer upsets him to the extent that he questions what he has already established. To answer this question he has to start constructing the graph again modifying the interpretation. This phenomenon may explain why it takes as long to formulate a second hypothesis as it did to formulate the first one.

Determining the stages is based partly on a logic, functional or even topological vision of the system. As the graph is seldom fully determined, this more often than not involves juxtaposition of parts of the graph. These parts are chosen empirically according to their estimated importance on the basis of deep knowledge. This type of activity is apparently the one which is the most commonly used in the course of the tests.

Model n° 3 : logical approach

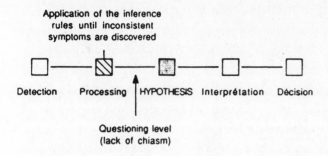

**Questioning level
(lack of chiasm)**

Characteristics :

This model describes a logical type of problem-solving by systematic application of causal rules, applied directly to the symptoms. This logic consists in following the circuit (importance of topology). The operator concentrates on the sensors. The actuators are only invoked as a cause or consequence of a change in a sensor status. Unlike the previous model, the aim is not to draw up a complete inference graph but to highlight an inconsistency (or several inconsistencies). The study of these chiasms determines a field of hypothesis. The approach then becomes inductive.

As a complete graph is not drawn up here to solve the problem, the operator seldom makes a full, systematic investigation of the situation. This is liable to give rise to errors and may prevent double faults from being discovered.

Assessment

A first result consists in showing the diversity of the processes and inferences implemented by the operators. Yet the impact of a software
aid system should differ according to the problem-solving process developed by the operator.

Each model developed to take account of the different types of process provides indications of interface modifications or specifications (software aids). We can thus sum up the elements which result from this preliminary study :

Model n° 1

This type of activity is based mainly on deep knowledge. It results in a considerable time-saving when the hypothesis formulated is suitable, but this is random. Modification of this type of activity involves training in terms of deep knowledge of the process. Software aids should not aim to eradicate this type of activity as the potential use of short-cuts and intuitions is one of the advantages man has over the machine.

However, all the relationships must appear clearly and the most likely hypotheses be highlighted to play on the overall impression. This means that the interface has to present the operator with summaries, comparisons of information, even if the latter is displayed elsewhere. In the images currently used, some decision-aid graphic systems play this role, for example side-by-side presentation of the temperatures in the heat exchanger 01mt/19mt. Comparison of this information directs the operator very quickly in the right direction to formulate his hypothesis.

Model n° 2

Training aims to establish "rational" processes which follow this model. In reality this type of process is confronted with two problems :
- other processes exist enabling "short-cuts" (which are more or less beneficial) to be made. This type of process is necessarily in conflict with the other types. If the process uses the short-cuts proper to the other models, it loses its rationality.
- yet this type of process or activity demands in most situations memorization capacities which the operator does not have, forcing him to use short-cuts.

Therefore, if this type of activity is to be favoured, the operator has to be provided with memorization aid systems (symptoms tables, inference graph in schematic form). But if the operator does not construct the interpretation of the situation progressively, will he be able to use this symbolic material ? Isn't progressive summary-interpretation indispensable to the problem-solving process ?

Model n° 3

The limit of this type of activity lies in the tendency not to explore all the logical reasoning paths and to restrict oneself to the first direction followed. This observation can lead to automation of determination of chiasms. The notion of logical reasoning paths, application of rules and discovery of contradictions brings us down to known abilities as far as programming is concerned. Automation of this reasoning sequence does not mean replacing the operators. Indeed, once the contradictions have been cleared up, the operator has to deduce his hypothesis : only the processing phase (establishing the inference path) would be taken over by the computer.

This brings up the essential problem : if the subject does not perform the processing himself, will he be able to draw up and test the resulting hypotheses ? What would the consequences of this assistance be as far as cognitive processing and therefore performance and reliability are concerned ?

It is apparent from these three studies that :

- the nature of the Man-System interface has a significant impact on the performance and cognitive behaviour of the operators
- this impact is subjected to the necessity of modulating the aid provided to suit the specific phases of activity
- the requirements in terms of aid system are varying. The aid system must therefore either overcome these differences or induce a common problem-solving mode.

4 OPERATOR AID SYSTEM SPECIFICATIONS

This preliminary study n° 3 enabled us to design a single aid system capable of meeting our objective of improving the interpretation process. We are therefore developing different aid systems which will be tested comparatively.

4.1 PROCESS ELEMENTS INVOLVED

What information can the operators get at interface level to interpret incident situations ?
  - directly available information
  - information accessible by analysis of the situation
  - information available only temporarily
Studies 1 and 2 aimed to organize the directly available information at the graphic layer level to improve their use. The desk recorders or historical accounts displayed in the monitor windows provide the temporary information continuously.

This leaves the information accessible by analysis of the situation which is costly for the work load and which moreover require the use of deep knowledge of the process.

This is the case in our situation of causal relationships between the process variables which the operator has to master to interpret the situation.

The aid systems which have been developed try to favour establishment and use of these causal relationships according to the needs identified in the course of preliminary study n° 3. The use of a qualitative model to develop these systems is justified by the explanatory role of this model (Caloud, 1988). Based on the notion of intervariable influences, it enhances display of the causal behaviour of the system on a given variable, using an operator protocol to be defined.

In what way should this information be made available to enhance interpretation ? To provide the elements to be able to answer this question, these relationships first have to be characterized more specifically in terms of space and use of the inferences.

Defining the space of the inferences

The potential relationships (inferences) between information are analyzed in terms of :
- the nature of the relationships
- the state of this relationship with respect to the system model

Nature of the relationships

There are basically 3 types of relationships which correspond to knowledge the implementation of which in situation assumes a specific representation.

Automatic actions : inference (sensor -->-->--> actuator)

A control channel or a safety device create a more or less complex relationship between a sensor and an actuator : a change in the sensor status results in an action. Within the limits of the actuator the initial change is controlled and therefore masked. In one of the incidents, the first of these relationships is never identified as the change is slight and rapidly controlled, but it nevertheless has repercussions on the system as a whole.

The knowledge connected with the relationships is well indicated and accessible. However its implementation in a disturbed situation represents a heavy mental load : the incident situation diverts the automatic action from the initially scheduled context.

<u>Direct effect</u> : inference (actuator -->-->--> sensor)

Each actuator has a direct if not immediate effect on one or more specific sensors. The action of a valve on a flowrate, or of a pump on a pressure, are classic examples. Different actuators may act on one and the same sensor in accordance with priority rules. This can lead to inversions in the status change of sensors which the operators will only be able to understand by identifying these contradictory direct actions. In study n° 2, for 80 % of the tests with incorrect operation the relationships between these contradictory direct actions were not detected.

<u>Indirect effect</u> : inference (sensor -->-->--> sensor)
For the interface, a distinction has to be made between two types of indirect effects :

- Propagation effect of a variable without change of unit :
  E.g. : temperature propagation (pressure or flowrate) down-stream on a single line. A good representation of the direction of the flows solves this relationship. The topological "point of view" is effective here. In 90 % of the tests the temperature propagation (outside the heat exchanger) is not used.
- Effect of a passive or active component (change of unit) :
  E.g. : storage : effect of a flowrate on a downstream level; power transfer : effect of a flowrate on a temperature downstream from a heat exchanger.
  In the case of a heat exchanger the Flowrates =====> Temperatures relationships do not have a single solution. Classically the temperatures are measured and the operator has to make hypotheses on the flowrates. This type of hypothesis involves a large memory and attention load. A latency time and/or hypothesis questioning and/or backtracking follows the drawing up of this hypothesis in 93 % of cases.

<u>Effect on (or from) a non-measured variable</u> : (XX ---°---> YY)

The operator is led in an incident situation to reason on non-measured variables ("virtual sensors"). This then involves an inference of a strategic type requiring extrapolation and establishment of the connections between the symptoms.

These virtual sensors are verbalized 30 % by experts (shift supervisors/ operators) against 3 % for "non-experts" (assistants/technicians).

<u>Inference status</u>

In situation, any inference may comply or not with the process and therefore with the relationship expected by the qualitative model. In the inference space, this may constitute an alarm. A non-complying inference is of great potential informative value. It constitutes an element which is directly usable to build up a hypothesis (cf study n°3 model n°2).

4.2 PROTOTYPE AID SYSTEM SPECIFICATIONS

<u>Behaviour components involved</u>
What problems do the operators encounter to process the inferences necessary to solve the incident situation ?
In the course of preliminary study n°3, various points arose :

- problem of memorizing information
- difficulty of working on symbolic material of the following type :
  use of virtual sensors
  development of working hypotheses
  examination of inferences according to a non-topological order
- different problem-solving modes :
  inductive : the hypotthesis is formulated very early and processing consists in backing it up (model n°1 and 3)

  deductive : the hypothesis is formulated very late and processing is the generator of this hypothesis (model n°2)

Each interface developed will specifically favour one of the above points.

<u>Prototype interfaces</u>

In the first sttudy the Chemical and Volume Control System of a 900MW Pressurized Water Reactor has been presented in terms of circuitry and instrumentation. In the new interface we will complete the interface with shematic relationships between sensors.
Problem formulation

We specify the problems to be formulated and the consequent interfaces.

The following two comparisons will be made :

1) The impact of an inference-processing aid system which reduces the memory load as compared to the impact of an aid system facilitating work on symbolic material.

2) The impact of an inference-processing aid system which favours a deductive problem-solving mode as compared to the impact of an aid system favouring an inductive problem-solving mode.

To this end three interfaces have been developed :

- Interface A : synthesized presentation of the complete inference graph adapted to the situation
- Interface B : fragmented presentation of the inference graph
- Interface C : presentation of information significant of the incident

1) Large memory load versus work on complex symbolic material.

Windowing and information distribution techniques are used. To test which is the most critical factor, the impact of interface A and interface B on the performance and behaviour of the operators will be compared.

Interface A presents the complete inference graph of the incident broken down into two diagrams :

Mass balance : flowrate inferences

Energy balance : temperature inferences

This graph is not directly connected to the system topology, but imposes a high abstraction and decontextualisation level making it costly from the symbolic work viewpoint. It does however enable all the information to be gathered together and memory load problems to be overcome as all the information required to solve the incident is present.

Interface B presents the inference graph in a fragmented windowing manner directly underneath the variables. This enables a construction activity favoured by a context known to the operator (looking for cause and consequence inferences of such or such a variable) and linked to the

system topology. The qualitative graph information layout will however increase the memory load.

What are the consequences of an aid system favouring one of these aspects with respect to the other ? This poses the problem of the real impact of an aid system which plays a part in a human problem-solving process, in other words the problem arises of the correspondence between the roles played by each system (man and machine) from the strategy and representation points of view, and also as far as tools and their limits are concerned.

2) Inductive approach be favoured with respect to deductive approach ? Filtering techniques were used :

The impact of interface A and interface C on the performance and solving mode of the operators will be compared.

Interface A presents the complete inference graph (25 inferences) and therefore requires a large amount of prior processing.

Interface B filters the information and only presents the "automatic action" inferences and the non-complying inferences which constitute essential elements for formulating the hypothesis.

Do these interfaces enable a different type of problem-solving model, or a specific model, to be favoured ? Do these interfaces have a different impact depending on the incidents and therefore on the situation implying that the problem-solving mode varies according to the situation ? These questions will be brought up in the course of this study.

5 CONCLUSION

Our studies have proved the necessity of adapting the interface to suit the activity of the operator, and have showed how design criteria can be defined.

Interface specifications must include real Man-Machine cooperation means. For this cooperation it is crucial to achieve a fit between the representations and strategies used by the two systems. Only then will the two participants be able to assist one another mutually (Samurçay, Hoc 1988).

The research developed on the use of existing systems is

useful to highlight faults in the design of this cooperation. But it is seldom possible to draw up new specifications which are sufficiently precise to correct these design faults. We are devoting our efforts to a systematic approach to decision aids, which can provide the operator not with a diagnosis, but with all the elements necessary for making the right diagnosis.

This is why we design simulations enabling the aid that can be provided by future systems to be assessed. We hope that we will thus be able to favour the design of interfaces whose knowledge representation and strategies would be more suitable for the users. A corollary of this approach is that activity analysis methods have to be improved. It is becoming indispensable to establish the bases and means of a real interaction between interface designers and specialists combining skills in cognition and in artificial intelligence.

The latter must promote the essential safety ergonomy of graphic interfaces : the place where Man-Machine interaction takes place, in all the fields where monitoring of complex dynamic processes exists.

REFERENCES

(1) BAINBRIDGE, L., (1983) Ironies of Automation - In Automatica n° 6 pages 775-779

(2) CALOUD, P., (1988) Raisonnement qualitatif. Application à l' aide à la supervision des procédés continus. Ph.D thesis, INP Grenoble.

(3) CACCIABUE, P.C., MANCINI G., GUIDA G., (1988) A knowledge based approach to modelling the mental processes of a nuclear power plant operator. International Conference on Man-Machine Interface in the Nuclear Industry. AIEA Tokyo.

(4) COUTAZ, J., (1988) From cognitive psychology to computer science: towards a method for designing and implementing interactive systems. ERGO-IA'88, Biarritz.

(5) DE KLEER, J., BROWN J.S., (1984). The origin, form and logic of qualitative physical laws. I n AJCAI pages 1159-1169.

(6) DE KLEER, J., BROWN J.S.,(1984). A qualitative physics based on confluence. In Artificial Intelligence vol 24.

(7) DORMOY, J.L., (1987) Résolution qualitative: complétude, interprétation et contrôle, mise en oeuvre dans un système à base de règles : BOOJUM. Ph.D thesis PARIS VI.

(8) FERRAY-BEAUMONT, S., (1989). Modèle qualitatif de comportement pour un système d'aide à la supervision des procédés continus. Thesis to be published. INP Grenoble.

(9) FORBUS, K.D., (1984) Qualitative process theory. In Artificial Intelligence vol 24.

(10) FOUCHE, P., CHARLES, A., BARTHES, J.P., MELIN, C., (1989). Un panorama de la physique qualitative. Journées internationales d' Avignon.

(11) HAYES, P., (1979) The naïve physics manifesto. Expert system in the micro electronic age. Michie Editor, Edinburgh

(12) JOLICOEUR P., GLUCK M.A., KOSSLIN S.M., (1984). Pictures and names : making the connection. Cognitive psychology, vol 16, 243-275.

(13) HOC, J.M., (1986). Aides à la résolution de problèmes. In R. Patterson (ed), Aspects de l'ergonomie en informatique. Bruxelles.

(14) KUIPERS, B., (1984). Commonsense reasoning about causality. Deriving behaviour from structure. In Artificial Intelligence vol 24.

(15) KOSSLYN, S.M., (1989). Understanding Charts and Graphs. Applied cognitive psychology, vol 3, 185-226.

(16) LEYVAL, L., FERRAY-BEAUMONT, S., GENTIL, S., (1989). Declarative modelling for process supervision. AIPAC.

(17) NODINE, C.F., KUNDEL, H.L., (1987). The cognitive side of visual search. In J.K. REGAN, A. LEVY- SCHOEN Eye-movements from physiology to cognition. North Holland.

(18) SICARD, Y., SIEBERT, S., (1988). Comparaison d'interfaces de conduites. Essais incidentels sur imageries graphiques. ITBM vol. 9 n° 1

(19) SICARD, Y., SIEBERT, S.,(1988) Control Interface Evaluation. Incidental tests on desk and graphic displays. I nternational Conference on Man-Machine Interface in the Nuclear Industry. IAEA Tokyo

(20) SICARD, Y., SIEBERT, S., THEBAULT, M.H., (1988): Comparaison d'interfaces de conduite. Essais incidentels sur pupitre et imageries graphiques. Le travail humain tome 51 n°1.

(21) SICARD, Y., SIEBERT, S., OUDIZ, A., THEBAULT, M.H., (1988): Improvement of incidental recovery performances on console by the use of synthesis images in the monitoring phase. International Conference on thermal reactor safety. Avignon.

(22) WELSON, K., (1983) The derivation of concepts and categories from event representation. In E.K. SCOLNICK (Ed)New trends in conceptual representation. New Jersey.

(23) WILLOUGHBY, A., (1989) : Making qualitative reasoning more quantitative. Journées Internationales d'Avignon.

C409/028

Some aspects of the quality assurance of personnel carrying out finite element analysis

P W DICKENSON, BSc, MSc, CEng, MIMechE
Nuclear Installations Inspectorate, Health and Safety Executive, Bootle, Merseyside

SYNOPSIS In this paper, the need to assess the competence of personnel carrying out finite element analysis is emphasised. In carrying out its regulatory role on behalf of the Health and Safety Executive, the Nuclear Installations Inspectorate (NII) must be satisfied that appropriate standards are developed and maintained by the licensee.

Since finite element methods have an important bearing on the acceptance of a safety case, it follows that relevant codes are adequately validated and the personnel applying the code are competent.

Attention is drawn to the work of the Quality Assurance Working Group of the National Agency for Finite Element Methods and Standards (NAFEMS) who are active in this area. The paper also considers the methods that are available to assess the competence of personnel engaged in finite element methods.

1. INTRODUCTION

The duty of the NII is to see that the appropriate standards are developed, achieved and maintained by the licensee to ensure that the necessary safety precautions are taken and to regulate and monitor the safety of the plant by means of its powers under the licence. In view of the above, there is a need for the NII to be aware of the developments in the field of Quality Assurance. This paper deals with one aspect of Quality Assurance, that is its application to finite element analysis. In preparing this paper the work of the National Agency for Finite Element Methods and Standards (NAFEMS) Quality Assurance Working Group (formally the Accreditation Working Group) is used extensively.

In this paper, the need to assess the competence of personnel carrying out finite element analysis is emphasised. Since finite element methods have an important bearing on the acceptance of a safety case, it follows that relevant finite element codes are adequately validated and the personnel applying a code are competent in its use.

Attention is drawn to the work of the Quality Assurance Working Group of the National Agency for Finite Element Methods and Standards (NAFEMS) who are active in this area. The paper also considers the methods that are available to assess the competence of personnel engaged in finite element methods.

2. APPLICABILITY

Finite Element Analysis has an important role in the safety of nuclear installations. Its wide spread use in the nuclear industry means that it is used as part of many of the safety cases that the NII receives. Whether it is in the design of new plant or fitness for purpose arguments the finite element analysis method may play a significant part in the acceptance or rejection of the case.

The analysis may originate from the licensee, contractor, sub-contractor or consultant. In all cases the application of a Quality Assurance System could be a useful tool to ensure that what is required from a safety case is provided by the analysis in question. The organisation producing the analysis should ensure that their Quality System covers the finite element topic within its scope of applicability.

The degree of rigor of the Quality Assurance system applied to any given situation will depend on several variables. These variables include, but are not limited to: the safety classification of the component; the degree of reliance on the analysis in the overall safety case; the degree to which product inspection, acceptance standards or other criteria affecting safety are dependent on the analysis; other commercial criteria outside the scope of this paper.

3. SETTING UP A QUALITY ASSURANCE SYSTEM

In respect to setting up a Quality Assurance System for those undertaking finite element analysis NAFEMS have produced two useful documents. The first document is Reference 1 and is a 'Quality System Supplement' to ensure that analysis procedures and software are validated to a degree appropriate to their purposes and applied in a consistent and controlled manner for analyses affecting product integrity. The second document is Reference 2 and sets out standards for defining minimum levels of competence of teams of people using finite element analysis in the design or validation of engineering products. Any System in operation should be part of the company's corporate Quality Assurance procedures and consistent with them.

The objectives of the system need to be clear to all the personnel working within its scope. To this end the system needs to be documented and available to anyone affected by it. Responsibilities need to be defined and agreed at all the management levels that have an interest in the Finite Element analysis.

The documentation should be in a form that allows it to develop with the system. The system needs flexibility so as not to constrict its applicability as circumstances change.

The Quality Assurance system should have as the prime objective of providing a reliable finite element service. This objective should be understood by all, implemented by those concerned and maintained for all categories of analysis without exception.

4.   MANAGEMENT RESPONSIBILITIES

The organisational structure related to finite element analysis needs to be identified to include the management structure and the technical expertise available to undertake the analysis required.

For any given analysis the personnel who collectively form the necessary and sufficient expertise to undertake the task need to be identified and their role within the analysis documented. This documentation should cover the management function, those who will carry out the analysis, those who will verify the work, those who will provide the software and all the interrelationships. The structure will not be static and so will change as the project progresses. The dynamic nature of the structure should be reflected in the documentation.

Those responsible for the correct selection of software prior to use in a safety case will need to specify the finite element codes to be used and which attributes need to be validated so that validation of the programs can be carried out in a controlled and consistent manner. Similarly, procedures and documentation will need to be defined to control software development and updating. In all cases the assumptions implicit in the programs need to be clearly stated and the limits of applicability defined. It is probable that personal programs will need to be accommodated within the system, that is, programs written by individuals to assist them in their work.

For a safety case, verification of the work carried out will be a vital aspect. The personnel and other resources required for the verification process will need to be clearly defined, whether internal or external to the organisation together with their necessary expertise. The independence of the verification process will have to be demonstratable to third parties.

For a given project personnel will have to be selected who collectively provide the required level of expertise. Where there is a short fall in the 'in-house' capability (of

capacity or skill) it may be necessary to use external organisations or consultants to fill the gap. The personnel external to the company must comply with the Quality Assurance system. Once the selection process is completed the specific responsibilities, the inter-relationships and authority of all the personnel who manage, perform and verify the analysis should be documented.

Where a project goes through various phases to achieve the required outcome there will be a need to review the progress at key points along the way to ensure that the final objective will be achieved. Similarly, where the design parameters alter in the course of the project reviews will need to take place. The Quality Assurance system must ensure that these reviews are carried out in a controlled manner and documented adequately. Where design development is required the investigative analyses need to be controlled and consistent with the Quality Assurance procedures provided for this purpose. Any assumptions and modelling approximations need to be clearly stated and consideration given to the effect they might have on the design alternatives. Critical features and analysis results that might have an effect on the outcome need to be monitored closely and results reviewed as necessary.

5.   CONTRACTED OUT ANALYSES

Where work is contracted out the Quality Assurance procedures of the sub-contractor or consultant will need to be reviewed to show that an adequate capability exists. The licensee will have to agree with the supplier:

a)   the category of importance of each analysis to be performed;

b)   the method of analysis, its qualification and validation;

c)   the validation of the finite element codes used;

d)   the format of the design report produced and the detailed content of the report agreed;

e)   the organisations involved in assessing the work and the level of access that such assessors will have to company confidential information.

6.   ANALYSIS TASKS

It would be helpful if each analysis task had a specification which defines:

a)   the purpose of the analysis and the output required from the analysis;

b)   the level of importance the analysis has (relative to safety for example);

c)   the source of the input data;

d)   the analysis procedure to be followed;

e) the output checking procedure;

f) the resource requirements.

7. REPORTS

The reports produced explaining the results from the analyses should be prepared in such a way that they show an assessment of their accuracy and engineering relevance to the project. A general description of the method of analysis and the procedure followed should be included. All computer programs used during the analysis should be fully identified and described. Any report produced should be capable of independent review.

8. PROGRAM VERIFICATION

It is important to adequately verify all software (regardless of source) before it is used for product analysis. The verification process needs to be planned, performed and documented. Care needs to be taken that where several versions of a code exist, only fully verified versions are available to the product analysts. In carrying out the verification consideration should be given to testing:

a) the fundamental theory and conditions required by the theory;

b) established appropriate benchmarks;

c) appropriate, well posed problems with established solutions;

d) for rejection of invalid problems or solutions.

Where ever possible, results appropriate to a given procedure must be confirmed by some independent means. The means of confirmation should be stated in the reports produced, or referenced. Where confirmation has not been obtained this should also be clearly stated.

Validation must extend to any pre-processor and post-processor used.

9. DESIGN CHANGES

Design changes to a product need to be formally assessed for their implication to the analyses that are planned for the product. This process needs to be covered in the formal change control procedures and revised documentation issued. Out-of-date documentation must be withdrawn from use.

10. DOCUMENTATION CONTROL

All the analysis activities need to be documented to assist work transfer, restart or modification. Analysis work plans, specifications, reports, validation analysis procedures and referenced validation analyses should be included in the documentation. Documentation should also provide an audit trail and auditable information.

Notification to documentation should be introduced through formal change control procedures.

11. BOUGHT IN PROGRAMS

Finite Element software bought or leased should be shown to meet the specified application requirements. The software supplier should be asked, where possible, to define the software's technical requirements including tests or conditions which demonstrate satisfaction of these requirements.

Software developers should be encouraged to provide evidence of their software Quality System and quality control documentation.

Documentation relating to purchased software should be maintained by the purchaser and supplemented where necessary.

12. PERSONNEL QUALIFICATION

Reference 2 provides a useful guide to the qualification of personnel undertaking Finite Element analysis. It sets out to provide guidelines for setting the standard for defining the minimum levels of competence of teams of people using the method in the design or validation of engineering products.

All contractors, consultants or assessment agencies carrying out finite element analysis in support of the integrity of structures and safety cases should ensure that the people employed on such tasks have sufficient expertise. The level of expertise required will vary depending on the importance of the analyses. Reference 2 defines three categories of importance for which minimum levels of competence are required.

A team of people will, in all probability, be required to provide collectively the necessary expertise for any given analysis task. Reference 2 refers to the need for a supervisor, analysts, and software specialists. It may be that one person can fulfil more than one of these roles.

Personnel requirements will need to be qualified in terms of:

academic or professional qualifications;
general analysis experience;
finite element modelling and problem experience specific to the analysis required;
finite element software experience specific to the analysis required.

The degree of experience required will vary with the category of importance of the analysis and must be relevant to the application. Formal training in finite element methods will be relevant to promoting personnel competence. Analysis experience accumulated in a lower category of work is considered by NAFEMS to contribute to qualification for tasks of a higher category.

Where the software expertise is not available within the organisation it may be necessary to contract suitable personnel from the software supplier. Conversely, where the organisation chooses to subcontract analysis to an outside body that is unfamiliar with the product, the necessary product expertise may be provided to the contractor.

Analyst training should be controlled in such a system by the task allocation process. The requirements for experienced personnel in the more important analyses forces inexperienced personnel to be used in lower category tasks initially until such personnel have gained sufficient experience.

Personnel records should provide a data base to be used to:

allocate tasks;
judge training course requirements;
indicate on the job training requirements.

The personnel records should as a minimum contain:

professional qualifications and years of engineering experience;
training courses attended;
finite element analysis experience.

13. DISCUSSION

In writing this paper the work of NAFEMS has been used to provide a source of additional information. This is because of the author's familiarity with the work of that organisation. The use of this source of information is not meant to imply that this is the only organisation active in this field. The reader may know of other bodies that can furnish her or him with suitable alternative reference material.

One of the aims of providing a Quality Assurance system to cover finite element analysis is to minimise errors in the analysis attributable to human factors. The following paragraphs indicate some areas where the application of Quality Assurance to finite element analysis should reduce the possibility of errors that could be due to human factors.

The Quality Assurance system should take due regard of the use of inexperienced personnel in the analysis of components important to the safety of nuclear plants. There is a tendency for some managers who are unfamiliar with finite element analysis to believe that the computer programs do all the work without the need for experienced personnel to drive them, or check their results, etc. A well designed Quality Assurance system that is capable of meeting international and industry peer review should promote the use of suitably qualified personnel to ensure the correct application of finite element analysis.

Analysis of important safety components in nuclear plant can take several years to complete. There is always the possibility that, if care is not taken over the specification of the analysis, the different parties with an interest in the final results can have different perceptions of what is to be achieved.

The Quality Assurance system should provide a mechanism to ensure that "minds will meet" throughout the analysis process.

Where an analysis is used to help set the standard for manufacturing inspection or in service inspection it will be important that the two distinct sets of professionals understand the requirements and capabilities of each other. The need to keep both parties up to date with the findings of the analysis should be reflected in the Quality Assurance system. This will ensure that where, for example, inspection validation is applied it is underwritten by the analysis performed.

When reporting the results from the analysis it is important that all the requirements of the relevant Design Code are shown to have been addressed. Also, requirements that are additional to the Design Code will have to be shown to have been met. Quality Assurance should ensure that report writers address this important aspect correctly.

14. CONCLUSION

The demonstration of the safety of a nuclear installation is an important role that a licensee has to fulfil. At the heart of many safety cases the use of finite element method has an important part to play. It is the belief of the author that the use of Quality Assurance in this area of analysis will assist the licensee in meeting his obligation to prove the safety of his plant. Where finite element methods are used the Nuclear Installations Inspectorate will require the licensee to demonstrate that the programmes are validated and the analysis results meet the relevant Design Code.

15. REFERENCES

(1) Quality systems supplement to ISO 9001, published by NAFEMS, National Engineering Laboratory, East Kilbride, Glasgow G75 0QU.

(2) Guidelines for assessing personnel competence in organisations carrying out finite element analysis, published by NAFEMS, National Engineering Laboratory, East Kilbride, Glasgow G75 0QU.

16. ACKNOWLEDGEMENT

This paper is published by permission of Mr E A Ryder, Chief Inspector of HM Nuclear Installations Inspectorate. The views expressed in the paper are those of the author and do not necessarily represent the views of the Inspectorate.

C409/028

C409/031

The management of interfaces between organizations involved with the construction of Sizewell 'B'

P H BUTLER, BEng, MIQA
Nuclear Electric, Knutsford, Cheshire
B H SALMONS, BSc, FIQA
Gilbert and Associates (Europe) Limited, Twickenham

1   INTRODUCTION

The overall organisation for the design, construction and commissioning of Sizewell 'B' is described, together with the specific responsibilities of the organisations involved. The paper describes how the parameters for each interface are identified, and how the formal arrangements for controlling transmission of information and material are handled.

Whilst each organisation will perceive quality achievement as the ultimate objective, the specific individual responsibilities may dictate different, and sometimes opposing mechanisms for implementation, due to different perceptions of priority. The PWR Project Group has the ultimate responsibility for building Sizewell 'B' to cost and schedule and to the specified quality, and the paper describes, with some examples, how the different perceptions are addressed in order to achieve the ultimate objective.

2   ORGANISATIONAL ARRANGEMENTS FOR SIZEWELL 'B'

The interfacing arrangements for Sizewell 'B' are as shown in Fig 1.

Nuclear Electric

Nuclear Electric, as Owner and Site Licensee retains absolute responsibility for the Project throughout its total lifetime.

Within NE a PWR Project Board (PPB) with its associated PWR Project Group (PPG) has been established to undertake the project management for Sizewell 'B'. The organisation is responsible for all design and safety requirements and project management to achieve satisfactory completion and commissioning to meet time, cost, quality and performance targets of the station.

The PWR Project Board

The PPB acts as Client for the project and determines policy for the management of the project consistent with the strategic objectives of NE. The PPB operates in accordance with NE's Directives and Procedures and will satisfy NE's quality, safety, reliability, contract and specification requirements.

The PPB has fully delegated responsibility from the Board of NE and supervises the PPG and monitors its performance. The Chief Executive and his PWR Project Group (PPG) report directly to the PPB. The membership of the PWR Project Board is shown as Fig 2.

The PWR Project Group

General Arrangements

The PPG is the executive arm of the PPB. The PPG undertakes the engineering, procurement, construction and commissioning of the station. It is responsible for preparing the safety case and for providing an operational engineering support service to NE up to, and including, the second refuelling outage. It is also responsible for managing the contracts which are drawn between NE and the contractors, which are executed in accordance with NE financial and contract procedures.

The PPG is led by the Chief Executive who reports directly to the PPB. The organisational structure of the PPG is illustrated in Fig 3 showing the division into Project and Engineering Departments. A typical organisational structure of a Project Team is illustrated in Fig 4.

Detailed Responsibilities

Chief Executive

The Chief Executive is nominated as the Responsible Officer for the Project charged with the task of ensuring the execution of the scheme.

He delegates the role of Responsible Officer for contracts, to either the Engineering Director, or the Project Manager, as applicable.

The Chief Executive has responsibility for all phases of the project up to the completion of station commissioning.

In particular, the Chief Executive is responsible for:

(i) completion of the project to budget and programme at the required level of quality.

(ii) ensuring that those conditions of the site licence which apply to the station are observed until such time as it is appropriate for this responsibility to pass in part or in total to NE Production.

Engineering Director

The Engineering Director directs activities of the Engineering Department and acts as 'The Engineer' for contracts covering design, manufacture and supply of equipment for the Project as designated by the Chief Executive. He is accountable to the Chief Executive for:

(i) The layout, civil engineering and plant designs for Sizewell 'B'

(ii) The integrity and production of the safety case and safety submissions for Sizewell 'B'.

(iii) The placing and the management of the contracts designated by the Chief Executive for the design, manufacture and supply of equipment.

(iv) The provision of information systems for PWR Project Group.

(v) The placing and management of contracts for the research and development in support of construction and licensing whilst keeping the PPG aware of all R&D.

(vi) Acting as the agent of Nuclear Electric for the purposes of the Nuclear Site Licence during construction and commissioning.

Project Manager

The Project Manager is responsible for the management of the total resources necessary for the client engineering and construction activities of the PWR power station and for completing the project to time, cost, quality and performance. He is responsible for the planning, financial, construction and commissioning activities of the project and for the engineering and contracting for the civil works and site related contracts.

He participates in the process of obtaining Consents necessary to construct the station. He acts as client to the Central Engineering Organisation for the work carried out on the project to ensure that project commitments related to time, cost and quality are met. In addition, he contributes to the formulation of policy within the PWR Project Group as a whole.

Quality Assurance Manager

The Quality Assurance Manager reports directly to the Chief Executive and is required to conform with NE QA policy. The Quality Assurance Manager has overall responsibility for monitoring the quality related activities on Sizewell 'B'.

This responsibility is implemented by monitoring the quality related activities of the project participants on a hierarchical basis, and ensuring that appropriate surveillance, inspection and audit activities are implemented throughout the total hierarchy of purchasers and suppliers of structures, systems, components and services. The QA Manager is also responsible for monitoring the quality assurance activities related to Independent Inspection Agencies, Inspection Agents and Inspection Validation Bodies, as necessary.
He is responsible for managing the QA Team which is independent of other PPG functions. He establishes quality assurance requirements and assures their effective implementation, verification and documentation. In practice this responsibility is carried out in conjunction with other responsible PPG managers.

The QA Manager therefore has the authority to recommend a stoppage of work when, in his opinion, continuation would jeopardise the quality of the equipment and plant.

Organisational Interfaces

The major organisational interfaces are illustrated in Fig 1.

External Interfaces

The major interfaces external to NE are:

(i) The suppliers for the plant and civil works.

(ii) Design consultants and assistance.

(iii) Inspection Validation Bodies (such as IVC)

(iv) Inspection Agents (such as the Automated Shop Inspection Contractor)

(v) The Independent Inspection Agencies.

(vi) Engineering Inspection Authorities
Board of the I Mech E (via HSD).

The above interfaces external to NE are
governed by commercial contracts and agreements
which clearly define the responsibilities
of the organisations and these are detailed
in the contract documents. The contracts
stipulate the form of documents that must
be transmitted between the contracting
organisation and the PPG, and identify
the submissions to be provided by the organisation, and the information required to
be provided by the PPG to the suppliers.
The procedures for communication between
the PPG and the supplier are specified
in the contract and form part of a hierarchical
system. Each supplier is in turn responsible
for:

(i) Establishing that each of his potential
suppliers has the technical capability
to supply the items and services required.

(ii) Ensuring that each of his suppliers
has acceptable quality assurance arrangements.

(iii) Monitoring the performance of each
of his suppliers against those arrangements.

The project arrangements include activities
which lie outside the hierarchical quality
assurance system as follows:

(i) Independent design assessment and/or
witness of inspections and tests of selected
items important to safety by Independent
Inspection Agencies. The IIAs may also
participate in the PPG's monitoring of
supplier QA arrangements or carry out their
own monitoring of such arrangements by
evaluation or audit.

(ii) Independent validation by appropriate
bodies of procedures, equipment and personnel
used by the suppliers for specified inspections
of selected primary circuit items, and
used by the appropriate Inspection Agent.

(iii) Independent evaluation and surveillance of the Quality Assurance arrangements
of specified items to enable the Engineering Inspection Authorities Board (EIAB)
of the United Kingdom Institution of Mechanical
Engineers (I Mech E) to issue a Certificate
of Authorisation to NE.

Internal Interfaces

The main interfaces within NE are the HSD,
NE Production and NE Corporate Function
groups such as Information Technology.
The method of communication with these
organisations is controlled in accordance
with a Project Procedure. The control
of submissions to the NII is through HSD
and is carried out in accordance with a
Project Procedure.

The QA arrangements for the PPG are subject
to independent monitoring and surveillance
by HSD. This independent activity is directed
at the QA arrangements for nuclear safety
related items of plant.

3   EXAMPLES

Every individual concerned with the design
and construction of Sizewell 'B', both
internal and external to NE, is subject
to influence by the three basic project
commitments cost, schedule and quality.
However, each individual, dependent upon
his specific responsibility, may perceive
different priorities in the achievement
of the ultimate target. For example, a
Project Manager may be more directly influenced
by cost and schedule than an individual
reviewing a Safety case in Safety and Technology
Group. The Quality System for Sizewell
'B' has been designed to ensure that within
this spectrum of perception each parameter
is given due consideration, and sufficient
checks and balances are built in to ensure
the objective is met. Some examples are
given below describing the controls introduced
in typical likely problem areas.

Document Review

Documents, both of internal and external
origin, are reviewed and approved within
PPG, according to specific procedures.
These procedures describe the arrangements
for distribution of the documents to affected
parties, and the collation and disposition
of review comments. There are occasions
when the person responsible for the document,
possibly influenced by cost and/or schedule,
may not be willing to accept the reviewers
comments. In such situations the procedure
requires that the contentious issue is
elevated via line management to a level
which ensures proper consideration of the
factors involved.

Tender Review

At the time of tender review, the tender
which inevitably attracts greatest project
attention is that which quotes the lowest
price. However, even though the tender
has arisen from a previously approved supplier
list, there may be aspects of the tender
which are not attractive with respect to
technical and/or QA considerations.

The procedures for tender review ensure
that again all affected parties are involved
in the review, and where there may be technical
and/or QA deficiencies, which cannot be
resolved at that time with the tenderer,
the deficiencies are given a comprehensive
review and weightings applied as necessary
to ensure that the contract is correctly
placed.

Engineer's Approval of Contractor Documents

The PPG specifies, in its contract documents, requirements for its contractors to submit categories of documentation for PPG information or approval. This has led to the submission of thousands of documents and drawings, of varying importance, for PPG review.

While the Quality Assurance standards, such as BS 5882, appear to suggest that client approval of documentation may be a requirement, this is a topic which requires careful analysis. It is a human condition that once a document is sent to someone for his approval he feels bound to make comments on it, even if it is already fit for its intended purpose. At best the item submitted will give rise to questions in the recipients mind and he will feel the need to comment in the form of questions to its originator. However many rules are laid down, or however much guidance is given, individual human beings will still feel injury to their pride if they allow items to go by without exercising their right to comment.

This leads to several different types of situation, none of which is desirable from a QA point of view, e.g.

- the iteration of comments between originator and commentor becomes protracted when measured against real time needs to fabricate or inspect items.
: result : items may be fabricated/inspected against documents which have imprecise approval, giving rise to the question 'What was done, to what criteria', without a clear or unambiguous answer being available.
: the records for the item do not clearly show a proper audit trail of how it was made, which will give rise to uncertainty as to its history when this is required at a future date.

- The receipt of voluminous comments by a contractor from his client creates frustration and extra work, especially when they are seen as duplicating or contradicting comments which the contractor has already made, or are of an interrogatory nature.
: result : the contractor loses heart in making his own judgements on technical matters and allows the client, who may not be best placed to make the technical judgements required,to make the judgement for him. This situation cuts across and blurs the responsibilities of the parties.

A typical example of this type of situation did arise with PPG's involvement in the Design Reports required by the American Society of Mechanical Engineers (ASME) Boiler and Pressure Vessel Code Section III, where Reports certified by the contractor personnel responsible as complying with the Code, were subject to routine comments in addition by the PPG and other Parties. This practice has now ceased.

Control of Design Changes

A change to a design is inevitably disruptive to the project programme, particularly if the construction is well under way, and hence could have major cost implications also. This finally can result in pressure from those directly concerned with cost and schedule not to change the design, despite the perceived necessity from the technical side.

Secondly, where a design change has been accepted there can be pressure to implement the change as rapidly as possible in order to maintain the project programme. To avoid this conflict, and others which can arise with respect to design changes, specific procedures have been developed and implemented.

These procedures assume firstly that design changes are categorised according to their perceived effect on nuclear safety considerations. Such design changes which affect safety are reviewed amongst others by the PPG Safety and Technology Group, who must be satisfied that the proposed change, or failure to implement it, will not jeopardise safety considerations. All proposed design changes are reviewed by affected PPG Engineering Groups and Project personnel, and agreement reached as to the need for the change or otherwise. Following PPG agreement, those changes which affect safety are further reviewed by HSD and NII, to enable those parties to be satisfied that safety has not been compromised.

Audit and Surveillance Inspection

Within the PPG the organisation which is most remote from cost and schedule consideration is, by definition, the QA team. The arrangements described for audit, both within the PPG and external, and for surveillance inspection of suppliers' activities give added assurance that the specified quality is achieved from design to commissioning. Significant non-conformances, normally from audit, are required to be brought to the appropriate level of management for resolution. The surveillance inspection activity on suppliers ensures that material is not released from the works until the QA team is satisfied, as evident by the issue of a Quality Release.

Summary

The major organisational arrangements and resultant interfaces have been described, together with the responsibilities for the control of project activities. Some examples have been given which describe those controls considered necessary where there may be conflict between cost, schedule and quality considerations. The examples given highlight the necessity for identifying and defining all significant interfaces both internal and external to the project team, and the controls required to manage these interfaces.

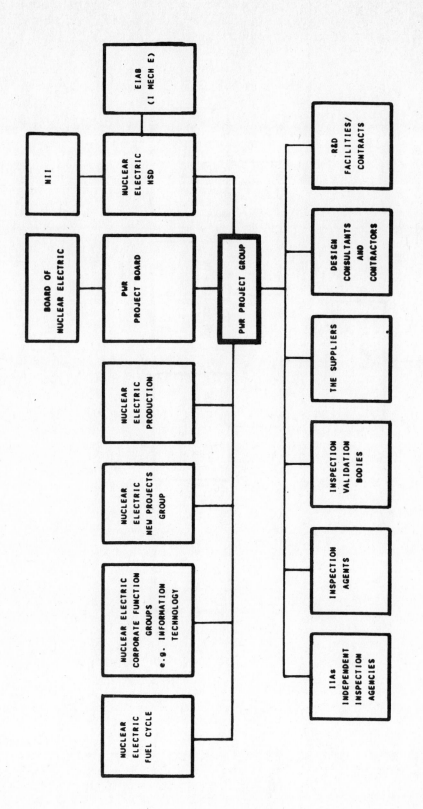

Fig 1   Organizations which interface with the PWR project group

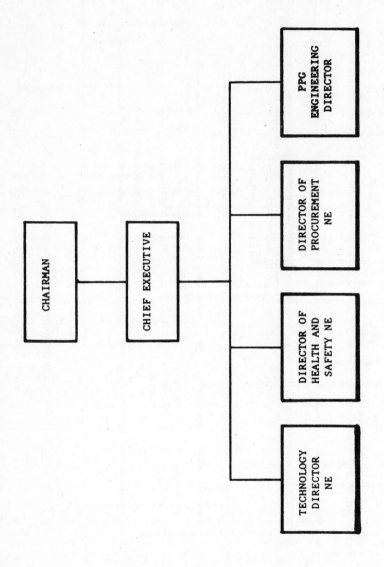

Fig 2   PWR project board

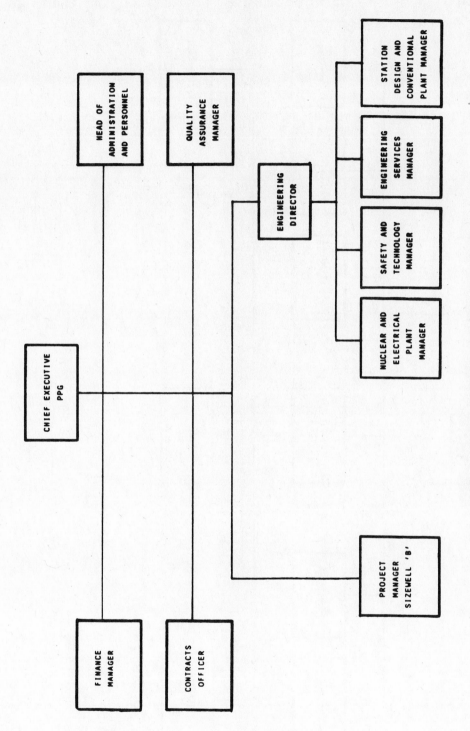

Fig 3   PWR project group management organization

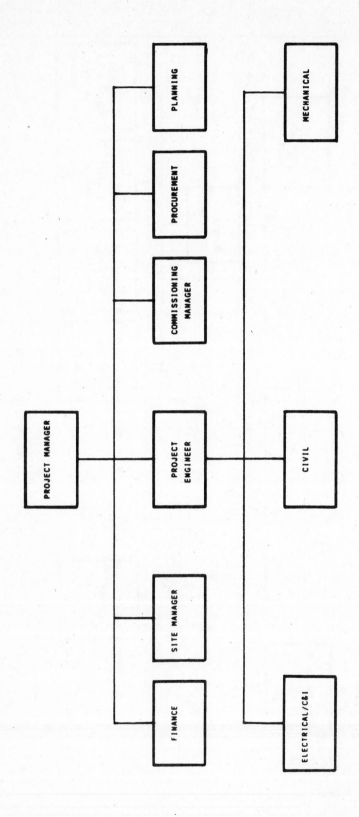

Fig 4   Project team

C409/003

The development of an ergonomics standard for the design of operator interfaces

B KIRWAN, J REED and **M LITHERLAND**
British Nuclear Fuels plc, Risley, Warrington, Cheshire

BNFL has realised the need to take a consistent approach to the ergonomic design of operator interfaces. Towards this aim, a design standard document has been produced under the direction of a principal design engineer based on the key ergonomics aspects of plant design. The standard was requested by the designers, and the original standard was produced by ergonomists working on BNFL projects. This standard was then reviewed by a large number of key design and operations personnel, and a series of multidisciplinary meetings produced the final version. The standard contains six sections (ergonomics requirements for the design of Control Rooms, Consoles and Panels Design, Labelling, VDU Systems, Alarm Systems and Colour Coding) containing approximately 180 guidelines in text format or supplemented by diagrams and tables. Each guideline is classified as either mandatory or advisory. A high proportion of effort concentrated on making the document usable by designers. The standard is not intended to be fully comprehensive, since the range of possible variations in the designs of interfaces makes such a task intractable at this stage. However, the document does ensure that account is taken of ergonomics throughout the design phase, and particularly in the early phases whilst design change is still cost-effective, and that designers are aware of the important issues and principles.

Background

BNFL is currently developing new plants which all, to a lesser or greater extent, involve interaction between operators and plant systems via a variety of operator interfaces. For some time BNFL has been aware of the importance of ergonomics, and has been involved in a number of multi-industry ergonomics support projects, such as the 'Short Guide to Reducing Human Error in Process Industries' (Ref 1), and latterly the more detailed longer version of this document (Ref 2), and was involved in early projects carried out by the Warren Springs Laboratory's human factors unit, which produced documents on various ergonomics aspects of complex VDU-based control systems. Such documents are aimed at reducing the impact of human error through the incorporation of good ergonomics practice in design, training, procedures, and management. It has been realised in BNFL that one of the critical aspects to get right in the design of the operator interface is the ergonomics of the design, as this can have a profound effect on human reliability and can give rise to otherwise unavoidable and undesirable operator errors. During the design stage of a plant, the design of the interface is a primary ergonomics 'degree of freedom' for reducing and avoiding the impact of human error. The other degrees of freedom, namely training, procedures, and management, are also important in reducing the likelihood of human error, and are fully addressed at the late design or commissioning stage.

However, although there is a good deal of ergonomics knowledge in industry, much of this knowledge is ill-fitted to the project design process. The design process is rapid and is subject to many criteria, largely cost and even aesthetics, as well as ergonomics. Designers need clear and unambiguous guidance, rather than statistical factual data which requires a good deal of interpretation and interpolation to apply to each individual interface design. Ergonomics is itself subject to many trade-offs between competing and occasionally apparently opposing principles which a designer may be ill-suited to attempt to resolve, and would have to go to seek ergonomics expert advice. This would be difficult given the usually large number of interfaces being designed at any one time, and the comparatively small number of ergonomists.

A further aspect of the problem of getting ergonomics guidance into plant designs is one of flexibility: some plants involve highly sophisticated systems, whilst others, appropriate to their nature, are fairly simple but robust operating systems. It would be non-productive, for example, to burden the latter systems with requirements for sophisticated 'user-friendly' and highly ergonomic computer VDU-systems when all that was effectively required for control was a panel with several pushbuttons and indicators Thus whatever mechanism implemented to achieve satisfactory ergonomics in plant designs must be flexible and sensitive to the different levels of complexity of different systems.

A final over-riding consideration was that, of the hundreds of ergonomics principles and data which could be subscribed, only the important principles should be adopted, again for reason of cost effectiveness.

The problem for BNFL was therefore to develop a mechanism for achieving high ergonomics adequately in plant design, within the following constraints:

i.   High priority ergonomics principles must be incorporated into the design process.

ii. Guidance must require minimal inter-pretation and be unambiguous, and deal with the so-called 'trade-offs'.

iii. The guidance must be flexible, recognising the different levels of complexity of the interface in different situations.

iv. The guidance should be resources effective, and not place too much additional workload onto the designer.

Approach

The ergonomists within the Safety and Technical Department in BNFL Engineering, Risley, developed document containing a set of some 300 detailed ergonomics checklist type questions which had been used by ergonomists for assessments on a number of plant designs (including existing plants). The design department then requested a review of such guidelines in order to develop a design-orientated check list. This approach was led by a principal design engineer.

It was further decided by the design office that the best way forward would be to extract from this assessment system the mandatory and significant advisory ergonomics principles and transform them into a formal design document. This document would then constitute a design standard. Such standards are used by all BNFL designers, and thus the development of a standard on ergonomics would mean that it would automatically be addressed by future design teams, who would be obliged to consult all existing relevant standards.

A number of design standards already existed on areas such as lighting and environmental factors, and since these design guideline documents deal with equipment, they do not cover aspects such as training and procedures (NB. less formal guidance on these aspects exists within BNFL).

The major ergonomics areas associated with operator interfaces on plants (inside and outside the control room) designated for the ergonomics standard were as follows:

1. Control Room Design
2. Console/Panel Design
3. VDU System Design
4. Alarm System Design
5. Colour Coding
6. Labelling

Within each area, the major principles were extracted from the 300 long checklist and reworded to read as precise recommencations. This was carried out by a project team consisting of a hybride group of desigers, a 'standards' representative, and two ergonomists. In many cases, figures and tables were used to condense the guidelines into more easily assimiliable forms. The original 'long' checklist remains in use as providing background information for ergonomists and designers.

The next stage was to divide the recommend-ations into two categories, those which were mandatory and should be implemented on every new plant design irrespective of the level of control system sophistication, and those which were advisory and hence could be omitted if extenuating design reasons existed in opposition to the principle. This categorization ensured that the major ergonomics principles would be incorporated into the design.

When all the principles had been categorised, a draft standard was issued for review to all plant managers at Sellafield and to many others involved in design, operations, and safety at all BNFL's sites. Every comment received was dealt with by the original project team which resulted in a number of both significant and minor amendments. After some months, a final design standard document was produced.

Tables 1-4, and figure 1, show some of the detail of the standard as it currently exists.

Concluding Comments

A mechanism for achieving high ergonomics adequacy in new plant designs has been developed and is about to be implemented. It is hoped that its progress can be reported on at the conference.

The task of developing an intra-company design standard on the ergonomics of operator interfaces has been non-trivial and sometimes difficult both in resolving technical disparities (eg. BS 4099 colour coding standard is, in some respects, not specific, and therefore can allow problematical colour coding systems to develop, Ref 3) and over-coming gaps in ergonomics guidance (eg. VDU screen display symbolic structuring and information density), and in creating a usable document which appears to offer some-thing of value to the designers which is neither enshrouded in jargon nor blatent common sense. Whether the document proves to be highly effective remains to be seen, but in terms of the degree to which it has inspired collaboration and closed communication and credibility gaps between designers, operators and ergonomists, the effort has been worthwhile.

References

1. Bainbridge L, Ball P, Eddershaw B, Hunns D, Kirwan B, Lihou D, and Williams J (1985), Guide to Reducing Human Error in Process Operation (Short Version). SRD Report R-347, SRD, UKAEA, Wigshaw Lane, Culcheth, Warrington, Cheshire.

2. Ball P, et al. Guide to Reducing Human Error in Process Operation (Long version). In Preparation.

3. BS 4099 Parts 1 & 2 (1986). Colours of Indicator Lights, Pushbuttons.

Acknowledgements

Acknowledgements are given to Tony Hayes of the Standards Department and Steve Wright of the Design Department who participated during the review of the guidelines at BNFL; and to S Whalley (RMC) and A Verle (W S Atkins) who participated in the derivation of the original assessment check list questions.

TABLE 1

CONTROL ROOM DESIGN REQUIREMENTS

1. Mandatory Requirements

   - Lighting SHALL minimise glare and reflections.
   - Control room temperature SHALL be 19-22°C with 30-60% relative humidity.
   - Control room noise SHALL be less than 65dBA.
   - Corridors or walkways SHALL allow easy and safe passage of personnel.
   - Furnishings SHALL NOT obstruct the operators view of control panels etc.
   - Equipment within the operating area SHALL NOT have sharp edges.
   - Writing or document reading space (480 deep - 750 mm wide - minimum) SHALL be horizontal and SHALL be provided in all operational areas.
   - There SHALL be communication facilities at all operating locations.

2. Recommendations

   - Operating areas SHOULD have a means of restricting visitor access.
   - Operating areas SHOULD be free from hazards, such as cables and pipes.
   - Supervisors offices SHOULD be an integral feature of control rooms.
   - Where possible, a window SHOULD exist in the control room.
   - Draughts SHOULD be avoided.
   - There SHOULD be storage space available in the operating area.
   - Storage space for operating information SHOULD be accessible from the console.
   - Storage space for protective equipment SHOULD be easily accessible.
   - The operator SHOULD be given a seated workstation if the task requires great precision or is of long duration.

C409/003 © IMechE 1990 75

TABLE 2

Recommendations for Control Selection

Required Control Function	Control Type
To access important or central functions at a high level in the system (not emergency safety functions).	Key switches
Standard on/off function	Pushbutton. Selector Switches
For immediate communication or action, frequently required	Pushbutton
Choice between three or more discrete positions	Pushbuttons. Selector Switches
For continuous variability	Control knob Thumb wheel Pushbuttons
Movement direction	Hand levers Joysticks Pushbuttons
Accurate control Precise movement	Handwheels Rotary selector switch Joystick Continuous adjustor knob
Alterations of speed	Direct positioning joystick Relative position of joystick Piezoelectric/strain gauge joystick Hand lever Foot pedal Pushbutton (the type that takes note of force)

TABLE 3

VDU System Design

Mandatory Requirements

a. Hardware

- The system SHALL contain enough VDU's to display all the relevant information required for a decision.

- There SHALL NOT be perceptible flicker on screen.

- Brightness level SHALL be adjustable.

- Character height SHALL be a minimum of 5 mm, and preferably 7 mm.

- Character width to height ratio SHALL be of the order of 0.7:1 to 1:1.

- The numeral character width to height ratio SHALL be 3:5.

- Flash SHALL ONLY be used to gain the operator's attention to important information.

- A flash frequency of 2-3 Hz SHALL be utilised.

- Keyboards SHALL NOT be fixed down.

- VDU monitors SHALL be located below eye height.

- Input devices SHALL be 'trackerball' type, backup SHALL be by alphanumeric keyboards.

- Response time SHALL be 0.1 seconds eg. for keyboard depression (parameter entry).

- Response time SHALL be a maximum of 2 seconds for indicating a response to a request.

b. Information Presentation

- The overall screen display system SHALL be hierarchial in nature to facilitate understanding of the process. It SHALL be broad rather than deep, and not exceed five levels.

- Each screen SHALL have a unique and informative title.

- At each level of the hierarchy, a particular title format SHALL be used so that the operator always knows where he resides in the process.

- Display pages SHALL be consistent such that menus and titles are in the same place on each page.

- The operator SHALL be provided with a simple means to go back up a level.

TABLE 4

Colour of Indicator Lights and their Meaning

Colour	Meaning	Examples
RED	Danger/Alarm	Control system fault Radiation level high Excess load on crane
YELLOW	Caution	Crane in collosion zone Shield door open Movement of machine Approaching travel limit
WHITE	Information only	Locking bolt engaged Control offered Machine parked
BLUE	Information only Power on/Panel energised Control accepted	As for white but use sparingly to group/link items of information

Note: GREEN SHALL NOT be used a a colour for indicator lamps

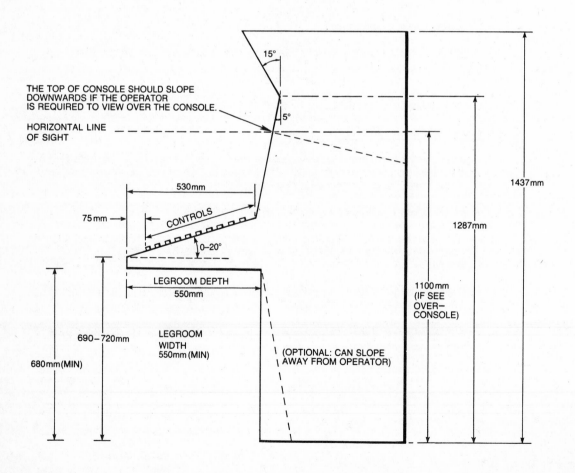

Fig 1   Seated console

C409/015

The development and implementation of a formal quality assurance system at an operating nuclear power station—Oldbury-on-Severn

N R REDMAN, IEng, MIQA, FIDiagE
Nuclear Electric, Bedminster Down, Bristol

This paper outlines the problems and difficulties encountered in implementing a formal Quality Assurance system on a power station that has been operational for 21 years. It describes the process of reviewing the existing documentation, developing a new document structure, the attitude change required to gain acceptance, the review and audit following implementation and the way forward.

1 INTRODUCTION

In 1982 the Executive of the Central Electricity Generating Board (CEGB) re-affirmed its policy on Quality Assurance thus:-

'It is the policy of the Central Electricity Generating Board that for all items of power generating and transmission plant and associated systems, there shall be in force appropriate arrangements for providing assurance of quality at all stages from design to decommissioning'.

In 1987 the Nuclear Installations Inspectorate issued a variation to each operating Power Station licence that required the licensee to establish and implement Quality Assurance arrangements for all matters affecting nuclear safety both on and off site. Heysham 2 had, from the outset of its design in 1979, a site licence requirement for formal Quality Assurance arrangements to be in place for the design, construction, commissioning and operation. Sizewell B has the same provision.

Other individual power stations had prepared their own site specific documents. It was CEGB policy under Regional autonomy to allow independent development. Consequently there was no overall co-ordination other than generic advice provided by a CEGB general guidance document and the requirement to comply with the content of British Standard 5882 (A Total Quality Assurance Programme for Nuclear Installations). The result was a diverse set of documents each one differing in content and style.

With the reorganisation of the nuclear power stations under one Director in 1987 it was decided that a common approach was required. A new philosophy using Quality Assurance principles as the central management system was developed and implemented utilising Oldbury as the lead station for the other CEGB locations. This was seen as an opportunity to 'take-stock' of the achievements and direction taken following an enhancement campaign inspired by Lord Marshall.

From the outset, it was recognised that a Quality Assurance system, incorporating internationally accepted standards, must be implemented with minimum disruption to station activities. This was accomplished by a process of participation and involvement by all levels of staff requiring Oldbury, not only to develop and implement a Quality Assurance system, but at the same time introducing the principles of TQM (Total Quality Management).

2 EXISTING DOCUMENTATION

For many years the CEGB has operated its power stations in a safe manner. There exist many well established systems and documents defining the methods and controls to be applied to the various activities.

Although these individual systems did not form part of a structured Quality Assurance system, they were considered adequate. These systems needed to be reviewed to ensure they met the requirements of BS5882. In addition enhancements identified within International Atomic Energy Agency (IAEA) and International Nuclear Power Operators (INPO) codes and guides were being considered for incorporation into the CEGB systems.

This review imposed some additional requirements on existing systems and no change to others. Several areas were identified as requiring specific attention such as:-

a) Document Control - A complete change in the culture of managing documents was necessary if the controls required by

BS5882 were to be applied by a central function within the station. The enhancements supported the need for Document Centres to be established to control centrally the preparation, review, approval and issue of documents produced within the station and also to ensure that documents received at the station were recorded, issued to the appropriate personnel and the necessary actions monitored through to completion.

b) **Stores Control** - The CEGB had, in the past, relied heavily on the final inspection of goods at the manufacturers works. Stricter controls needed to be applied to receipt inspection, the use of quarantine and bonded stores, and the physical storage conditions in order to prevent damage and deterioration of the purchased items.

c) **Maintenance and Operating Instructions** - An opportunity to standardise within the company on the format and content of working instructions was identified. Most of these instructions required revision to reflect the procedural requirements internationally accepted in the IAEA guide 50-SG-QA5 (Quality Assurance during the Operation of Nuclear Power Plants). These new formats are being adopted for all new and amended instructions following review. However, in view of the numbers involved, this is likely to be restricted to the higher QA graded activities.

d) **Records** - The culture of departments, sections and in some cases personnel retaining and storing records required addressing. Good record systems which provided for identification, collection, indexing, filing, storing maintenance and disposition and storage in facilities which provided a suitable environment to minimise deterioration, damage or loss needed to be developed. The document centre would provide the facility and controls to be applied.

The revisions of the systems and the subsequent implementation of a formal, structured management system required tactful co-ordination to ensure the minimum disruption to the station's activities.

3 NEW DOCUMENT STRUCTURE

The new site licence condition required that a formal Quality Assurance system be developed for the operating stations. A three-tiered system of documents had been identified as the generic model. Oldbury's selection as the lead station for development together with the proposed OSART visit gave the priority to enable the completion and implementation of the Quality Assurance documents within a challenging timescale.

The top-tier being the stations Operational Quality Assurance Programme which would define the Station Managers Quality Assurance philosophy for the managerial and procedural arrangements to be adopted to provide the necessary assurances. This document would be aimed primarily at the management team although it was mandatory on all Station Staff. The Quality Assurance Programme allocates responsibilities down to Departmental Manager and provides clear signposts to the middle and lower tier documents.

There were two types of documents comprising the middle tier. The first type being the departmental manuals which defined how each one of the four departments would be managed.

These manuals expanded on the requirements identified in the Quality Assurance Programme and clarified responsibilities and staffing levels. Also in the second tier were the central documents of the Quality Assurance system: the Management Control Procedures (MCP's). Twenty-seven MCPs have been identified to date. These MCP's define the responsibilities and methods for carrying out inter-departmental station activities. (A detailed listing is attached as Figure 1). They were in effect interface documents describing each department's specific responsibilities. The MCPs had to reflect the mandatory requirements of the CEGB procedures, the statutory requirements of legislation (both conventional and nuclear) and finally any enhancements felt necessary following the review of the best international standards.

The third tier comprised the various detailed instructions necessary to document the methods and controls to be applied to specific activities within a department. The third tier documents supported the generic requirements of the middle tier documents.

Many of these documents were replacements, in the new format, for existing documents and in other cases were specifying methods and controls to be applied to new systems. Irrespectively a system of introduction and implementation was devised to ensure a smooth transition. The intention was to start afresh by replacing the existing management structure with one based on Quality Assurance principles.

At a very early stage the station management adopted a policy for all new documents colloquially known as the '80-20 rule'. In simple terms when a document was considered to be 80% accurate it was issued. Approximately 80% of the production time, was being spent on getting the remaining 20% of each document correct. By adopting this policy documents could be issued and implemented to a much quicker timescale. Subsequently during implementation any problems or points of clarification were identified and the document revised and re-issued.

Other documents were generated to clarify responsibilities and to define training needs. Post Profiles would be generated for each managerial and supervisory post. They described the responsibilities of the post, reporting lines, qualification and experience requirements. Training profiles were developed to complement the post profiles by showing the training requirements (both formal and informal) necessary to fulfil the job function. Interface Agreements between the various CEGB departments and locations were developed to clarify responsibilities and to define how the interface would work in terms of methods and types of communication.

4 ATTITUDE CHANGE OF STAFF

It was necessary to give special consideration to the motivational/behavioural aspects of developing the new culture. It was evident at a very early stage that in order for the transition from the 'old' to the 'new' to be a success then staff awareness and acceptance had to be nurtured. The existing team spirit had to be taken to a level never before envisaged, without co-operation and willingness to accept change the transition would not succeed.

A training package was developed in order to make all staff aware of the Quality Assurance requirements and the new regime of management that was being developed. Three videos were commissioned by the CEGB to aid the presentation. One of these videos won a major international award at a prestigious American Festival. It was an amusing, yet thought provoking cartoon depicting Quality Assurance at the working level on a nuclear power station. The animator had visited Oldbury-on-Severn prior to drawing the cartoons. The video was highly successful in the training package, fully vindicating the decision to take a light-hearted approach. The same training package was given to all staff, irrespective of grade or responsibilities.

The biggest hurdle was fast approaching. Acceptance of the new systems including enhanced standards required an attitude change, not just by the work force but by the management team as well. There would be no return without an investment. So how could the management team promote a change in attitude and gain the co-operation of all? The philosophy that 'people are most willing to support any effort in which they have taken part or helped to develop' was adopted. Participation and involvement were to be the key.

It was recognised that the staff would not be motivated towards improvement in the absence of

- Commitment to quality from the management
- an organisational quality climate
- a method of approaching quality problems

These three factors are focused essentially at enabling people to feel, accept and discharge responsibility. Comments such as 'we know this is not the best way to do this job, but if that is the way management want us to do it, that is the way we will do it' make it clear that the expertise which exists at the point of operation has not been harnessed. The staff do not feel responsible for the outcome of their actions. Clearer responsibilities and accountabilities would foster pride, job satisfaction and better work. The station management recognised that before staff could adopt a change in attitude their commitment would have to be evident.

The station had an additional 'benefit' in that a complete restructuring of the nuclear power stations had been implemented. New jobs and titles enabled responsibilities to be more clearly defined. Responsibilities would be retained until such time as the responsibility was 'claimed' by another post holder. Restructuring also enabled the management to review its style and method of operating. Improvements soon became evident one example being a simplified, hierarchy of meetings all with fully defined aims, objectives and attendees.

The first stage of the attitude change was to encourage from the workforce ideas and suggestions aimed at improving relationships, quality and the environment within the station. A specialist consultant was commissioned to construct a four week programme to promote the generation of ideas and suggestions. The programme was called 'H.I.T' (Housekeeping Ideas Thanks). After a rather bumpy start the campaign gained momentum. Staff involvement, after being initially cautious, was overwhelming. The consultant had stated at the outset that participation of 70% or greater would be very successful - the station recorded better than 90% participation and created over 2500 sound ideas in the four week period. This gave the management a further problem - implement some of the ideas very quickly or run the risk of a loss of credibility. The ideas were required where possible to be of a scale that could be implemented by staff themselves thus minimising the involvement of management and maximising the number that could be quickly implemented. Immediate response indicated the commitment of management.

People's attitudes clearly can be influenced by communication. The essence of changing attitudes to quality is to gain acceptance for the need to change, and for this to happen it is essential to provide relevant information, convey good practices and generate ideas and awareness through a two-way communication process. In the CEGB like most other large organisations this is possibly the most neglected part of operation, yet failure to communicate effectively creates unnecessary problems resulting in confusion, loss of interest and eventually in declining quality through apparent lack of guidance and stimulus. In introducing the major changes in culture and attitude at Oldbury it was essential to have good communication.

A system named 'Team Talk' was introduced which allowed rapid, accurate dispersement and feedback of information to all staff levels. The workforce were being involved and in some cases consulted to feel part of the change in culture. Team Talk is essentially a regular gathering of teams where explanations of what has been done, what has to be done and what else is happening are communicated. The programme provides for a minimum of a half-hour briefing every four to five weeks on subjects that are relevant to each team. The briefing to be carried out by the immediate 'boss' of the team.

Most of the staff at Oldbury had worked for the CEGB for many years. They therefore found it difficult to make comparisons with the way other utilities and similar industrial organisations were operated. The station was faced with another problem how could it engender or promote improvement without the knowledge from exposure to international standards and practices.

A series of visits for a wide cross-section of staff to see for themselves how others operated Nuclear Power Stations was planned. Approximately 250 staff benefited from visits to utilities within Europe. The benefits to the CEGB in terms of return for the investment were immeasurable. Again it demonstrated the commitment of management to the cultural change with an additional benefit of a second-wave of enthusiasm from the workforce. With the encouragement of the management team the staff recognised the combined threats arising from public concerns about privatisation, failure to display 'excellence' to the public and the possible implications of a single European Market in 1992, following the theme of our former chairman - Lord Marshall - it was a battle for survival. The desire to be as good if not better than the foreign utilities quickly filtered throughout the station.

Changes in the working environment by enhancing housekeeping standards by improving lighting, painting and cleanliness would also promote a change in attitude. Painting a turbine hall basement white and at the same time improving the standard of lighting might appear to be the psychology of a madman. The result proved the opposite. It engendered a sense of pride and ownership never encountered. Incidents of untidy workmanship would be more evident and therefore reduced.

Trip and accident hazards were reduced to a minimum and the maintenance and enforcement of the higher standards again demonstrated a commitment from all staff.

In the comparison between the internationally accepted content of working instruction and the long established CEGB type of working instructions, enhancements were identified.

The psychology of how the instructions could be enhanced and accepted by the workforce required careful consideration. The solution was apparently simple - utilise the craftsmen to rewrite the working instructions to the enhanced standard at the same time giving them the opportunity to rationalise the detail to a more acceptable level. This philosophy had never been tried before, would it be acceptable to the craftsmen? The enthusiasm that had been engendered by good communication and participation made the idea readily acceptable to all. The craftsmen were delighted to be involved in rewriting 'their' work instructions. They felt part of the team. The craftsmen were supported by technical authors who ensured the format was acceptable and, where necessary, improved the quality of the text. Whilst this eased the demands on the craftsmen it introduced a need for second checking to ensure no corruption had occurred prior to submission for approval to the station Engineering Department.

It was necessary to establish ownership of the Quality Assurance system. It could not be with the Quality Assurance section, nor the Station Manager, the system had to belong to the station and every member of staff. Quality had to be managed into every employee's job, consequently all members of staff were encouraged to anticipate problems at the same time

they were given the power, via the document control system, to propose changes to processes to prevent errors.

The concept of right first time, every time had been introduced during Quality Assurance training. Implementation of this system had created an environment which sought perfection in all operations, a management attitude that encouraged the workforce to ask why an error had occurred, and a desire to track down the root cause of a problem and either take or propose an action to prevent it from happening again.

Collectively all of the above items contributed to and caused the change in attitude of the workforce at Oldbury-on-Severn power station. The station management had nurtured a sense of professionalism and ownership within the station staff.

5 REVIEWS AND AUDITS

In simplistic terms an internal audit sets out to establish whether the quality management system is being operated according to the written procedures. A review addresses the much wider issue of whether the quality system actually meets the requirements and aims to determine the system's effectiveness. The results of quality audits are used in the reviews for if the procedures are not being operated according to plan, it may be that improvements in the system are required, rather than enforcing adherence to unsuitable methods.

Oldbury-on-Severn power station implemented a system of reviews and audits when the quality system was introduced. The quality audits were initially perceived by the staff as a management tool, a means of reporting to the manager, the station 'thought police' coming to check what they were

doing. The success of auditing was very much dependent on the approach of the auditors. To adopt the fundamentalist approach was not feasible, acceptance would be obtained by adopting a pragmatist approach. Carrying out the audits in a constructive way led to their acceptance by all staff. With the introduction of many enhanced systems the audit process was also regarded as an educational process for the auditees. Initially there were many corrective actions which either resulted in a change to the documented requirements or staff having to become more compliant with the existing requirements. Corrective action implementation requires commitment from the management and the right attitude from the workforce. Despite the normal workloads of the various departments the attitude towards the commitment made was positive and was re-inforced by the senior management discussing each audit report plus any outstanding corrective actions at the monthly management meeting.

The station Quality Assurance section had developed a computerised corrective action tracking system that provided a monthly management overview on the status of implementation and also provided a prompt for the auditees implementing corrective action. The system tracked the corrective action implementation of all audits carried out at the power station. The efficiency of the system served to enhance the credibility and acceptance of the audit process.

As in the development of all quality assurance systems the documentation at Oldbury-on-Severn power station was subject to a comprehensive document review by all affected parties. The system required that all procedural documents had a nominated person to be responsible for the document with a defined review frequency. Work Instructions were reviewed following:- incidents on plant items at Oldbury-on-Severn and other power stations, modifications to the plant or from feedback of inadequacy by the user. The willingness and speed with which documents could be amended was another contributory factor in their acceptance.

One other key activity was the annual review of the quality system for adequacy and effectiveness which was carried out by each of the four managers for their area of responsibility with the Quality Assurance section providing an overview report. The review considered the results of audits and reviews plus any other perceived quality problems. The report generated quality improvement in many areas.

The most significant factor was that the quality system could be amended, revised and improved, it was not cast in tablets of stone.

6 THE WAY FORWARD

The theme adopted at Oldbury to improve the practices and management was 'Management through Quality and Participation'. All efforts had to be directed on the Quality of the business as a whole. Quality at Oldbury is becoming an integral, strategic issue, affecting the whole of the station's attitudes and behaviour towards the way the station should be operated. Many people call this comprehensive approach 'Total Quality'. Total Quality concerns everything that occurs with the aim being to provide customer satisfaction at a profit.

The station still has some way to go to complete the enhancement plan. The management team are continually looking at ways of improving quality and efficiency with the move towards Total Quality the benefits of which are generally recognised as

- Greater assurance of safety
- Improved company image
- Improved productivity
- Cost reductions
- Improved certainty in operations
- Improved morale
- Improved management

The benefits of Total Quality are the lifeblood for the continuing success of the nuclear industry within the United Kingdom. The newly appointed chairman Mr J G Collier has stated that 'Our task over the next few years is straightforward - to regain public confidence in nuclear power. We have to demonstrate by actions, not words, that nuclear power is not only safe and environmentally clean, but also economic - in this country just as it has proved to be in other parts of the world'.

7 BIBLIOGRAPHY

1. 'The use of quality as a basis for improved management' - a paper presented at the IAEA symposium entitled 'Quality in Nuclear Power Plant Operation' held in Toronto 10-14 September 1989.

   Author D Joynson (Station Manager, Oldbury Nuclear Power Station)

2. 'The coordinated implementation of Quality Assurance Programmes across diverse CEGB Power Stations' - A paper presented at the IAEA symposium entitled 'Quality in Nuclear Power Plant Operation 'held in Toronto 10-14 September 1989.

   Author M T Hardy (Station Manager, Heysham 1 Nuclear Power Station

3. 'Total Quality Management' - Author J S Oakland. Published 1989

MCP 1 Allocation of responsibilities for compliance with the nuclear site licence conditions

MCP 2 The form and content of station documents

MCP 3 Document control

MCP 4 Graded application of quality assurance

MCP 5 Management of station records

MCP 6 Quality assurance review and audit

MCP 7 Arrangements for dealing with organisational interfaces

MCP 8 Establishment and use of station plant and apparatus inventories

MCP 9 Identification and labelling of items and systems

MCP 10 Selection qualification and training of staff

MCP 11 Significant operational activities

MCP 12 Establishment of the operational state of plant and apparatus

MCP 13 Surveillance and routine testing of plant items and systems

MCP 14 Safety

MCP 15 Management of nuclear fuel

MCP 16 Management of solid, liquid and gaseous waste

MCP 17 Environmental monitoring

MCP 18 Operational experience feedback

MCP 19 Management of maintenance work

MCP 20 Work control system

MCP 21 Plant modification

MCP 22 Control and calibration of measuring and test equipment (M&TE)

MCP 23 Procurement of items and services

MCP 24 Materials and spares control

MCP 25 Control of security and access

MCP 26 Contingency and emergency arrangements

MCP 27 Housekeeping

Fig 1   Management control procedures

C409/026

Quality management of human factors technology applied to Sizewell 'B'

J C WILLIAMS
Nuclear Electric plc, Knutsford, Cheshire

SYNOPSIS The integration of human engineering principles into the design, commissioning and operation and maintenance of a PWR plant, is described. Indication of successes and failures are outlined so that others may benefit from the experience gained.

1 INTRODUCTION

A major objective of the Sizewell 'B' PWR is to generate power at lifetime costs that are comparable to or better than those associated with a similarly sized power plant. In order to achieve this objective steps have been taken to ensure that the design is a proven derivative capitalising fully on the experience of many international engineers and operators.

As well as taking account of international design, operational and support experience, it has been necessary to build up an in-house architect engineering capability that can handle contractual affairs and the licensing contributions necessary to support, develop and finally substantiate the safety case. For this project it was considered appropriate to build a safety and technology function that could service the widely varying demands of the engineering and licensing processes. Within the Performance Group of the Safety and Technology Branch an Ergonomics Sub Group has been in existence for the last five years. This Sub Group facilitates the achievement of safety, operating reliability and maintainability by applying a human factors engineering technology programme across a wide range of project activities.

The programme is designed to take full account of the potential for human error and its possible impact on reliability and availability. It has four principal components, analysis, verification, validation and support. These components represent a collection of a wide range of activities which are designed to assemble information for design input, assessment and support to the pre-operational safety case.

2 COSTS AND BENEFITS

Safety is not achieved without effort, and it is important to reflect on the cost of such effort when compared to the overall added value that may be expected to accrue to a project's life. Although it is not wholly obvious human factors engineering applications can make a substantial contribution to project value. Not only is the contribution made via the licensing process, and the assurance of safety, but there is also a gain to be made by means of human factors audit and design input that can result in improved operability and availability.

The efficiency of this process and the effectiveness of the investment are contingent upon the quality, timeliness and effectiveness of the human engineering input. Quality is assured in a number of ways, for example, high standards of staff qualification, skills and levels of attainment. Timeliness is a function of awareness, management commitment and a determination to succeed, all ingredients which are abundant in the PWR Project Group, and effectiveness is a function of the perceived value of assessments, recommendations and design approaches. A measure of the effectiveness of the Ergonomics Sub Group's contribution would be the extent of the demands made on its resources for immediate judgements on a wide range of design, assessment and licensing issues, and the strong desire of the engineering team to maintain these resources at high levels.

Involvement in the engineering design and development process is required as part of the project's procedures. Design documentation relating to a wide range of project features such as controls, displays, layouts, procedures, reliability assessments, principles, equipments and facilities, is reviewed at an early stage.

Human engineering guidelines, criteria and standards are created and applied. Design audits and operability studies are performed and documented and the results form a data base from which extrapolations can be made regarding the anticipated gains in operability and reliability that may be claimed as a contribution to project success.

+ Now with Technica Limited.

3 METHODS

As indicated above, a very wide range of techniques has been used to collect the necessary information to achieve and sustain both high operational reliability and maintainability.

The methods have included task analysis, mock-up walk and talk through, human engineering design review, concept verification and validation, human reliability experimentation and assessment.

3.1 Task analysis

To ensure that the quality of the station design has been well supported, a variety of task analytical techniques has been developed and employed as appropriate to the needs of the project. A hierarchical form of task analysis was performed with respect to the total station mission in order to ascertain whether there were any particular topics that would merit individual attention, over and above those already identified by the licensing authorities. Several areas, particularly those concerned with communication, whether it be shift-to-shift, man-to-man, or room-to-room commended themselves for further scrutiny. The mission analysis also showed that most of the planned verification and validation techniques would be more than likely to confirm that the provision made within the design process would meet the human interface/functional interface requirements. It therefore reassured the designers and assessors that an independent station mission analysis could assure completeness and indicate areas which might benefit from further explicit effort.

In order to develop a task analytical methodology relevant to the needs of the design development and licensing support processes it was necessary to undertake a number of preliminary exploratory runs. These experiments provided the information necessary to produce a technique that was accurate, thorough, specific and usable. A start was made on a study of the inventory control function of the Chemical and Volume Control System. It quickly became apparent that although there was a general understanding of intent, there was no wide familiarity with the purpose or applicability of task analytical techniques, and so after considerable debate it was decided that a generic task analysis of a cooldown and depressurisation would be performed to familiarise a range of personnel with the types of techniques to be employed, and demonstrate the range of information that could be collected for application to the design, training, procedures and error analysis process.

This duly accomplished, it then became clear that for the range of Pre-Construction Safety Report-claimed safety actions it would be both necessary and appropriate to develop a standardised method for analysis of each claimed safety action. This was done with a particular view towards ensuring that the findings of each analysis found ready application to the project design and development process, without sacrificing the essential features of the analysis, which were to ensure that the task(s) required was well within the capability of the anticipated user group, even under the most onerous prevailing conditions.

The task analysis programme has been integrated with the Station Operating Instruction (SOI) Programme which is concerned with the creation of procedures. The SOI Programme also requires some understanding of task requirements in order to facilitate the successful development of procedures. This programme integration has achieved best use of resources, and the work undertaken has started from identified needs supported by a number of affected units such as the Fault Analysis Group and the Generation Division. A crucial feature of all of this work has been the desire to support the design/development process.

A very high degree of integration has been possible. For example, many easily-implemented design and procedural recommendations have been generated, with obvious early project benefit. A number of specific engineering and operating philosophy questions have also been posed, and with suitable adaptation to the analyses, it has been possible to answer these at a time when the freedom to choose from a variety of low-cost design and operational options existed. This, too, has obvious advantages from a quality management viewpoint.

3.2 Verification

Throughout the project design/development phase, considerable documentation has been generated concerned with principles, specification, implementation and procurement. In company with other groups the Ergonomics Sub Group has reviewed copious volumes of such documentation from a human engineering perspective. This activity ensures that, when delivered, all equipment affected by human factors issues, and subject to such review may be expected to operate in conformity with user expectations. Human factors audit processes at this stage have involved comparison of proposed designs with human engineering design principles, such as supplying feedback rapidly and directly from the affected component, and ensuring that force, reach etc requirements are well within the ability of the user group.

A substantial amount of walk through/talk through exercising has also been undertaken during this phase to ensure that the components and procedures are organised in accordance with user expectations and requirements from the points-of-view of ready and rapid association of ideas/action and general matching with the operators' models of process and plant organisation. This activity highlighted a substantial number of human engineering discrepancies which have been recorded and resolved. The discrepancies ranged from gross model mismatch, such as might be caused by completely unexpected placements of equipment or flows doubling back on themselves, through to relatively trivial examples such as the mimic depiction of an 'East' tank being inadvertently placed to the left of a 'West' tank.

To assist the resolution of some of the observed discrepancies further human engineering principles were enunciated to ensure that there was overall consistency across the plant. Rigorous policing was also undertaken to ensure that not only were appropriate design modifications made, but that they themselves did not introduce or constitute unforeseen complications to existing design principles.

This part of the process required high level negotiating skills on the part of the human factors analysts and proved highly effective. Practically all outstanding issues were resolved to the satisfaction of all concerned and this success demonstrates also the effectiveness of the formal quality assurance procedures which required mutual satisfaction or documentation of unresolved issues for the attention of the various engineers responsible.

Although understandably much of the verification process focused on the demonstration of compliance of the main control room with human engineering principles, it also involved very substantial verification of other parts of the plant such as the radwaste control room, local control panels and many mechanical handling interfaces such as the waste store manipulator and fuel cranes.

Apart from the hardware side of the verification process there was in addition a major review of the data processing software system design documentation. This review necessitated an in-depth knowledge of the alarm and information presentation system principles and an ability to imagine how system display techniques might be expected to operate and interact with each other in practice. Twenty-seven major documents were reviewed in detail to achieve this coverage. Not only was it necessary to visualise how the man-machine systems might work in practice but also how the hardware itself might relay, process and combine data. During this process it became apparent that several features had been misnamed, omitted or introduced in a sub-optimal fashion.

In a manner comparable to the hard panel verification, it was then necessary to document all potential human engineering discrepancies so identified and suggest appropriate remedial measures to resolve any outstanding concerns. Again, it was a tribute to the quality management process that the discrepancies were identified and formally recorded for resolution, so that despite the pressure of work a full auditable trail exists showing the concerns identified and the actions taken.

3.3 Validation

Whilst verification processes can be viewed as demonstrating that appropriate features have been incorporated into design and development processes, they cannot give the assurance that, when integrated and operated for real, the features that are relevant to operators will indeed give the correct information, at the right time, to an appropriate degree. To satisfy this part of the quality assurance equation another distinct activity has to be undertaken, namely validation.

Validation is concerned with demonstrating proofs of principle or operational worthiness. For Sizewell 'B' human factors engineering validation is regarded as constituting experimental or synthesised evidence that when integrated in real-time all relevant system dynamics will be conducive to the attainment of high levels of human reliability.

Some of the validation work necessary has already been performed. It involved the simulation of an important fault condition and the assessment of an integrated data and alarm presentation system when utilised by a representative sample of users. In all, three studies have been performed to date. The latest one involved the study of three basic parameters as they interact with the proposed design concept. First a check was made to determine whether the use of alarm lists as an adjunct to the integrated display system would help or hinder fault diagnosis and alarm handling. Secondly, a check was made to determine whether the rate of alarm arrival would affect the quality of information processing and thirdly, a check was made to determine whether the physical location of the VDUs and their keyboards would alter the processing of information in any material way.

These studies were conducted and analysed as systematically as circumstances would permit. Being an industrial prototyped environment, equipment and personnel did not always perform quite as desired. Thus, the research was not of a publishable standard. However, it was adequate to pin-point broad conclusions and the need for further development effort.

The data and alarm handling validation research showed that the new system was certainly no worse than the existing system, and had the added advantage that operators could choose how they would prefer to handle alarms, subject to prevailing circumstances. It showed that although there was a slight effect on alarm handling behaviour associated with increased arrival rates, these were not sufficient to cause major disruption over the range investigated. Although a behavioural difference between the two basic equipment layouts was observed, it was small, and in the context of the total task of alarm and information handling, sufficiently small that it could be discounted as constituting a major obstacle to the successful deployment of equipment in either configuration.

It is probable that the human factors engineering validation process will extend through the commissioning phase to power raise. However, for practical purposes the process is currently confined to securing confidence that the re-defined data-processing system will continue to perform to user expectations, thereby minimising search times, retrieval error and inappropriate behaviour. An exercise is planned to ascertain whether the hoped-for amounts of alarm reduction can be claimed with confidence, and further checks are planned to ensure that the alarms are presented in an understandable fashion in appropriate contexts.

Although prescriptive measures have been taken to ensure that audible alarms will possess high intrinsic meaning, minimum startle and maximum discriminability, the resulting audible alarm media will be evaluated from both the points-of-view of quality assurance verification, and their usability as judged by a panel of users (should the need arise).

An important requirement of the plant design is to ensure that, in the event of its becoming uninhabitable, control can be transferred from the main control room to the auxiliary shutdown room in order to achieve and maintain a hot shutdown condition. Another human factors engineering validation exercise is planned, therefore, to ensure that the necessary communication, both man/man and man/machine, will be conducive to successful and highly effective transfer of such control under these unlikely circumstances. It is likely that this exercise will involve simulation and role playing, with video recording as appropriate, similar to that used to evaluate the integrated data and alarm handling system.

3.4 Related support

None of the work described so far can have much credibility if it doesn't relate to the total work programme of the PWR project. This integration has been achieved via a series of measures, ranging, from the outset, via seminars, liaison groups, through design working groups to specific actions to support the design/development process to maximum effect.

Throughout the project development, there has been a strong coupling between the activities of the PWR Project Group and those of other formations such as Generation Division. This is exemplified by the original work of the PPG, executed on its behalf by the Projects Division of Nuclear Electric, to develop a checklist to guard against cognitive/conceptual error. Errors of this sort can arise when there is a mismatch between the state which an operator perceives a plant to be in, and its actual state. This checklist has been developed with the PWR training function in mind as primary client, but also with a view to its being applied elsewhere in the developmental process.

Similar input may be made to the Fault Analysis, Station Operating Instruction and

Control and Instrumentation activities. In addition, advice has been, and continues to be given to the Fault Analysis Programme, particularly with regard to the operationalisation and assessment of human reliability assessment methods.

Within the domain of support, there are several other activities of the Ergonomics Programme that need to be taken into account. Studies of operator stress and a preliminary assessment of maintenance facilities and procedures are being undertaken to determine the extent to which they will fulfil human engineering requirements, as is an assessment of local panel designs.

In addition, it has proved possible to assess the Quality Assurance Programme from a socio-technical viewpoint, and accordingly the Ergonomics Programme has not only assessed the format of QA procedures, and contributed to the methods for retrieving relevant QA procedure information, but it has conducted a detailed study of the climate within which the QA system itself is operated. It is believed that this may be one of the first studies of the QA process itself as it relates to the successful implementation of the requirements of a QA process and the way it is perceived by an organisation.

It should be no surprise to those concerned with the quality management of personnel in the nuclear industry that the assessment of the climate within which such a QA system operates is generally conducive to the achievement of high levels of human reliability both within the design/development process and the adherence to the requirements and exhortation of the Quality Assurance process.

4 CONCLUSIONS

From the Sizewell 'B' experience, it can be stated with confidence that the human engineering process works, as does the QA system within which it operates. Also it can be stated that the QA system itself functions well to provide the environment in which safety, reliability, operability and availability go hand-in-hand.

Thus, it will be seen from this experience that a properly integrated human factors technology programme coupled with effective project management principles can, and does, lead to a successful infusion of quality management in the nuclear industry.

ACKNOWLEDGEMENTS

This paper has been prepared with the encouragement of Dr Richard Garnsey, Safety and Technology Branch Manager of the PWR Project Group, typed by Jane Askey, and is published by permission of Nuclear Electric plc.

C409/027

A framework for the management of human reliability in quality management

D E EMBREY, BSc, PhD
Human Reliability Associates Limited, Dalton, Lancashire

SYNOPSIS Human error is a primary cause of quality failures in nuclear power and other industries. Many approaches have been developed for assessing and reducing error in the context of safety, and these can also be applied to quality. This paper describes an approach to optimising human performance from two perspectives. The first of these is the application of techniques to predict errors and to analyse their causes. These analyses provide the basis for the development of specific error reduction strategies. The second perspective is the implementation of management policies which will create an appropriate culture for minimising errors.

1 INTRODUCTION

Over the past twenty years, a considerable amount of work has been done in the nuclear power industry in developing techniques to evaluate and assess human error in nuclear power operations. However, the bulk of this work has been applied in the context of the responses of individual human operators to emergency situations, particularly from the perspective of providing inputs to Probabilistic Safety Analysis (PSA). More recently, the application of approaches from cognitive psychology has emphasised that the higher level functions of the human in nuclear power operations such as problem solving, decision making and fault diagnosis also need to be addressed (1). Nevertheless, the majority of work has been directed at modelling and improving human performance at the operational level, largely from the perspective of safety concerns.

In contrast to the considerable resources devoted to human reliability from the safety perspective, virtually no research has been carried out with regard to the implications of human error for quality. This is surprising, given that an erroneous human action is just as likely to have implications for quality as it is for safety. The influence of human error on the quality of operations can be seen in areas such as maintenance errors, the initiation of unnecessary trips, and in recovery failures where preventable trips could have been averted had appropriate actions been initiated in time. In all of these areas, human performance deficiencies are likely to lead to loss of availability, and degraded quality of operations.

In recent years, the approach of achieving safety and maximum availability by the use of quality standards such as BS5750 and its international equivalent ISO 9000 has been supplemented in many industries by the application of a series of a top-down management orientated approaches known as Total Quality Management (TQM). TQM draws heavily on the work of a number of Japanese and American gurus such as Taguchi, Ishikawa, Deming, Crosby and Juran. Although some of their approaches are primarily statistically orientated, almost all of them emphasise the importance of human error as a prime cause of quality lapses. Rather than attempting to blame the individual for such errors, however, one aspect of TQM focuses attention on root causes of errors and the solutions to eliminate them.

In this sense it is possible to see a convergence between the TQM philosophy and the approach which is being increasingly employed by researchers in the field of human reliability and human error research. Recent papers, e.g. (2), (3) have shown that most major system failures stem from a combination of multiple human errors that have their origins in preconditions created by policy failures at various levels in the organisation. Similar considerations apply to quality lapses. Punishing the individual who makes an error leading to a quality failure is at best a temporary solution or at worst a waste of time. Unless the underlying organisational causes are addressed, the quality (or safety) lapse will simply recur. Having said this, it is important that any top down management driven initiatives designed to improve quality by the reduction of errors should employ systematic methods and techniques which can be applied at the operational level.

Systematic methods for the assessment and control of human error have been developed by human reliability researchers, and these methods in combination with the approaches advocated in TQM, provide a comprehensive framework for the improvement of human performance leading to enhanced quality levels. The purpose of this paper is to indicate how a synthesis can be achieved between the human error reduction methods developed primarily in the context of system safety analyses, and the approaches used in TQM. We would emphasise that this paper concentrates on those aspects of TQM that are concerned with error reduction. Nevertheless, this is a fundamental aspect of the TQM philosophy. In terms of Statistical Process

Control (SPC), human error is the primary source of the 'special causes' of process variability described by Shewhart and Deming. In addition, when major quality lapses are analysed, human errors are almost invariably identified as a primary cause, although the antecedent conditions that give rise to these errors are usually a result of a failure in the design of the quality system.

We have developed a general philosophy for assessing and reducing human error which comprises three elements. The first of these is an integrated framework which considers the detailed technical methods which can be applied at the operational level. The second element considers the management framework within which these methods are implemented. The final element takes into account the characteristics of the organisational culture which may support or impede the introduction and the long term effectiveness of quality management initiatives. Each of these aspects will be discussed in turn in subsequent sections.

2 THE SYSTEM INDUCED ERROR MODEL

Most of the techniques that we have developed for assessing and managing human error at the operational level take as their starting point the System Induced Error model shown in Figure 1. This states that all individuals have certain built in error tendencies related to the way in which we handle information in a complex and sometimes unpredictable world (4). When these error tendencies are combined with error inducing conditions (for example distractions, stress, inadequate time to consider Figure 1 all the available information etc.) then an error is likely to result. For the error to give rise to a significant consequence for either safety or quality, an unforgiving environment has to exist. An unforgiving environment prevents or reduces the likelihood of error recovery. It also involves a vulnerable system state, which in combination with the unrecovered error causes the final undesirable consequence to occur, be it a quality lapse, an injury to an individual or a major system disaster such as Three Mile Island or Chernobyl. An error which gives rise to a vulnerable system state, but which does not in itself produce a significant consequence, is called a latent failure. Latent failures can arise at management levels (e.g. failure to schedule sufficient time and resources to carry out the required activities) or during operations (particularly during maintenance work). An error which combines with the vulnerable system state to give rise to the undesirable consequences is called a triggering event or active failure. Failure to recover an active failure (given that recovery is possible before the consequences ensue) is called a recovery failure.

A major premise of our approach is that many error inducing conditions arise from organisational and management policies that are outside the control of the individual who makes the particular active failure that initiates the quality or safety lapse. In these situations the attribution of blame is far from clear. In the past, the individual at the end of the chain of causality has usually been the recipient of blame and punishment. In recent years there has

been an increased realisation that the person who makes the last mistake is often no more than the 'snowflake that starts the avalanche' (5). Organisational and management policies may have created a situation where quality or safety failures are at some stage inevitable.

3 A SYSTEMATIC FRAMEWORK FOR REDUCING HUMAN ERRORS AT THE OPERATIONAL LEVEL

The technical aspects of the framework are illustrated in Figure 2. The control of error using this framework involves both proactive and retrospective activities.

3.1 Proactive aspects

Proactive activities are used to eliminate the underlying causes of quality failures before they occur. Proactive approaches can be further subdivided into design and audit activities. In this context 'design' refers to all aspects of the system design which might influence quality. Thus, it encompasses the design of the job, communications, procedures, training, work scheduling and the systematic elimination at source of deficiencies in these and other areas which could give rise to human caused quality lapses. Design activities occur during the development or upgrading of new or existing systems. A number of techniques are available for analysing at the design stage the anticipated role of the human in the operation of a system and for predicting where errors leading to quality lapses might arise. On the basis of these analyses, the characteristics of the system which could induce these errors can be eliminated from the design.

The other form of proactive activity to identify error inducing conditions is the use of audits. Audits are systematic appraisals of an existing system to identify characteristics which could induce quality failures. Audits can be carried out at varying levels of detail. Where time and resources are limited, an audit will be confined to an evaluation of systems such as training, procedures design, communications, supervisory roles etc. from a top down perspective. A more detailed audit will involve the application of audit checklists to specific operational activities where errors can have significant quality implications. The results of both types of audit will generate recommendations for strategies at the level of both policy and operations to eliminate the underlying causes of potential quality failures.

3.2 Retrospective aspects

The other approach to the elimination of quality failures is the reactive or retrospective approach. This involves the detailed analysis of quality lapses that have occurred in order to identify generic root causes that could give rise to similar problems in the future.

Retrospective analyses can be divided into several types. The first of these is the in-depth analysis of major incidents where significant losses have occurred. The investigations that are carried out in these cases should attempt to address not only the immediate human causes of the loss, but also the organisational policies which have created the preconditions for the incident.

As will be discussed in a later section, it is essential that investigations of major incidents are carried out in a blame-free environment. Ideally, the investigation team should comprise individuals who are seen to be primarily interested in establishing root causes to prevent a recurrence of the problem rather than attempting to assign blame. A number of tools are available to support such investigations. For example, the fishbone or cause and effect diagram popularised by Ishikawa can be helpful in delineating the various causal factors which have given rise to an incident. However, it is very important that such cause and effect analyses do not terminate at the immediate causes of an incident, but also consider the organisational policies that create these preconditions. Discussions in this area may expose the management of an organisation to awkward questions by individuals at a lower level in the organisation who may be involved in the investigation. It is important that such questions are dealt with frankly by management, and that the recommendations that emerge are implemented. If this is not the case, the whole investigative activity will rapidly lose credibility, and will be seen as an exercise to assign blame rather than to develop remedial strategies to prevent a recurrence of the incident.

Apart from the analysis of serious incidents, it is important that a monitoring system exists for collecting data on more frequently occurring but less serious quality lapses. The purpose of such a system is primarily to identify unique or frequently recurring underlying causes so that appropriate remedial strategies can be developed.

In designing such a system a number of issues have to be addressed, as identified in (6).

(a) Nature of information collected

This factor covers such aspects as whether the data is descriptive or causal, whether the system concentrates on reports of significant events, accidents and injuries or if it includes near misses, and whether the data is collected using a written report or through a standardised questionnaire.

(b) Help provided in gathering information

This includes factors such as the nature of any job aids, training for the analyst, and ease of use of any methods for determining causal analysis.

(c) Use of the information

Items here include: the nature of feedback from the system, what functions this information serves, and whether the system is used to generate specific error reduction strategies or other quality improvement strategies.

(d) Nature of organisation of scheme

Factors such as whether the system is plant-based or centralised, whether it contains voluntary or mandatory reporting, and whether it is computerised or paper based are covered under this heading.

(e) Acceptability to personnel

This final category looks at whether personnel have a 'pride of ownership' in the system, whether data is collected by known personnel, and the nature of any introductory training provided.

The third category of data that can be collected to assist in the reduction of human errors leading to quality lapses are near-misses. A near-miss in this context refers to an incident where there was little or no financial loss because an intervention by the operator (or another individual) recovered an error which would otherwise have had significant consequences. This type of retrospective analysis is particularly valuable for several reasons. There is abundant data to suggest that both near-misses and significant quality losses originate from the same root causes. Whether or not an error has a serious consequence depends more on when or where in a process that it occurs, rather than to any intrinsic differences in underlying causes. Thus, a 'no consequence' or a recovered error tells us as much about root causes (which may be implicated in a variety of failure scenarios), as an incident involving major losses.

Another advantage of near-miss data is that in almost all systems many more near-misses occur than significant quality incidents. Thus, there is potentially a larger pool of data available from which recurrent root-causes of quality lapses can be deduced. Near-miss reporting provides an early warning system which allows error causes to be identified and rectified before a major loss occurs. Otherwise, the insights that emerge from a structured analysis of incidents that have already occurred have to be paid for by the actual losses associated with these incidents.

3.3 Specific techniques: the SCHEMA framework

Human Reliability Associates have developed a number of specific techniques which can be applied during the proactive and retrospective phases of the analysis. These form part of SCHEMA (Systematic Critical Human Error Management Approach) framework. SCHEMA comprises three modules, as illustrated in Figure 3. These are the analysis module, the screening and risk reduction module, and implementation and feedback module.

(a) The analysis module

The first stage of the process involves identifying the specific functions that the operator is required to perform. These functions are translated into a detailed description of the operations and task steps required to achieve the functions by means of a systematic process of task analysis. The method of task analysis preferred in SCHEMA is Hierarchical Task Analysis (7). This has the advantage that it addresses the plans which control the sequencing of task elements as well as allowing the analyst to vary the level of detail of the analysis as required. Consideration of plans allow errors in both planning and execution to be evaluated in the subsequent error analyses. The example of Hierarchical Task Analysis shown in Figure 4 illustrates the use of varying levels of task redescription depending on requirements, and the delineation of plans.

The process of performing a task analysis will provide the analyst with many insights with regard to how errors might arise. However, it does not represent a systematic search strategy for identifying errors that may have significant safety or quality implications. The Human Error Analysis phase of the analysis module provides such a strategy. Human Error Analysis (HEA) is a generic name for a wide variety of techniques intended to systematically predict human errors which lead to quality lapses. The predictive HEA which is implemented in SCHEMA is described in detail in (8). HEA is intended to identify the following categories of error:

- Action Errors: Examples include actions which are too long or too short, right actions carried out on the wrong object, actions omitted, etc.

- Checking Errors: Omissions of required checks, carrying out the wrong check on the right object, etc.

- Retrieval Errors: Errors concerned with the retrieval of information from visual displays, procedures or memory.

- Transmission Errors: Errors which occur during the transmission of information between individuals.

- Selection Errors: Errors in situations where an object has to be selected or a choice made when there are alternative objects which could be erroneously chosen.

The task steps which are selected for evaluation are first subjected to a pre-analysis to eliminate broad classes of errors which are ruled out by the specific task conditions. For example, if no checking is involved during a task step such as closing a valve, then a checking error is not possible. The detailed analysis then asks the analyst a series of questions relating to each of the task steps in order to identify whether any of the error modes specified in the error classification described earlier is possible.

Although it is feasible to perform the task analysis manually, the Human Error Analysis requires computer support in order to be carried out in a reasonable time scale. Both the HTA and the HEA procedures are implemented in a computer program called THETA (Top-Down Human Error and Task Analysis). The HTA module of THETA allows the successive decomposition of tasks from their higher level functions to specific task steps. Those task steps for which a human error analysis is required are flagged during the HTA and are then entered automatically into the HEA module when this

option is selected.

(b) Screening and risk reduction module

This phase of the SCHEMA process is first used to specify the errors identified in the previous modules which are likely to constitute significant threats to quality if they occur. This evaluation is made by considering the likelihood that the errors will occur, and their consequences if they are not recovered.

Having identified errors which could cause significant quality lapses, a series of candidate strategies are considered to reduce the likelihood of their occurrence. Typical strategies might include the development of improved procedures, better information presentation or a revised training programme. These alternative strategies are then subjected to a cost benefit analysis and the chosen approach is then implemented as part of the final SCHEMA module.

(c) Implementation and feedback module

During the last stage of the SCHEMA process, the selected strategy to reduce the incidence of human caused quality lapses is implemented, and the results evaluated. The monitoring process is achieved by means of the data collection system discussed in section 3.2. This enables the effectiveness of the strategy to be assessed by identifying reductions in the incidence of the quality lapses (or associated near misses) that the strategy was designed to address. If the strategy does not achieve its objectives, then alternative approaches are applied until the required quality objectives are achieved.

4   THE MANAGEMENT AND ORGANISATIONAL CULTURE REQUIREMENTS FOR THE MINIMISATION OF ERROR

The techniques and methodologies discussed in the previous sections constitute a comprehensive set of tools for analysing errors and their causes due to those characteristics of human performance likely to have a significant impact on quality in nuclear power and other systems. However, these tools are unlikely to be effective unless they are applied within a systematic management directed programme designed to produce a quality orientated organisational culture. In the remainder of this section we shall discuss how such a culture can be achieved by considering the various components of a successful quality management initiative.

4.1 Commitment to change at all levels in the organisation

No quality management initiative will be successful unless commitment to change is engendered at all levels in the organisation. This can only be achieved if the commitment of senior management is demonstrated explicitly in terms of the resources (time, money and exposure) that they are prepared to devote to the initiative.

4.2 Recognition of existing cultural characteristics and needs

All organisations have existing cultures and subcultures which need to be taken into account for the successful implementation of quality initiatives. In this context the term 'culture' refers to the shared values, traditions and customs which exist in an organisation and which determine how things are done and how information is interpreted. Many attempts to introduce TQM approaches have foundered because programmes developed in other cultural environments (different industries, countries or even sites within the same organisation) have not been adapted to take into account the specific cultural characteristics of the organisation in which they are being introduced. It is therefore advisable to gain a thorough understanding of the cultural norms at all levels in an organisation before attempting to implement a quality management programme.

4.3 Consistency and continuity of purpose

From the perspective of the workforce, approaches such as TQM are likely to be viewed as being just the latest in a series of management fads. It is therefore essential that a quality programme is planned so that it can be administered over a realistic time scale (a minimum of two years) in order that continuity is established. Equally important is the maintenance of a consistent philosophy to quality and the avoidance of conflicting messages to the workforce from different levels of management in the organisation. For example, if line management are not committed to the philosophy of quality being the most important objective, they may condone or encourage practices which 'cut corners' to meet throughput requirements at the expense of quality standards. These practices can only be eliminated if senior management ensure that their commitment to quality is reflected by managers at all levels in the organisation, but particularly at the level of first line supervision.

4.4 Development of a blame-free culture

It is necessary to develop a culture which focuses on the system induced causes of quality lapses, rather than relying on blame and punishment to control human performance. Until a blame-free culture is developed, individuals will inevitably conceal the information that is necessary to address the root causes of human performance problems leading to quality lapses.

The achievement of such a culture is primarily dependent on an extensive education programme in the system induced error approach discussed in section 2, and on a consistent management attitude which avoids disciplinary action as a control measure except in the most extreme cases. These principles are well summarised by the quality guru Deming, when he emphasises the need to 'Drive out fear' (9).

4.5 Participation by the workforce in the quality improvement process

A major emphasis of the TQM philosophy is that the workforce should be 'empowered' to 'own' the quality improvement process by active involvement in activities such as error cause

identification and removal programmes and the investigation of quality lapses. In the past, techniques such as those described in Section 3 have been employed by a 'technical priesthood' and the recommendations then imposed on an uncomprehending and frequently hostile workforce. By involving the individuals whose jobs are likely to be changed in the analytical processes required to improve quality, they are more likely to be committed to the changes that may result from such exercises. Training in the techniques described in Section 3 should form a central part of the extensive quality education programme which should precede a major quality initiative.

5   CONCLUSIONS

This paper has attempted to show that in order to achieve an integrated approach to the human reliability aspects of quality management, it is necessary to address both technical and organisational issues. The first part of the paper described a framework for systematically identifying possible human errors with significant quality implications and for controlling such error tendencies by means of appropriate error reduction strategies. These proactive approaches are complemented by data collection systems which provide a feedback mechanism for reducing the incidence of quality lapses by identifying their root causes. The second part of the paper has discussed some examples of the cultural and organisational factors that need to be taken into account in order to successfully implement quality management initiatives.

It can be seen that the technical and organisational perspectives on the human reliability aspects of Total Quality Management are essentially complementary, and a successful programme to enhance quality needs to contain elements from both areas.

REFERENCES

1.   Pew, R.W., Miller, D.C., Feeher, C.E. Evaluation of proposed control room Improvements through analysis of critical operator decisions, 1981, Research Report NP-1982, (Electric Power Research Institute, 3412 Hillview Avenue, Palo Alto, California 94304, USA).

2.   Reason, J.T. Management risk and risk management : research issues. Human Reliability in Nuclear Power, London, 1989, (IBC Technical Services, Bath House, 56 Holborn Viaduct, London EC1A 2EX).

3.   Embrey, D.E. The management of risk arising from human error. Human Reliability in Nuclear Power, London, 1989, (IBC Technical Services, Bath House, 56 Holborn Viaduct, London EC1A 2EX).

4.   Reason, J.T. and Embrey, D.E. Human Factors Principles Relevant to the Modelling of Human Errors in Abnormal Conditions, 1985, Report no. EC1-1164-B7221-84-UK, (European Atomic Energy Community, Brussells, Belgium).

5. Woods, D.D. Technology Alone is Not Enough. Reducing the Potential for Disaster in Risky Technologies. Human Reliability in Nuclear Power, London, 1987, (IBC Technical Services, Bath House, 56 Holborn Viaduct, London EC1A 2EX).

6. Lucas, D.A. Human Performance Data Collection in the Nuclear Industry in : Human Reliability in Nuclear Power, London, 1987, (IBC Technical Services, Bath House, 56 Holborn Viaduct, London EC1A 2EX).

7. Shepherd, A. Issues in the training of process operators. International Journal of Industrial Ergonomics, 1986, 1, 49-64.

8. Lucas, D.A. and Embrey, D.E. New directions in qualitative modelling in : Human Factors and Decision Making : Their Influence on Safety and Reliability edited by B.A. Sayers, London, 1988, (Elsevier).

9. Deming, W.E. Out of the Crisis, Chapter 3, 1986, (Cambridge University Press).

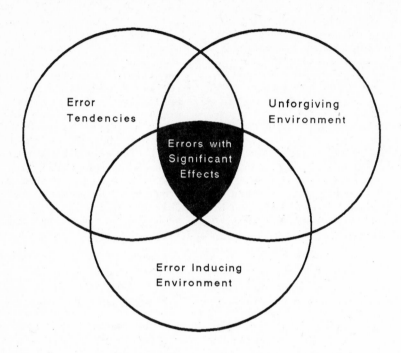

Fig 1   The system induced error model

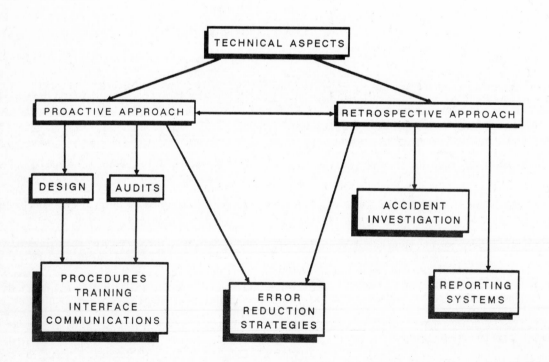

Fig 2   A framework for controlling error at the operational level

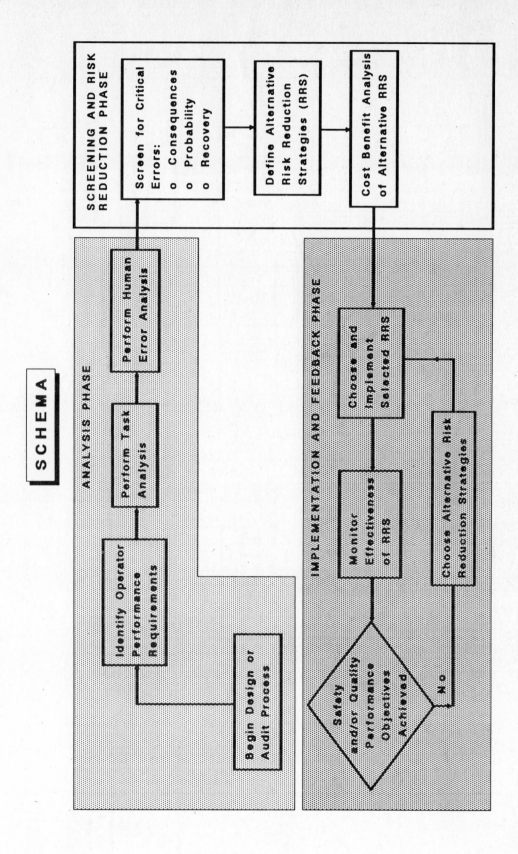

Fig 3   An integrated approach to the identification and management of system induced errors

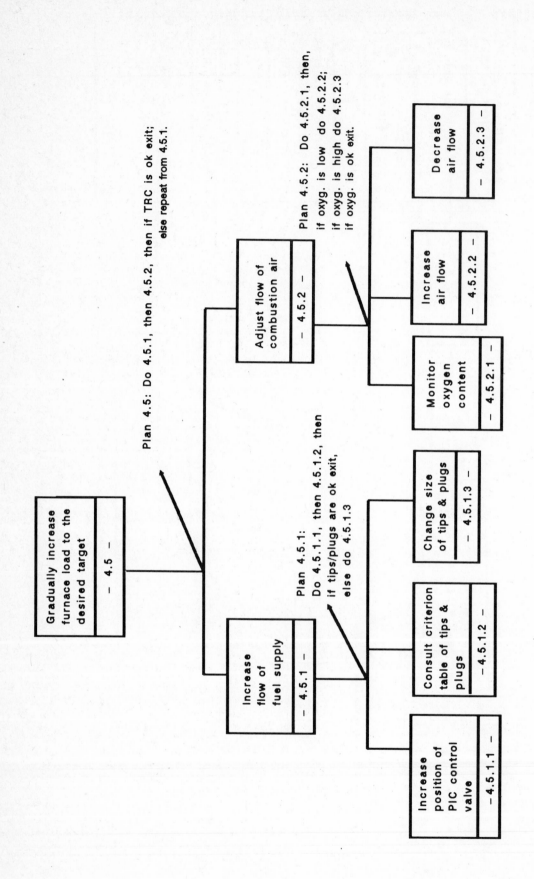

Plan 4.5: Do 4.5.1, then 4.5.2, then if TRC is ok exit;
else repeat from 4.5.1.

Plan 4.5.2: Do 4.5.2.1, then,
if oxyg. is low do 4.5.2.2;
if oxyg. is high do 4.5.2.3
if oxyg. is ok exit.

Plan 4.5.1:
Do 4.5.1.1, then 4.5.1.2, then
if tips/plugs are ok exit,
else do 4.5.1.3

Gradually increase
furnace load to the
desired target

— 4.5 —

Increase
flow of
fuel supply

— 4.5.1 —

Adjust flow of
combustion air

— 4.5.2 —

Increase
position of
PIC control
valve

—4.5.1.1 —

Consult criterion
table of tips &
plugs

— 4.5.1.2 —

Change size
of tips & plugs

— 4.5.1.3 —

Monitor
oxygen
content

— 4.5.2.1 —

Increase
air flow

— 4.5.2.2 —

Decrease
air flow

— 4.5.2.3 —

Fig 4   Hierarchical task analysis

C409/013

Combining task analysis into the design process in order to ensure compatibility between operating personnel and their equipment

S P WHALLEY, BSc, PhD, MErgS
R M Consultants Limited, Garrett Field, Warrington, Cheshire

SYNOPSIS The aim of this paper is to introduce a model for incorporating task analysis into the system design process from day one, right through to checking human performance once the system is running. It will demonstrate how information gained early in the system concept stage can be expanded as the design progresses which will ensure that task analysis is a cost effective process.

If the full task analysis procedure is followed through all phases of a system's life cycle, quality assurance of personnel performance can be provided with fully documented evidence. Task analysis makes explicit that which many people may already be considering implicitly and hence decisions and assessments can be audited.

1 INTRODUCTION

Task Analysis is not in itself a new concept (1) (2) but the term Task Analysis can be defined in a number of different ways, with the major distinction being between the use of the term to describe a technique, versus its use to describe a method. Task Analysis in this context is being used as a term to describe a method, supported by a range of possible techniques. Most system designers implicitly consider the role of people within the system but, for large complex systems, such as those within the nuclear industry, the lack of a written description or 'blue print' may result in misunderstandings, inconsistencies or communication problems between members of a design team. This can be a particular difficulty when the design passes from the initial functional specification to the detailed design phase and when different specialists are involved, e.g. mechanical design engineers and instrument design engineers.

Task Analysis formally extracts information and (using collection technique) records (using representation technique) what will be expected of the people who work within the system and hence the demands that will be made upon them. This record of expectations can be used as a source document in a similar way to an equipment functional specification (e.g. engineering flow diagrams) and, as more information is known, detailed drawings. In addition, it can serve as a quality assurance document since all task assumptions are auditable and hence task accomplishment can be ensured.

As the system design progresses, initial task analysis can be expanded, extended and re-iterated with any changes in task requirement formally noted. By matching task goals to the task requirements that are needed to achieve the goals, individual items of equipment and areas of plant can be linked to specific tasks. Once this link is established, it can be checked that the design is adequate for personnel to successfully complete their tasks, i.e. to ensure generic compatibility between operating personnel and their equipment. Subsequently, this can be followed up during commissioning and operating by checking on the actual performance of human tasks when interacting with the system. This ensures that tasks are being performed as required and expected, and checks the specific compatibility between equipment demands and human capability. The emphasis is on extending task analysis (TA) through all phases of a system's life cycle.

By starting TA early in design, a formal two-way communication channel can be established whereby knowledge of human limitations can be included in design decisions, rather than the equipment automatically indicating specific personnel requirements and training. The latter are only too often used as a method of coping with over-demanding designs. It is worth pointing out that the increasing problems with personnel selection caused by a shrinking labour pool (an abundance of choice will not be a feature of the 1990s!) can be minimised through consideration of equipment demands in relation to task goals and human capability during the design phase.

2 HUMAN FACTORS ISSUES

Good design is achieved by the consideration of a number of human factors issues: Who will be performing the tasks? Which goals should be given to control systems and which to people? Can tasks be divided between team members? Are information and control mechanisms suitable? Can personnel use that which is given to them? Will personnel training and support be possible? Are opportunities for errors avoided as far as possible?

These human factors issues are sometimes referred to as; person specification, allocation of function, workload and organisation, work needs and human limits, skills and knowledge acquisition, performance assurance.

2.1 Person specification

A person specification details the characteristics needed by individual workers including; physical and mental capabilities, qualifications, personality traits and experience. Rather than producing a person specification in response to a design, it is possible to think about the pool of potential workers and their characteristics, using this as a means of influencing the design. The system can be designed so that peoples' tasks do not demand capabilities that they do not have or will be unable to get through training. This may be a particularly important method of ensuring compatibility between people and their equipment, especially if personnel will be transferred from other installations or there are likely to be labour/ skill shortages in the market place.

2.2 Allocation of function

This commences by dividing the system sub-goals or 'tasks' between equipment (control systems) and people and extends to placing responsibility for task performance on different individuals within the team. Some tasks are best performed by 'machines', e.g. monitoring, repetitive tasks, and others by people, e.g. pattern recognition, fault diagnosis. It is important that people are not included as a 'safety net' to mop up forgotten tasks and those too difficult or expensive to specify for equipment, or for equipment to achieve. People need to be properly integrated into the system design and this can be properly achieved only by formal analysis of system goals and the associated operations.

2.3 Workload and organisation

The amount of input required from personnel should be established following, or in combination with, the allocation of functions and must influence the design of the system. Alternatively, the group commissioning a design may limit the number of personnel to be involved with the system, for example; if the intent is that no more than two operators shall be required per shift and an assessment indicates that there is too much work allocation for this number, then either the design must be changed or extra staff made available. It is also important to assess the process time available against the time necessary to complete the tasks, resulting in an appropriate input to the design. If a team of people will be required to work within the system then the design needs to include adequate communication methods. The actual location of equipment and its ease of use will influence task time and the co-ordination of activities, for example; if associated equipment is positioned close together, then movement times will not need adding to task times, and one individual may be able to cope.

2.4 Work needs and human limits

Designers of equipment should respond to the identification of information requirements including system response feedback and to the identification of controls that will be required to successfully complete each task. Having identified the task needs, it is then possible to consider how to provide for these needs via the 'operator interface' in order to ensure that the user can function with the equipment within the intended environment and workspace. This is the major check point for compatibility between equipment and operating personnel.

2.5 Skills and knowledge acquisition

It is important to ensure that design does not preclude operator support supplied through procedures, fault diagnosis aids, manual handling aids, checklists, etc. nor prevent the success of training. Both can be used to overcome design deficiencies but only to a limit; if design is good they can act as enhancers. Particularly poor design cannot be effectively eliminated by aids and training. Traditionally, and somewhat ineffectively, problems identified during HAZOPs or other hazard assessment methods have automatically had an action noted such as 'provide operating instructions', 'ensure adequate training' and similar.

2.6 Performance assurance

The implications of any incompatibility between personnel and their equipment can be checked through error identification and quantification. The final check for compatibility can be achieved during commissioning and operating via performance checking. It is important that if any personnel selection requirements were logged as necessary for compatibility with the design demands, these personnel characteristics should be looked for during the operational phase of the system life cycle.

3 THE SYSTEM LIFE CYCLE

There are a number of identifiable stages within a system's development. These can be considered as possible target points by which stage a certain level of task description should be reached. This will ensure that the best use is made of the task information available. These life cycle stages are as follows:

3.1 Concept

A product or service need is identified with consideration of the market requirement, for example, the need for additional regional electricity supply. The basic inputs and outputs of the system are defined and a philosophy decision should be made regarding the role of people. At this point, it is possible to document whether it is hoped the system will be automatic, semi-automatic or manually controlled and whether past designs with their human roles will be used or modified.

3.2 Functional specification

At this stage, the process or system units are defined (unit operations) linked together and associated with system sub-goals. If a new design, then the feasibility of the process is determined. The system is represented as a flow sheet or process flow diagram. It is possible to document the major sub-goals of the system and to estimate the time slots necessary for fulfilling each goal, hence, a high level system activity plan can be prepared. Tight time limits dictated by the system or process may immediately preclude operator involvement.

3.3 Preliminary design

Specific methods are selected for material transfers and communication structures. These are recorded as Piping and Instrumentation Diagrams or Engineering Flow Diagrams. The need for specific items of equipment and control mechanisms are detailed. At this stage, further thought should be given to human involvement. Should valves be manually operated, locally operated or operated by software control logic or the state of the system? (e.g. pressure control valve, level control valve). What information do people require to monitor the system and ensure its productivity and safety? Are there any goals that must be accomplished but without there being suitable technology? Are there any unknowns about the system chemistry? Is the technology complex and in need of a significant amount of understanding? All these aspects can be addressed during task analysis and documented using a TA representation technique, for example Hierarchical Task Analysis (see Table 1). This task information should be used to provide human factors guidelines for the instrument and mechanical design engineers and draughtsmen. At this stage, hazard assessment and Hazard and Operability Studies can be carried out. Such teams should include human factors specialists or people knowledgable of the discipline to check for human involvement and potential problems in order to prevent or minimise problems during detailed design. For example, if the wrong valve could be opened, ensure that it has coding elements within its design (e.g. handle type and size or button design if remote), its labelling and positioning. If appropriate, consider the use of interlocks.

3.4 Detailed design

This phase establishes the layout of equipment and the choice of specific items. System equipment is positioned and drawn to scale, labels are designed and located, the control system is finalised and instrumentation provided. At this point, the task description should be almost complete with sufficient level of detail to feed forward into the design of operating instructions.

3.5 Construction

Construction often occurs in stages. Sections that have been designed in detail and approved are built whilst other areas are still being finalised. Problems can often emerge at this point resulting in deviations from the design, which can possibly break down the compatibility with human capabilities. It is necessary to check that the task analysis assumptions remain valid. If not, the implications of change must be addressed.

3.6 Commissioning

As a final pre-operational phase, the system is tested and checked for functioning and any necessary modifications can be made to instrumentation and control. This is the first chance for checking the realism of the task analysis and its ability to be left in place as a QA document.

3.7 Operating and maintaining

The system is now running and fulfilling its role, with maintenance work ensuring that this situation continues for as long as the system is required. The task analysis process can now act as a monitoring function, ensuring that the personnel requirements identified for successful compatibility between people and equipment are maintained and that plant modifications do not alter the design in such a way that new demands are created.

4 THE TASK ANALYSIS PROCESS

Human factors issues are best assisted by re-iterations of task analysis with information collection and representation taking place through each stage of the system life cycle, building on the stage before. This is because the amount of detail available increases as the system design is refined. In addition, check points can be established for ensuring that earlier suggestions have been incorporated. Every human factors issue cannot be considered from day one; as indicated, certain issues can be raised and checked but others have to wait for more detail. Conversely, if human factors was left out of the design process, it may be found at the commissioning or operating stage that the resulting system is badly flawed and inoperable, or unable to be maintained, or that significantly more personnel are required to make things work or to ensure safety.

The task analysis process has two dominant features:

(a) The feed forward of an increasingly detailed task profile. This acts as a QA document and ensures that everyone working on the project has the same understanding of the expected level and type of human involvement.

(b) Exchange of information relating to different human factors issues and their requirements, with design decisions based on a knowledgeable trade-off between human and engineering requirements. Potential problems with one aspect of human factors may be overcome by provisions relating to another.

Figure 1 demonstrates the interactions needed between the different human factors issues through the plant life cycle in order to achieve compatibility between personnel and their equipment. The detailed steps, required to cover each issue, indicate the role of task analysis. As a whole, these steps need to be covered within the time span indicated, but in themselves may vary in time commitment and life cycle stage.

The solid connecting lines demonstrate how a task description can feed forward between human factors assessments, developing more detail and accuracy as the system design progresses. The dotted connecting lines indicate information flows between the human factors assessments so that design decisions based on one issue can influence the others.

Figure 2 indicates the QA decision loop that should be entered at each life cycle check point, and at regular time intervals during the operational phase. This ensures that the TA process does not continue in isolation but that the information and implications for human factors are transferred through to designers as well as operations.

To support this general task analysis process, the user will need specific task analysis techniques. The task analysis sub-group of the Human Factors and Reliability Group identified in the region of forty useable techniques that supported task data collection, task representation or both. This group is currently producing a Task Analysis Handbook (see Acknowledgement) documenting a sub-set of these techniques and demonstrating how they support the Task Analysis Process.

5   SELECTING TASK ANALYSIS TECHNIQUES

A loose distinction is made between TA techniques used to help the assessor collect information (for example; activity sampling, verbal protocol analysis) and those used to document or represent the information. Certain techniques are acknowledged as facilitators of both (for example; link analysis; signal flow graph analysis, state space action diagrams).

It is important to point out that not all the TA techniques can be used at every stage in the system life cycle, nor do they necessarily facilitate coverage of all the human factors issues. Based on this understanding, it is important to select specific techniques capable of assisting with the task analysis process. There are no specifically right or wrong techniques that help to document a given system's human tasks. In fact, it has been shown that most TA assessors modify existing techniques to suit the particular situation they face - hence the large number of techniques published within the literature (3) (4). A sample of these techniques is presented in Table 1.

Two techniques, in particular, tend to be used as a focus for task analysis; the first is hierarchical task analysis (Figure 3) and the second is task decomposition or tabular format technique (Figure 4). The reasons for their dominance is that the former provides the iterative process necessary to pursue a design's evolution from day one and the latter gives the analyst scope to record important supporting information. HTA starts with major task goals which are then divided into sub-task goals and eventually specific physical and mental actions. HTA also ensures an understanding of how the different sub-tasks fit together via task plans which help when considering time dimensions and workload levels. Tabular format methods can be used to provide additional information to the HTA or can be produced directly for procedural type tasks. HTA and tabular format can be used at all stages within the system life cycle and for addressing all the human factors issues.

Other techniques are at their best when used as supporting techniques, to pursue particular problem areas or particular human factors issues.

6   TO CONCLUDE

The design of any large or complex system, of which nuclear plant are prime examples, will benefit from engineering for equipment capability and human capability. To help ensure a compatible design, personnel task demands and needs must be formally analysed and documented. This explicit information can then be updated in the same way as engineering documentation and drawings, and be used as a tool by design engineers. The complete task analysis process can be implemented as part of an auditable quality assurance procedure, extending from concept to operations, in order to design and maintain the compatibility between system equipment and personnel. This should ensure that the system can operate at its optimum in terms of safety and production. There is some evidence that this is starting to occur within the nuclear industry (5).

ACKNOWLEDGEMENTS

Many of the ideas that are expressed within this paper have evolved through working within the Task Analysis Working Group (TAWG) of the national Human Factors and Reliability Group. Currently, this group is developing a Guide to Task Analysis which introduces the concept of the task analysis process, detailed descriptions of 25 task analysis techniques and supporting case studies.

TAWG can be contacted via the author or via: HFRG, SRD, AEA Technology, Wigshaw Lane, Culcheth, Warrington, Cheshire WA3 4NE.

REFERENCES

(1)   Miller R B   A Method for Man-Machine Task Analysis WADC Tech Rept, 53, 137 Wright-Patterson Air Force Base, OH, 1953.

(2)   Annett J and Duncan KD   Task analysis and training design Occupational Psychology, 1967, 41, 211-221

(3)   Shepherd A   Analysis and Training of Information Technology Tasks   In Diaper D (ed) Task Analysis for Human Computer Interaction, 1989, (Ellis Harwood, London).

(4)   Wilson JR and Corlett EN Evaluation of Human Work : A practical ergonomics methodology Parts I and II, 1990, (Taylor and Francis, London).

(5)   Reed J et al   Design of Emergency Shutdown Panels in Contemporary Ergonomics 1990 ed E J Lovesey, 1990, 393 - 398, (Taylor and Francis).

Table 1: The two major Task Analysis Techniques plus a range of Subsidiary Task Analysis Techniques

Technique	Life Cycle Stage	Human Factors Issues	Role	Summary
1. Hierarchical Task Analysis (HTA)	ALL	ALL	Representation	A method of recording system goals and task sub-goals, with their order of performance, that can be re-described to the necessary level of detail. If recorded pictorially it looks like a tree with branches and sub-branches.
2. Decomposition or Tabular Format	ALL	ALL	Representation	A set of short descriptions is produced for the task elements, with additional information presented according to a set of pre-determined sub-headings.
3. Activity Sampling	Operating and Maintaining	Performance Assurance	Collection	Real-time human actions are observed and recorded at a selected sampling interval. Sampling frequency should be at least twice the frequency of the behaviour of interest or at random intervals for routine repetitive tasks.
4. Checklists	ALL	ALL	Collection	Used to check that a system complies with pre-determined standards. This may be designed as a form for approval prior to a project moving forward to the next phase.
5. Confusion Matrices	Detailed Design Onwards	Performance Assurance	Representation	This is a tabular plot of stimuli (displays) against potential responses. Actual task responses are recorded on the grid squares with the diagonal showing the frequency of correct responses.
6. Link Analysis	Detailed Design Onwards	Workload, Work Needs, Performance Assurance	Representation	A diagrammatic representation of visual or physical movement between system components. This includes frequency and importance information and is accompanied by a tabular data sheet.

Table 1 Continued

	Technique	Life Cycle Stage	Human Factors Issues	Role	Summary
7.	Operator Action Event Trees	Functional Specification Onwards	Performance Assurance	Representation	A representation of success and failure routes through an action sequence. This can take place at any level of task detail. A failure probability can be attached to each stage so as to produce an overall probability of success/ failure for the complete event.
8.	Operator Modification Surveys	Commissioning Onwards	Work Needs, Performance Assurance	Collection	The assessor enters the workplace and looks for any temporary modifications made by the workers. These are recorded under three headings; memory aids, perceptual cues and instrument grouping. This can be used to establish areas of difficulty.
9.	Operational Sequence Diagrams	Preliminary Design Onwards	Workload, Skills and Knowledge Acquisition, Performance Assurance	Representation	Tasks are represented diagrammatically often in the form of a flowchart making use of standard symbols and showing the links between operations and their normal sequence. These are supported by a text description. It can be used to illustrate relations between personnel, equipment & time
10.	Simulation	Preliminary Design Onwards	Work Needs, Skills and Knowledge, Performance Assurance	Collection	The task activities take place on a representation of the equipment or information and controls. This may be of high (equipment) or low (paper) fidelity depending upon the reasons for undertaking the simulation.
11.	Verbal Protocol	Commissioning Onwards	Work Needs, Skills and Knowledge Performance Assurance	Collection	An expert carries out the task whilst providing a running commentary of thoughts and reasons for actions. Useful for identifying knowledge requirements and mental proces- sing necessary for successful task completion.
12.	Walk Through, Talk Through	Commissioning Onwards	Skills and Knowledge, Performance Assurance	Collection	Workers who know the system demonstrate their tasks either on the plant or a representation of it. At the same time, they are prompted to describe and explain the actions and methods. Movements and comments must be recorded and analysed.

104

© IMechE 1990 C409/013

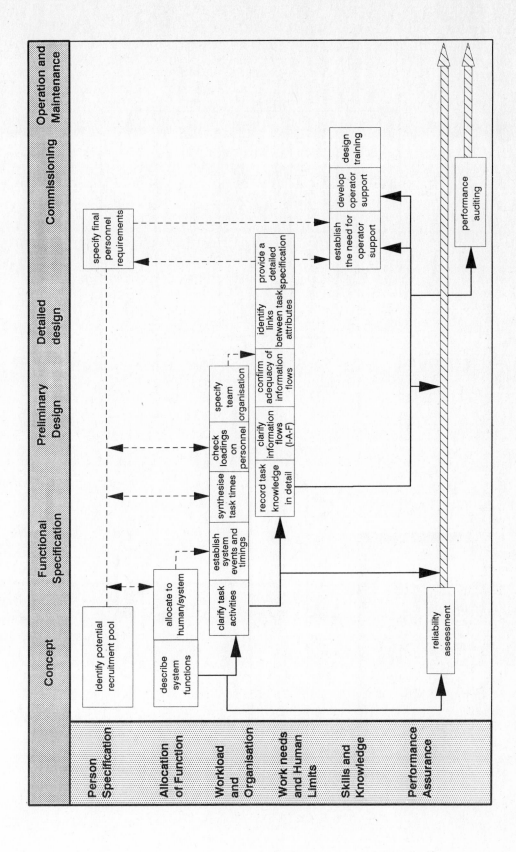

Fig 1   Integrating task analysis during system design

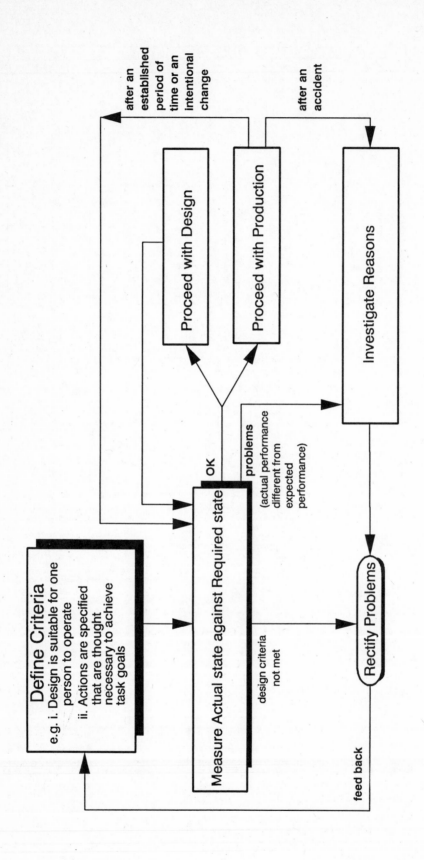

Fig 2   Quality assurance decision loop

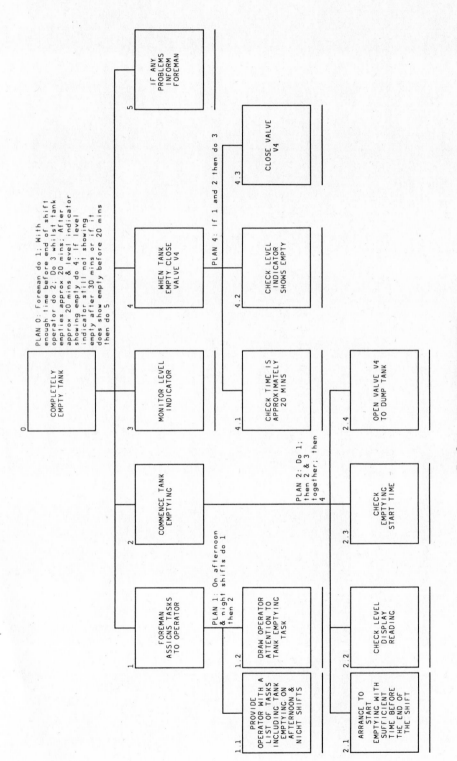

PLAN 0: Foreman do 1; With
enough time before end of shift
operator do 2; Do 3 whilst tank
empties approx 20 mins; After
approx 20 mins & level indicator
showing empty do 4; If level
indicator still not showing
empty after 30 mins or if it
does show empty before 20 mins
then do 5

| 0 | COMPLETELY EMPTY TANK |

| 1 | FOREMAN ASSIGNS TASKS TO OPERATOR | | 2 | COMMENCE TANK EMPTYING | | 3 | MONITOR LEVEL INDICATOR | | 4 | WHEN TANK EMPTY CLOSE VALVE V4 | | 5 | IF ANY PROBLEMS INFORM FOREMAN |

PLAN 1: On afternoon
& night shifts do 1
then 2

| 1.1 | PROVIDE OPERATOR WITH A LIST OF TASKS INCLUDING TANK EMPTYING ON AFTERNOON & NIGHT SHIFTS | | 1.2 | DRAW OPERATOR ATTENTION TO TANK EMPTYING TASK |

PLAN 2: Do 1;
then 2 & 3
together; then
4

| 2.1 | ARRANGE TO START EMPTYING WITH SUFFICIENT TIME BEFORE THE END OF THE SHIFT | | 2.2 | CHECK LEVEL DISPLAY READING | | 2.3 | CHECK EMPTYING START TIME | | 2.4 | OPEN VALVE V4 TO DUMP TANK |

PLAN 4: If 1 and 2 then do 3

| 4.1 | CHECK TIME IS APPROXIMATELY 20 MINS | | 4.2 | CHECK LEVEL INDICATOR SHOWS EMPTY | | 4.3 | CLOSE VALVE V4 |

Fig 3   An example of HTA

Sub-Task	Information Needs	Actions Required	Feedback	Potential Errors	Consequences

Fig 4   Example of tabular TA format headings

C409/014

Quality assurance of human error modelling in a major probabilistic risk assessment programme

H S RYCRAFT, BSc, MSaRS
British Nuclear Fuels plc, Sellafield

SYNOPSIS A method of incorporating the consideration of operator error within a major PRA exercise is described along with the quality assurance procedures employed to ensure a quality product.

1 INTRODUCTION

British Nuclear Fuels (BNFL) Sellafield is an integrated irradiated nuclear fuel handling and reprocessing site on the West Cumbrian coast. Its prime functions are to receive and treat about 1000 t per annum of 'Magnox' type uranium fuel from reactors in the UK and abroad, and to receive and store uranium oxide fuel. The site includes fuel storage ponds, chemical reprocessing plant, plutonium and uranium finishing lines, high and medium active liquid storage facilities and liquid effluent clean-up facilities.

During 1986 the Nuclear Installations Inspectorate (NII) carried out a safety audit at Sellafield. Following this, the NII required BNFL to prepare a "fully developed Safety Case" (fdSC) for each of the approximately 50 existing plants. The fdSCs had to replace any existing safety assessments with extensive qualitative and quantitative assessment covering both routine work and fault conditions. The safety of both the workforce and the general public had to be examined.

Senior safety managers at Sellafield decided to identify hazards using the structured HAZOPs technique and then to assess the risks associated with these hazards using probabilistic risk assessment (PRA).

The incorporation of quality into an assessment of a plant's safety has many facets eg:

- quality of information available for assessment
- quality of procedures and management employed in carrying out the assessments
- quality of personnel carrying out the assessments.

To assess the risks posed by a plant, the assessors had to quantify the risks and evaluate the results against common criteria. The risk criteria chosen for the PRA already existed, having been developed by BNFL some ten years earlier, mainly to provide design targets for a new generation of plants.

This paper concentrates on describing the methods employed to assure the quality of human error modelling and quantification which formed an integral part of the PRA.

2 THE QUALITY OF INFORMATION

Following a few HAZOP meetings for each plant, it became obvious that with standard guide words suitably modified with operator interaction in mind, along with the advice from the operator representatives on the team, the HAZOP method was capable of broadly identifying where an error by an operator or supervisor could lead to a potentially hazardous situation. Similarly, consideration of the operating instructions identified crucial steps in a task where a mistake could lead to an untoward event. With all the teams using the same method, the PRA management could assure themselves that the majority of fault sequences along with the potential operator involvement, were identified. These potential error situations were then recorded and forwarded to the PRA analysts for assessment in more detail.

The PRA analyst would first calculate the potential consequences of the identified faults, and if they were close to or exceeded the criteria consequence level, the frequency of the fault had to be calculated. These calculations were undertaken using fault tree analysis which had to contain appropriate human error modelling.

3 THE DEVELOPMENT OF HUMAN ERROR ASSESSMENT IN THE PRA

The quantitative analytical tool called 'fault tree analysis' is widely used in industry for the examination of systems and plant safety. However, carrying out a PRA is not straightforward, the uncertainties inherent in both the system under scrutiny and the PRA methodology can affect confidence levels in the final risk figure, which must be appreciated before the results may be used.

To carry out such assessments of these plants without addressing human error would have been easier and would be similar to comparable large PRA exercises carried out in the past by other organisations. It was

obvious, however, that to omit the consideration if the human operator in the system
under review could lead to optimistic or misleading assumptions about the risks posed.
This was particularly true of the older
plants at Sellafield which have many manual
systems and/or require operator intervention
in the event of a malfunction. So a PRA
study for Sellafield that did not consider
the human operator as part of the system
would have been at best incomplete, and at
worst, misleading in terms of risk. This was
unacceptable to the management organising the
assessments and this led to the development
of the method described in this paper.

The system developed integrated operator
error probabilities with the consideration of
equipment reliability, allowing the overall
system to be assessed. At no time at this
initial assessment stage was the operator
component separated from the equipment reliability. This integration is believed to provide a more realistic model of the system's
risk than if the two components were separately assessed.

A survey of the quantitative methods for
assessing operator reliability revealed that
the most widely accepted international method
was the "Technique for Human Error Risk Pre-
diction" (THERP) developed in 1978 by Swain
and Guttman in Sandia Laboratories (1). The
technique had advantages in that it was well
known and had been used on many nuclear plant
studies (primarily in the USA), and its
weaknesses were also known and could be taken
into account when using its data.

To use this method on its own had two
major disadvantages. The error data did not
cover some of the routine activities undertaken at Sellafield and comprehensive
application of the technique required many
trained human factor specialists.

The first disadvantage was dealt with by
substituting reliability experience gained at
site, and using 'expert judgement' (a recognised technique for allocating human error
probabilities (2)). The probability data
base used was therefore a hybrid of THERP
and expert judgement values. A basic data
base already used for the design case for the
new Thermal Oxide Reprocessing Plant (THORP)
being built at Sellafield, formed the core of
the data base. This data base (called HED
(3)), derived from WASH 1400 II (6), already
had expert judgement probability values
produced by safety professionals at the
design stage of the new plant. To use the
data base the design assessor had to
reference all human errors to a similar item
in the data base, or a new human error
probability and its description had to be
entered within the data base. Thus HED
contained simply a set of error descriptions
and associated probabilities. It was not as
decompositional as THERP and had no specific
model of dependency. The HED database was
further modified during the human error
modelling for the Sellafield PRAs, by
incorporating operational experience from
the plant under examination so that each
plant eventually had its own tailored human
error data base.

Experience had shown that most of the
operator errors occurring in the fault trees
were simple lapses and slips. To assess

these all in detail, using a resource intensive technique such as THERP was not considered necessary. There were also benefits to
be gained by integrating the operator error
treatment within the same broad approach as
equipment reliability, and radioactivity
release modelling. It would also have been
very difficult to recruit the number of
necessary personnel able to resource a THERP
approach. We expect that this will be little
different from any other company which uses
PRA for risk assessment.

Any quantitative treatment of human
error would be by trained PRA analysts with
guidance from a few experienced human factors
specialists. Human factor specialists were
already available within the department as
other work carried out by the section proved
to have the necessary pool of skilled
personnel with access to information and
developed techniques, eg Task Analysis, to
support the quantitative assessment of human
reliability within PRAs.

To produce a standard human error
assessment procedure, the THERP methodology
was examined and simplified by taking primary
elements of the method without the detailed
combination methodology. This created a
unique procedure that was usable by non
specialists by providing an effective level
of guidance based on a straightforward
decision chart. The decision chart led the
analysts by a series of questions to a
suggested probability. This probability
would then be modified (if necessary) by
consideration of any additional performance
shaping factors and/or dependency rules, as
detailed in the assessors' guidance notes.
In this way the analysis achieved an accuracy
which was acceptable for the PRA's use.
Using this method released the human factor
specialists to concentrate on those PRA's
that required complex modelling or in depth
analysis in order to identify the factors
which, with improvement, would reduce the
error likelihood.
The use of one assessor to carry out the
assessment (ie equipment and human error)
with advice from specialists has advantages.
The analyst will have an overall appreciation
of the fault sequences within an assessment
and can concentrate effort and resources on
the part of the assessment which reveals the
sequences that are of greatest importance, ie
post the greatest risk. Similarly, the limited resource of the human error specialist
can also be selectively concentrated on the
cases which are more complex or prove to have
a significant impact on safety.

The assessment procedure also required
the assessor to model the operator and time
dependencies within the system. This consideration proved to be the most difficult to
model and included 'common cause' considerations. A method was developed with the
adoption of a Human Performance Limiting
Value (HPLV). This was invoked when an
assessor had to combine operator error probabilities in their fault trees through an
AND gate, ie requiring the probabilities to
be multiplied. Most operators' actions are
affected by dependency within a system. A
reliability exceeding 1 E-4 for an operator
system must be rare and require the highest

training, optimum conditions and well designed man-machine interface. Only where true independence could be argued, eg different line management, could a probability of less than 1 E-4 be countenanced. The maximum most plants have is 30 years operating experience and when considering the opportunities for error, the most reliable operator dependent system still had probabilities emerging in the range 1 E-4.

This is where the modelling of an error sequence is very important in that the consideration of multiple and parallel errors involving the operators associated with the error sequence have to be weighed against the circumstances on the plant which provide the opportunity for the errors to occur, eg the relative difficulty of performing the error actions.

For example the assessment of an operator error involving the inadvertent operation of an inaccessible damper on a ventilation a system. Given the consequences of such an error in the given situation, then the task had to be examined in more detail to identify ways in which the probability of operator error could be reduced. Review of routine damper operations by the analyst established the opportunity for the error. At the end of the review a judgement had to be made as to whether further consideration and inclusion of the error advances the PRA of the plant and truly reflects the relative risk of the plant. For one such case, the consequences were not acceptable at the derived frequency. The solution adopted was to reduce the human error by removing the damper operating mechanism, ie an equipment modification creating a further physical barrier to the operator error.

In each case the analyst has to record an adequate explanation of the error being modelled, the performance shaping factors that affected the probability chosen and any known dependencies in the system.

Effectively the human error assessment could be thought of as a screening method whereby the human errors affecting the system/plant could be assessed and their relative importance to the safety of the workforce, general public or environment determined.

4 QUALITY OF PERSONNEL AND ANALYSIS

The analysts employed were a mixture of BNFL and contractor staff. A minimum acceptable standard of training and/or experience was predetermined and personnel were recruited against a specification.

Before an analyst was allowed to produce the assessments, they had to attend a detailed training course on all aspects of the work. This training course was produced by safety management and the lectures were given by appropriate specialists. The training detailed the method of carrying out an assessment and the reasoning behind the risk criteria adopted. As part of this course, instruction on how human errors were to be included and modelled in the assessments were given and the analysts were introduced to the human error probability data base. A manual was issued which supported the analyst's training and formed the basic reference for the analysts throughout their work. Part of this manual contained human error modelling guidance notes.

The analysts were not tested on completion of this training, as many of the assessors gained a working expertise by using the technique and their progress and approach to competence was closely monitored by reviewing the quality of the first draft/ initial assessments. If any analyst, on producing an assessment, showed a lack of expertise in any area, appropriate individual coaching was given.

The training and experience of the analysts have been an essential part of ensuring the quality of modelling within the PRA and hence the estimation of the total risk posed by a plant or system.

The management system of selection, training of the analysis, and the provision of a detailed assessment procedure manual, provided the baseline to assure a consistency of approach to the PRA. The procedure manual details the methods acceptable for undertaking the analyses, provided the associated assessment data bases, ie release fractions, equipment reliability, human error probabilities, and outlined the format(s) for presenting the results of the analyses. This provided a robust framework within which the analyst could assess the diverse risks under review and in so doing, attain an appropriate standard of quality.

5 SUPPORTING HUMAN FACTOR WORK WITHIN PLANT SAFETY ASSESSMENT

Since 1983, Plant Safety Department at Sellafield has been developing practical assessment techniques to assess in-situ the safety of the procedures and equipment used by the operators. Much of this involved standard Quality Assurance techniques in that observed procedures were judged against legislative and company policy requirements.

By 1987 this system, called Operating Safety Reviews, had already used standard ergonomic assessments and Task Analysis in determining by in-situ observation and testing the understanding of operators, the standard of safety practice on selected plants. Again the development of the system into the area of Man Machine interface and procedure/operator interface was a natural progression for the improvement of safety advice to management. In 1989 the Operating Review method was adapted to form part of a "Divisional Safety Audit" method required by Company Policy. Further methods of safety auditing are being developed for 1990 which aims to provide management with an accurate assessment of the practice of safety on their plants. Methods of assessing organisational safety, including evaluation methods for assessing 'safety culture' on plants will be examined. Emphasis remains on the assessment of safety practices as observed on plant.

Another area of importance was that of error recognition and knowledge of error sequences involving both equipment and operator. Sellafield has always kept a record of the accidents and incidents that have occurred on the site, and the records include the investigations, some dating back to 1950. Since 1971 the Nuclear Site Licence under which Sellafield operates, requires certain accidents, incidents and minor events to be recorded. As part of this record the proceedings of any investigation have to be kept. In 1984 Plant Safety Department at Sellafield were required to set up an analysis system of all radiological recorded accidents, incidents and events, in order to identify common contributory factors and root causes (4). This system has subsequently provided much insight into operator and management errors, and common organisational problems.

In summary, this expertise incorporating plant knowledge in human reliability techniques, methods of analysing incident scenarios and the knowledge of past accidents, incidents and minor events, was common to all the human factors specialists. These lead assessors were therefore assessed as being competent to act as the advisors to the PRA analysts.

6 SENSITIVITY ANALYSIS

High quality PRA includes sensitivity analyses in which possible variations of system reliability parameters, are determined. Such analyses will often show that human error rate assumptions have little effect on the hazard frequency. Where it can be shown that increasing the human error rate by an order of magnitude, or for high failure rates using unity, has little effect on the hazard frequency, then detailed analysis of the error is clearly unnecessary. Where such changes have a marked effect on the hazard frequency, more detailed analysis is necessary. In such cases the human reliability assessment was extended either by a human factor specialist or under their guidance.

These task/error sequences were modelled in more detail using Task Analysis, THERP and any other appropriate associated method, to identify whether or not the original modelling was reasonable and whether the choice of probabilities were realistic. Depending on the findings of the detailed assessment, the assessment was remodelled accordingly.

Where the system risk was shown to be "unacceptable", ie close to or breaching a Risk Criterion, the plant management were consulted and a qualitative human error assessment using task analysis was carried out. On the basis of this, operating procedures or management\supervisory procedures were improved and in some cases it was possible to identify equipment modifications that would reduce the likelihood of an operator error or improve the management supervision of a task, thereby reducing the overall risk.

A second check of the error sequences was required, ie the review of all relevant recorded incidents in order to determine whether the error sequence (or part error sequence) had occurred in Sellafield's history. This was to determine whether the assumptions made in the assessment were reflected by history.

For example, if the error was assessed at a frequency of 1 E-4 year and yet it had happened in the plant's (or equivalent plant's) history, then the fault sequence and procedural safeguards were carefully re-examined to establish whether the low figure could be justified or the error sequence required remodelling. Conversely, if the frequency assessed was very high, ie 1 E-1 and the historical review did not reveal the error sequence (or part of the error sequence) then the model was considered to be suspect and was carefully reviewed.

Using incident histories in this way gave only a crude calibration, but it gave some confidence that gross underestimation of an error was unlikely to occur and incorporated plant operating histories into the consideration of their risk. Due to the variable quality of such information, the incident histories were not used directly to derive frequencies of operator error. However, methods have been developed by BNFL and it is expected that derived data will start to become available in the near future (5).

7 VERIFICATION

Finally, in order to consolidate the quality of the assessments, they all had to go through a quality checking procedure. A number of trained and experienced personnel (a quality review team) had to scrutinise each assessment for:

- completeness
- accuracy of plant and process descriptions
- the use of the appropriate release fractions
- the use of the appropriate methodology and logic
- mathematical accuracy
- the use of the appropriate equipment reliability data
- the appropriate modelling and use of human error probabilities.

Each reviewer was identified by reference to their training and experience and their area of competence indicated in the procedure manual.

Each reviewer was authorised by the Head of Plant Safety Department before undertaking this work.

Each assessment was passed to authorised reviewers and only when it was judged to have attained the appropriate standard in each area was it issued. The PRA analyst had to obtain each quality assessor's signature to provide a record for subsequent quality assurance auditing.

8 SUMMARY

In summary, the method employed and refined by BNFL Sellafield for use in their major PRA programme for the incorporation of quantitative treatment of operator error, does not rely solely on one data source or technique.

The initial quantitative assessment is approximate, but the quality checking procedures employed assures a standard of consistency across the safety cases. This initial assessment, coupled with sensitivity analysis effectively identifies the operator errors which are critical in the fault paths, and ultimately to the risk posed by the plant. This therefore targets the more in depth analysis assessment to the errors that matter.

The assurance methods employed to ensure the quality of the person undertaking and guiding the assessments is the bedrock of the technique. The past experience and training of the analysts is relevant, but the training and guidance of the analysts during the PRA has proven to be of primary importance.

The use of this method and the human factors specialists selectively, has allowed a large number of assessments to be effectively carried out with an adequate precision at an acceptable cost.

The method is under continual review and development of the system continues, eg error modelling for diagnosis and decision making.

REFERENCES

(1)   SWAIN A D, GUTTMAN H E. Handbook of Human Reliability Analysis with Emphasis on Nuclear Power Plant Applications. NUREG/CR-1278.

(2)   COMER M K, SEAVER D A, STILLWELL W D, CADDY C D. Generating Human Reliability Estimates using Expert Judgement. 1987. NUREG/CR-3688. Vol 1 Main Report.

(3)   KIRWAN B. Comparative Evaluation of Five Human Reliability Assessment Techniques. SaRRS '88'. Altrincham.

(4)   BALL P W, RYCRAFT H S. Analysis and Reporting of Incidents at a Nuclear Fuel Reprocessing Plant. IAEA Conference. Vienna. October 1987.

(5)   KIRWAN B, MARTIN B, RYCRAFT H S, SMITH A Human Error Data Collection and Data Generation. 11th ARTS Conference, Liverpool. April 1990

(6)   WASH-1400. Reactor Safety Study - An Assessment of Accident Risks in US Commercial Nuclear Power Plants. NUREG-75/014

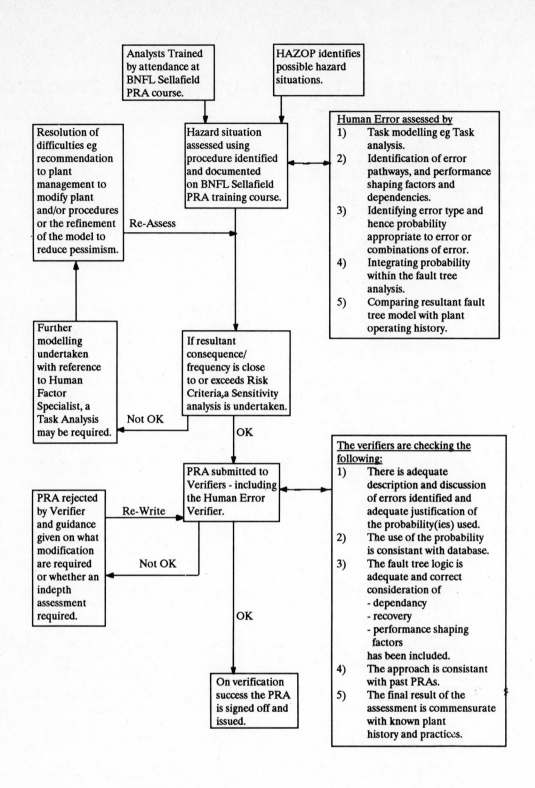

Fig 1   Flow diagram of probabilistic risk assessment procedure incorporating human error probabilities

C409/012

Human factors in the design of the advanced gas cooled reactors

Rev J E NEWELL, BSc, CEng, FIChemE, ARCS
Nuclear Electric, Gloucester

SYNOPSIS   Human error in the design process for the AGRs has contributed to delays, cost over-runs, depressed output capacities and unsatisfactory availabilities. A research programme jointly with a university will explore the nature of these human errors and the lessons to be learned from them. A few examples are given which illustrate different aspects of human error in the design process.

1.   INTRODUCTION

The programme of AGR construction in Britain has been marred by design changes, extended construction times and cost over-runs. There have been depressed output capacities and unsatisfactory availabilities. Yet there is no single factor which identifies the AGR as being fundamentally unsound. Behind the numerous design problems lie problems of human fallibility in the form of decisions taken and in the environment surrounding those decisions.

Human error has been recognised within the CEGB for many years. Emphasis has been placed upon operator error - i.e. active human failure - and upon the ergonomic procedures for reducing it. However, the AGR design experience raises human factors issues of a substantially different nature. The most significant faults have been in decisions taken or not taken and those faults have generally remained latent for considerable periods. The triggers which activate these latent faults may emerge in the course of assembling or testing components; in the process of establishing safety and reliability cases; or in operation of the plant.

Quality Assurance of the design process has hitherto concentrated upon procedures at the level of the designer to reduce the frequency of errors. This paper takes examples from selected plant areas in the AGR programme to explore why people take wrong decisions and how the quality of decision taking can be improved. Technical failures often have their roots in contract philosophy, relations between contractors, resourcing decisions, programme planning, safety perspectives and in the personal qualities of the designers themselves.

2.   BACKGROUND

The CEGB programme of Magnox stations saw a start of construction in 1957 at Bradwell and Berkeley and a completion of construction in 1971 at Wylfa. In general terms, the design and construction went relatively well, although there were some cost over-runs and some delays to programme. There were a number of design faults, by far the greatest being a failure to account for the high rates of corrosion of carbon steels in carbon dioxide coolant gas after oxide breakaway. In consequence, all of the stations except Berkeley had to be operated with gas temperature restrictions and these greatly reduced the output of the units.

In 1965, the AGR programme started with Dungeness 'B'. This new system would use the full steam temperature and pressure of the 660 MW turbines and would achieve high thermal efficiency. It was foreseen that the advanced gas cooled reactors would represent the great breakthrough to plant which would produce electricity consistently at a cost well below that of coal fired or oil fired plant.

Now, a quarter of a century later, that vision has not materialised. After significant delays, Hinkley Point 'B' and Hunterston 'B' have come near to design output for several years. Heysham II and Torness were commissioned in remarkably short time and showed themselves able to generate at above their design capacity. More recently, that capacity has been greatly curtailed by difficulties with refuelling equipment. Hartlepool and Heysham I were severely delayed, were expensive and have only slowly been raised to high loads as faults have been corrected. Dungeness 'B' has the worst record, although its future looks better than its past.

Major causes of some of these problems lie in the field of construction contract structures and site industrial relations. They are outside of the scope of the present paper. Clearly they accounted for much delay and expense. However, if they were the sole problem areas then, when construction was eventually completed, the plant should have worked as intended. Often this was not the case. The plain fact is that, when they were needed, some of the designs were wrong.

One possibility could be that the concept of the AGR was itself wrong. Had this been so, then, across all of the stations, there should have been a small number of major recurrent problems. An example could have been a consistent failure of cores to provide sufficient reactivity. Another example could have been a generalised large deterioration of corrosion behaviour due to unexpected effects of radiation. In fact, there were no systematic faults of this magnitude which would have shown the AGR system to be fundamentally defective. It is significant that, in critical nuclear areas, the AGRs have shown few major problems, whilst nearly all of the design deficiencies have arisen in the areas of complex general engineering. It is not only in the case of the AGRs that major projects have experienced multiple design deficiencies as a result of human error. Research into the nature and mechanisms of the human error processes therefore offers the prospect of yielding large benefits to society in the future. Such research is being planned as a joint Nuclear Electric/University project. This paper is able to give a preliminary discussion of the issues.

3. THE NATURE OF ERROR

The fact that the problems of the AGR designs have not been grounded in some immutable limitation in physics means that they are most probably attributable to incorrect decisions. As will be seen, these decisions may lie at various different levels. Known examples include macro political/industrial decision errors down to an error of design judgement in the size of a small dowell pin. Collectively, they are human errors.

Of course, human error has been present throughout human history. Attempts to combat it are evident in the regulatory requirements and building codes which existed several thousand years ago. Ancient codices bear the certification marks of QA auditors, who tried to ensure accuracy.

In modern industrial terms attention to human error focussed first upon errors in the production line. These are generally active failures i.e. the operator error has immediate consequences and the relationship between the error and the effect is apparent. Of course, there may be delayed effects revealed as subsequent product failure. Analysis of that failure is used to re-define production line facilities and procedures for future use. However, at the production line itself, the emphasis is upon the avoidance of active human failures. (There is a parallel activity to avoid mechanical failures.)

These active errors may be of several types. They may be unintentional deviations, either in what is done or what is not done. They may be deliberate deviations, usually in the form of habitual malpractices so as to involve the use of least effort or in response to an indifferent environment. They may also result from inadequacies in the planned and defined actions.

It is a natural development from treatment of human error on the production line to dealing with active errors in the power station control room. This is an area which has received substantial effort in the electricity industry, especially during the past two decades.

Design deficiencies are usually different in nature. A mistake will typically have no immediate consequences. In the case of a major project, the latent error may lie dormant for years until some set of circumstances triggers a plant failure. Cause and effect may be difficult to correlate and emphasis tends to be focussed upon the immediate trigger rather than upon the underlying design fault. Moreover, the time lapse between cause and effect may mean that history has lost the details surrounding the cause. Even worse, a search to establish commercial blame and hence financial liability may obscure the evidence for the real cause. Often an inquiry may establish either cause or blame, but not both.

As with active errors, causes of latent errors may lie in unintentional or deliberate deviations on the part of the designer. Deficiencies in planned and defined actions are even more likely to be important as causes of latent errors, compared with the causes of active errors.

4. SCOPE OF THE DESIGN PROCESS

It is tempting to define the design process as starting when (figuratively) the draughtsman first puts his pencil to paper. Yet many of the design faults have their roots at an earlier stage than this. It is a design decision to determine how many designers shall be engaged on each stage of the design and how much time they shall have. Equally, the quality of the final design is influenced by decisions on designers' facilities, such as computers, etc. Other precursor design decisions include the location, type and size of plant to be installed and its intended operating regime.

Major impacts upon the final plant design can come from political decisions on public perception and public acceptance. Decisions on financial framework have a large impact upon design, as emphasis shifts between capital expenditure and revenue expenditure.

It is thus preferable to consider the design process as including all of those decisions in which human error may be the root cause of an inadequate design of the plant.

5. THE DUNGENESS 'B' DECISION

One of the largest examples of human error in the AGR design process was the decision to place the Dungeness 'B' contract at the then prevailing state of design development. It was indeed a complex political, commercial and economic decision, some details of which may not emerge until the release of the 1965 Cabinet papers at the end of 1995. An outline concept of the plant was available which was expected to yield a more effective and economic station with 20% more output than the designs of competitors, but that concept had only been produced late in the process of tendering.

Within the Atomic Power Construction Company (APC), decisions were taken that resulted in the submission of a priced tender for a plant design which had not been developed. Assumptions were made that, during the course of construction, the design would evolve in such a way that the plant would meet the performance requirements and that it would be constructed to time and within the contract price. Those assumptions were not realised; APC went into liquidation; full load has not been achieved after a quarter of a century from the start of construction and availability has been poor.

People do not readily take such risky decisions as this. It runs against the normal tradition of engineering and commercial prudence. However it is equally surprising that the tender was accepted and that Treasury authorisation was given for the investment of public funds. Politically a reactor system was demanded, and demanded rapidly, which would not produce international dependence for technology. Strong views were raised in favour of a British-developed reactor. Its prospects would stand stronger in the public eye if it were shown to be economic. Yet the more developed designs did not look cost-effective and a gamble was taken on a undeveloped, but seemingly more economic design. These considerations appear to have placed pressure on the decision takers to depart from usual prudence and to proceed without waiting for more complete designs and corresponding economic analyses. This was a monumental case of human error and it merits research to analyse the mechanisms which produced it.

Unavoidably a project as large as a nuclear power station must involve decisions at a political level. It impacts upon national budget and international balance of trade; perhaps on national security and political trading preferences; certainly upon employment, regional investment and infrastructure; inevitably upon company profitability. Decisions which appear to be engineering or industrial in nature may have to be taken right outside of the engineering domain. Yet they need to be taken with a full comprehension of engineering and commercial reality. Reduction of the risk of human error involves the development of a 'quality plan' which defines who shall take each type of decision, according to which criteria and upon the basis of which inputs. Even now there is little evidence to show that this lesson has been learned. Unfortunately, it sometimes appears that only the most important decisions are exempt from QA!

6. THE CONSORTIUM DECISION

Another macro decision had dramatic effects upon the design of the AGRs. The design of the early reactors at Calder Hall and Chapel Cross had gone well. Hinton wished that the following civil reactors should be handled in a similar manner. This would have meant that the design would have been by one single organisation under his direct control. Construction would then be undertaken by companies under contract. However, the Government insisted that there must be commercial competition for complete contracts, in the belief that competition would yield a better end-product at a more economic

price. (This is, of course reminiscent of opinions current today.) As a result, five consortia were set up, to tender in competition with each other. In consequence, each station differed from the others. This same approach carried forward into the AGR programme, with the exception of Heysham II and Torness.

There is no doubt that the consortia had the ability to construct major plants, whether nuclear power stations or different industrial processes, provided that the designs were available. That ability could provide the scope for construction competition. Such competition would apply whether or not the total project contracts were made 'competitive'. The same was not true of design. The nuclear power industry has demanded an inordinately high proportion of the nation's top quality technologists. The Government, apparently unknowingly, took a design decision. It was to subdivide the available technologists into several groups competing with each other for designer resource, such that none of the groups was fully adequate for the job. In imposing its decision, the Government seems not to have realised that this was a design decision which would prove to be a major error.

7. THE HARTLEPOOL/HEYSHAM I BOILER CLOSURES

Another set of decisions which involved very costly errors was that relating to the Hartlepool/Heysham I boiler closures (although even these costs are small compared with the Dungeness 'B' decision and the Consortium decision).

The Magnox stations had, in the main, relied upon steel for the primary pressure circuit. For the two final stations and for all of the AGR stations, reinforced concrete pressure vessels (RPVs) were used. These have the advantage that their strength lies in large numbers of steel tendons, thus providing substantial redundancy against tendon failure.

For Hartlepool and Heysham I a novel form of boiler was used. These are cylindrical in shape and are lowered into eight cylindrical holes in the RPV. It would be a large and unacceptable accident if one of these boilers were to be blown out of the RPV, so that the form of boiler closure and its retention are critically important. Recognising that steel pressure components had been acceptable for most of the Magnox stations and that steel pressure vessels were acceptable for PWR stations throughout the world, the plant vendors designed a steel closure head for the boilers. The design was such that the critical features in these components were in compression and the safety of this design was approved by the vendors and by the CEGB. No objection was raised at that time by the Nuclear Installations Inspectorate (NII).

When construction was well advanced, the Inspector raised objection to the use of steel for the closures, even although it was in compression. Construction work had to be halted for many months whilst a new design of concrete closure head was developed. The result was a long delay to construction and a large cost penalty.

More recently, with the introduction of the PWR, the Inspectorate has adopted the world opinion that steel may be used for the primary circuit, even although it is used in tension.

For the purpose of this paper, it is not of first importance whether the error was in believing the steel closure to be safe, or in believing it to be unsafe. One or other was erroneous and the change of mind was very costly. The NII exercises a large influence upon the final design and it must therefore be seen as a part of the design process. A variety of human factors contributed to this costly reversal of policy. They range from the resourcing of the NII, through the pressures upon the designers, to the decisions upon proceeding with construction. It is now recognised that, as far as is possible, the safety authorities should accept the design as early as is practicable and certainly before major fabrication or construction commences. Even so, it must be recognised that new information may cause that endorsement to be modified or rescinded.

8. THE NII PSYCHE

Whether or not the boiler closure change was necessary, it did draw attention to a psychological factor which is believed to have applied on occasions as a cause of design change and programme delay. If the inspectors are to be effective in their appraisal of design safety, then they must be the intellectual equals of (or superiors to) the original designers. Thus, they cannot be satisfied psychologically with mere checking, but require a creative input comparable with that of the designers. This means that they must show, even if only to themselves, that they have achieved something of a magnitude compatible with their abilities. Absence of detected errors in design may well lead to the imposition of subjectively conditioned changes. A growing Inspectorate must understandably be keen to exercise its muscles and its staff must wish to establish themselves. Failure to allow for human nature in this way should be expected to lead to change and delay.

9. DESIGN CONTRACT STRATEGY

It is only necessary to have read the technical and popular press over the years to see claims that AGR deficiencies are due, on the one hand, to the CEGB interference in the Contractors' designs or, on the other hand, to the inadequacy of the Contractors' efforts, despite hand-holding by the CEGB. Those who have been intimately involved in the design process see truth in both claims, but deplore the drum beating which has sometimes taken place. The reality on a day to day basis is that engineers and technologists from the vendors and the customer work closely together.

The mere fact that images of conflict have been promulgated does reflect upon the nature of contracts for design, although the approach to Heysham II and Torness was different. For most of the AGR stations, responsibilities during the construction activities tend to be fairly well defined. On the other hand, there was inadequate definition of relationships during the design activities. This might have been a satisfactory arrangement if the Contractors had been liable for all costs arising from deficient design, including all operating penalties. In such a case, the purchaser would only need to make such checks as related to his legal liabilities and safety.

As the CEGB would be liable for the vast majority of the costs of defective design, it was necessary for them to have a substantial staff to monitor designs and hence to limit their commercial risks. Indeed, there has always been a strong case for the Hinton view. This would have meant that the design would have been done by the organisation which carried the penalties for any deficiency in that design. However, because of the Government decisions, large teams of scarce people were placed with both the vendors and the purchasers.

Recognising that the contract cannot place the main commercial penalty upon the contractors for design fault, then the purpose of the design contract can be questioned. Is it in fact a contract to design a nuclear power station? Alternatively, is it a contract to combine a large number of highly skilled people in the most effective way in order to design a nuclear power station? The first form of contract would be based upon an outline performance specification. The second would be based upon human interactions. This human contract has not hitherto been used for power station design and it needs research in order to develop it. Failure to do this has sometimes resulted in the alignment of people into adversarial groups rather than an integrated team.

10. BOILER DESIGN

With all types of nuclear power station, boilers have caused substantial loss-of-production problems. In America, they have frequently been called the Achilles' heel of the PWR. In Britain, the boilers on the gas cooled reactors have contributed their substantial share to loss of production. The problems of the British units were discussed at length in two special issues of Nuclear Energy (5 & 6) in 1986. The present Author wrote the introductory paper under the heading "'Twixt core and conventional plant". Herein lies the root cause of many of the shortcomings. The high technology of the reactors attracted a large pool of the best available human resources. The conventional plant was fairly traditional and attracted a suitable resource.

Boilers lay between these two. There was an
inadequate perception of the level of innovative
technology and science required in their design,
development and usage. This was reflected in
the approach to human resourcing and particularly in the small effort contributed by the
CEGB. The cost of learning by remedial research
instead of predictive research has been very
high.

The most outstanding example has been on the
boilers for Hartlepool and Heysham I. The
concept showed great originality. These units
are very compact and represent an effective use
of heat transfer surface. The helical design is
more than usually tolerant to temperature
maldistributions across the diameter of the
reactor. Yet the human resources applied and
the decisions taken were insufficient to
understand the ways in which they would behave,
the instabilities which they would develop and
their sensitivity to dimensional tolerances.

11. FUELLING MACHINERY

One of the largest causes of lack of output
capacity in recent years has been the fuelling
machinery. The AGRs were all intended to refuel
on load, yet this intent is not realised. Some
of them may achieve low load refuelling whilst
others will remain with off load refuelling. At
some of the stations, refuelling rates are still
slow, so that reactivity and output have been
limited. As in the case of the boilers, root
causes lie in human resourcing at the design
phase and in the timing of the use of those
resources.

12. DISCUSSION

The examples mentioned in this paper are just a
few representatives of technical problems in the
AGRs whose root causes are to be found in human
factors. It may be said that only rarely is bad
design the root cause of plant failure or of
design-related delays and cost over-runs. Much
more frequently the root cause is human error in
the design process - this process being
understood in the wider sense, which includes
the designer, his environment and the management
decisions which surround him. The cost to the
nation of human error in the design process is
enormous. Yet the research which is put into it
is small compared with the research effort
devoted to human error in other fields. This
brief review gives some background to the
programme which Nuclear Electric and a
university propose to follow over the next few
years.

smg/JEN/Report/435

C409/011

Goal-oriented failure analysis—a systems analysis approach to hazard identification

A B REEVES, BSc, BA, CEng, IChemE, J DAVIES and J FOSTER
AEA Technology, Culcheth, Warrington, Cheshire
G L WELLS, BSc, CEng, IChemE
Department of Mechanical and Process Engineering, University of Sheffield

SYNOPSIS Goal-Oriented Failure Analysis, GOFA, is a methodology which is being developed to identify and analyse the potential failure modes of a hazardous plant or process. The technique will adopt a structured **top-down** approach, with a particular failure **goal** being systematically analysed. A **systems analysis** approach is used, with the analysis being organised around a systems diagram of the plant or process under study. GOFA will also use **checklists** to supplement the analysis – these checklists will be prepared in advance of a group session and will help to guide the analysis and avoid unnecessary time being spent on identifying obvious failure modes or failing to identify certain hazards or failures.

GOFA is being developed with the aim of providing a hazard identification methodology which is more efficient and stimulating than the conventional approach to HAZOP. The top-down approach should ensure that the analysis is more focused and the use of a systems diagram will help to pull the analysis together at an early stage whilst also helping to structure the sessions in a more stimulating way than the conventional techniques. GOFA will be, essentially, an extension of the HAZOP methodology.

GOFA is currently being computerised by S&R using a knowledge-based systems approach for implementation. The Goldworks II expert systems development tool is being used.

1   INTRODUCTION

Hazard and Operability Study (HAZOP) is a technique which is used extensively in the chemical process industry and nuclear industry for identifying **'what can go wrong'** on hazardous processes. The overall exercise is known as **hazard identification**, which is the first stage in a **risk assessment** study. Subsequent stages in risk assessment are frequency analysis (ie 'how often'), consequence analysis (ie 'how bad'), with the final computational stage being the calculation of risk levels to exposed persons.

Although HAZOP is widely used it still suffers from serious inadequacies; these are discussed further in Ref 1, with the most serious problems being:

-    time-consuming and therefore costly

-    tedious

-    ineffective computerisation to date

-    poor brain-storming with current approaches

The aim of the GOFA project is to provide a PC-based tool that will improve on the existing HAZOP methodology for hazard identification applications, by providing a more stimulating and efficient tool.

2   BACKGROUND

2.1 General

The GOFA project has its 'roots' in research work which has been undertaken at S&R into the use of expert systems technology in the domain of hazard identification (Ref 1). The research has concentrated mainly on the use of a top-down reasoning strategy and supporting checklists for hazard identification.

The application of this approach on risk assessment projects within S&R led to the innovation of using a systems diagram as a basis for the hazard identification exercise. The use of a systems diagram was first applied on a hazard analysis on an emergency shutdown system, on an offshore oil and gas platform. The technique has since been applied on other hazard identification exercises.

S&R are currently computerising the GOFA methodology using a knowledge-based systems approach.

2.2   The HAZOP Methodology

HAZOP is a technique for systematically considering **deviations** from **design intent** by the application of a series of **guide words** such as **MORE, LESS** etc to process **parameters** such as pressure, temperature, flow etc. The **Causes** and **Consequences** of each deviation are then sought. Ref 1 gives a detailed description of the HAZOP methodology.

The HAZOP methodology is intended for use in group sessions which comprise of multi-disciplinary experts for the plant or process under study. A HAZOP team would typically have between 4 to 8 members.

The important features of a HAZOP study are therefore:

- Design Intention
- Deviation
- Causes
- Consequences

Ref 1 also includes an analysis of the strengths and weaknesses of HAZOP. The current problem areas encountered in the use of the technique are:

- time-consuming and laborious
- lack of knowledge
- hardware orientation
- combinatorial failures
- documentation

It is intended that GOFA should provide significant benefits in all of these areas.

2.3   Objectives of the GOFA Project

Following the detailed examination of the strengths and weaknesses of HAZOP, it has been recognised that the fundamental reasoning process which is used within HAZOP is both succinct and very general, ie forward and backward examination on the cause and effect of **a deviation from a design intent**.

The main limitations and weaknesses with current approaches to HAZOP have been recognised as problems associated with the actual **implementation** of the technique and not the fundamental methodology. The GOFA project is therefore concerned with **implementing HAZOP in a more efficient way**. The means for achieving this are the use of knowledge-based programming techniques, the provision of a graphical/windows environment, and the use of a systems diagram approach.

The aim of the GOFA project is:

To develop a PC-based tool which provides a more efficient and stimulating environment for a hazard identification study than conventional approaches to HAZOP. GOFA will, essentially, be an extension of the existing HAZOP methodology.

3   A SYSTEMS DIAGRAM APPROACH

The GOFA analysis will be applied in a systematic fashion on a formal system description of the problem under study. It is anticipated that it will be feasible to develop a number of generalised system paradigms for various types of GOFA analyses, eg for the analysis of failure goals such as:

- major disaster on a chemical plant
- loss of reaction control in a reactor
- transport accidents
- failure of protective systems
- failure of emergency plans

The Systems Diagram will be created at the outset of a session by the users and will be specific to a chosen failure goal. By selecting a particular failure goal for analysis the capability then exists to select only sub-systems and components that are pertinent to that goal. This is in contrast to the existing methodology of taking a P & I Diagram and attempting to identify all possible failure scenarios for all components, which is invariably a very long and tedious task.

In addition the Systems Diagram approach will allow other factors to be included in the analysis, hitherto not possible. This immediately opens up opportunities for management and operator actions to be included in the identification process, as well as other system influences that are not illustrated by a P & I Diagram.

Due to the general nature of the GOFA technique it should be applicable for the analysis of any failure goal for a system which can be represented on a systems diagram.

Figure 2 shows the basic format of a systems diagram. The main assembly within the **system** boundary is called the **system** and this has been sub-divided into **sub-systems**. Each sub-system is further divided into **components**. These components can themselves be a system in their own right. If analysis of the current failure goal indicated that a particular component warrants further analysis, then a separate GOFA analysis could be carried out on another system diagram which represented that component.

Components can also occur outside the system, in the surroundings: components that interact with the system make up what is normally called the **environment** in systems analysis terminology. Due to a conflict with risk assessment terminology here, the term 'environment' is avoided for GOFA and **external factors** is the preferred terminology for these components.

An external factor is defined as a component that can influence the system, but which cannot be controlled or influenced by the system itself. Components that can strongly influence or control the system should be included within the system boundary - such components would affect the performance of the system if they were to be removed from it.

As indicated on Figure 2, relationships between components can be indicated on the system diagram. Figure 3 shows a system diagram which was used as a basis for studying how an emergency shutdown system on a large pipeline could fail to operate during an emergency (say, a large fire) on an off-shore Oil and Gas platform.

A particular plant or process could be represented on a systems diagram in a variety of different ways. It is essential that it should contain all important and relevant components and sub-systems whilst not being over-complicated. The diagram will subsequently be used for 'steering' the GOFA study in a systematic way into the required areas of interest.

The systems diagram can be supplemented with generic checklists for various types of failures associated with particular types of equipment.

It is envisaged that the final GOFA tool may need the facility to 'chain' together a number of system diagrams in order to rationalise the analysis.

The advantages of a Systems Diagram approach are summarised as:

(i) The additional types of information that can be represented on a systems diagram compared to a P & I diagram, eg operator and management factors

(ii) In a GOFA study the hazard identification process will be focused on a particular failure goal, the study should therefore be more efficient, with less consideration of unimportant events.

(iii) GOFA will provide a more **general** tool than conventional HAZOP, any system which could be represented on a **systems diagram** and for which **deviations from design intent** can be examined would be amenable for analysis.

(iv) The use of a systems diagram should help to clearly define the problem under study and 'condense' the basic information requirements for the study into a more manageable form.

4   A KNOWLEDGE-BASED SYSTEMS APPROACH

The implementation of GOFA in a knowledge-based environment provides two important advantages over conventional programming approaches involving the use of languages such as Fortran or 'C';

- generic knowledge on component and system failures can be readily incorporated and integrated with the systems diagram

- the relationship between sub-systems and components can be defined and corresponding failures determined; this also raises the possibility of the determination of 'common-mode' effects, and also inferencing on failure modes.

The current approach is to use **object-oriented** programming techniques to define these relationships between items on the systems diagram.

The development of the prototype is being carried out using the Goldworks II software package; this an expert system 'hybrid toolkit' produced by Gold Hill Computers Inc.

Goldworks has been chosen since it has the following features and capabilities:

- runs on an IBM-PC with 8mB of extended memory

- portability onto workstation platforms, ie SUN, VAX etc.

- runs under Microsoft Windows and therefore provides the facilities for the graphical interface requirements for GOFA

- supports frames and object-oriented representation

- low cost run-time licences

- fully integratable with LISP code thus providing added flexibility for developers

5   THE GOFA KNOWLEDGE BASE

The GOFA knowledge base is required to support four basic types of information:

- guideword specifications

- checklists

- system definition, with components and relationships

- GOFA analysis user input knowledge

5.1   Guideword Specification

The HAZOP team, in particular the team leader, must have a clear understanding of semantic definitions of the guidewords which are central to the HAZOP technique. Also the team should identify a list of such guidewords that may be appropriately associated with specific system properties in order that all possible deviations with respect to that property will be considered.

It is important that these guideword semantics and property associations are agreed upon by the HAZOP team before analysis begins. Therefore a function of GOFA will be to offer the user a list of appropriate guidewords relative to the properties of that component. The user should be able to add or delete items from this list which is then assigned to the appropriate property. In this way a parameter/guideword relational database could be maintained.

5.2   Checklists

Checklists provide a useful information source during traditional paper HAZOP sessions as a suitable aid-memoire to prompt team brainstorming beyond the 'blank-sheet' stage. Such checklists are predominately domain specific and consist of generic cause and related consequence, preventative action data relevant to common failure events previously encountered and remedied. Sources of this data pertains to specific industries eg chlorine, nuclear, oil/gas etc and are usually the result of previous risk assessment efforts.

This checklist expertise represents **generic knowledge** and will be encoded to form a suitable add-on supplement within the GOFA generic knowledge base. The GOFA users would be able to pull information direct from these checklists into their current analysis on request.

It is important to note that the amount of generic failure information which is available to the users during a GOFA session needs to be carefully controlled. There is a danger that too much information could have a tendency to stifle brainstorming. User feedback on the use of GOFA will be needed to get the balance right.

5.3   System Definition

The GOFA analysis information should be structured during the system diagram building and analysis stage of GOFA. Both frame-based and graphical representations of real-world system objects, and influencing factors external to the system objects, will be created and saved in some meaningful configuration to user defined files.

One feature of GOFA is for the users to be able to pick up a generic system diagram file and modify it to suit the problem under study. A range of generic system diagrams (ie system paradigms) therefore need to be developed; it is intended that some of these could be developed during evaluation of the prototype on 'real-world' applications.

5.4   GOFA Analysis User Input Knowledge

During analysis users will need to enter text describing particular event scenarios, ie event cause, consequence, etc. This will be represented graphically in the activation of a scenario window which may be iconised to display its relationship with the event under consideration. At appropriate moments users should be able to reactivate scenario windows from their iconised state for editing or reference purposes.

A frame-type structure will also be created for inferencing purposes where cause text etc is asserted directly into slot-values of the corresponding event instance in the Goldworks II object environment. Hence the GOFA system would again be automatically structuring the users knowledge (brainstorming efforts) in a form suitable for expert system inferencing purposes. Possibilities for such inferencing are discussed later.

6   GOFA PROTOTYPE

A GOFA prototype is currently being developed using Goldworks II. Following an evaluation phase for this prototype the final tool will be developed. Figure 1 shows the software development life-cycle which is being followed for the GOFA project.

The GOFA prototype aims to provide a deliverable, usable tool as stated in the design objectives. To achieve this the design of the GOFA Hazard Identification Tool has been broken down into a number of modules. There are three main reasons for this:

(i)   To ease the problems of tool development beyond the prototype stage.

(ii) To aid maintenance of the final system.

(iii) To allow different developers to design and implement parts of the system with a minimum of conflict with other system modules.

In selecting the modular approach it is hoped that the **Systems Diagram Builder** can be used independently of the rest of the tool so that further paper exercises using the GOFA methodology can be undertaken. It is also feasible that having produced a systems diagram using the tool this might be applied to different techniques for comparison purposes.

7   FUTURE DEVELOPMENT OPTIONS

During the prototyping stage a number of further design options are to be considered, ie

(i)   Brainstorm Tool - a tool to assist the user in defining a systems diagram for a particular application.

(ii) Scenario Builder - a tool which can inference on the knowledge base to deduce multiple-event scenarios.

The concept of a Scenario Builder for a narrow domain has already been demonstrated as feasible during a current SRD/HSE project, ie the SAPPHIRE (CIMAH Safety Report Expert system) currently being undertaken for the HSE by AEA S&R Knowledge Engineering Section. A Scenario Builder for a chlorine plant has been developed using the expert system tool XiPlus. The feasibility of extending this concept for inclusion within a **general** tool, however, has not yet been demonstrated.

(iii) Form-filling - the requirement to provide a conventional form-filling type option within GOFA needs to be addressed, ie the ability to carry out a GOFA analysis without the system diagram approach. This could make the final tool even more flexible in its potential application areas.

(iv) Guideword Thesaurus - the broader range of entities that might constitute systems subject to GOFA risk analysis will not be able to utilise standard HAZOP guidewords,

eg MORE, LESS etc. In order to develop meaningful deviations for essentially non-quantitative entities, eg entity = 'operator' suitable deviations might be generated by applying guidewords such as FATIGUED, TIME, PANIC, BOREDOM etc. Liaison with human factors experts within S&R will be undertaken to identify suitable guidwords for such entities.

The HAZOP team must firstly identify all entity properties they wish to consider as potentially contributing to risks. The GOFA system might then consult a Guideword Thesaurus and suggest suitable guidewords based loosely on the quantitative nature of the property. Novel properties which the system has not previously encountered could be compared semantically with a relational knowledge base of such properties and associated guidewords. The main requirement would be for a set of simple parsing rules to interpret the attribute nouns in the context of the entity they apply to.

8   POTENTIAL PROBLEM AREAS

One of the likely problems which will ultimately be encountered with users of GOFA will be the construction of a systems diagram. Hazard analysts who are unfamiliar with systems diagrams concepts are likely to struggle with the new concepts embodied within GOFA. They are likely to meet problems with deciding on:

-   which components should be included within a certain sub-system

-   what is an external factor?

-   is this a system component or an external factor?

-   defining the MAIN FAILURE GOAL of the system

-   defining design intent for a component

-   defining relationships between components

In short, the use of a systems diagram approach for hazard identification is a NEW CONCEPT and considerable experience in applying the technique needs to be built up before potential problem areas can be fully identified and resolved.

9   GLOSSARY OF TERMS

Common Cause Failure

The failure of more than one component, item or system due to the same cause.

Common Mode Failure

The failure of components in the same manner.

Failure Goal

The system failure which is of interest for the GOFA study, eg catastrophic failure of a chlorine bulk storage tank.

Goldworks II

A commercially-available software tool for building knowledge based applications. The tool is produced by Gold Hill in the US and marketed by Artificial Intelligence Ltd in the UK.

Guidewords

A list of words applied to system items or functions in a **hazard** study to identify undesired deviations.

HAZOP (Hazard and Operability Study)

A study carried out by the application of **guidewords** to identify all deviations from design intent with undesirable effects for safety or operability.

Hazard

A physical situation with a potential for human injury, damage to property, damage to the environment or some combination of these.

Hazard Identification

The identification of undesired events that lead to the materialisation of a **hazard**.

Knowledge Based Systems (KBS)

A system which incorporates the problem-solving expertise of a **domain expert**. The knowledge is represented in a computer in such a way that the computer can approximate the expert's ability to solve a particular class of problems.

Knowledge Elicitation

The process of obtaining the problem solving knowledge from the **domain expert** by the **knowledge engineer**.

Knowledge Engineer

The person who is skilled in acquiring the knowledge from the **domain expert** and manipulating it into a form suitable for inclusion in a knowledge based system.

10   REFERENCES

(1)   REEVES A B. "Studies on the Application of Knowledge-Based Technology to Hazard Identification", PhD Thesis (draft), Department of Mechanical and Process Engineering, University of Sheffield, July 1990.

(2)   DAVIES J A. "Modelling Systems and Experts", MSc Dissertation (draft), Faculty of Technology, Polytechnic of the South West, August 1990.

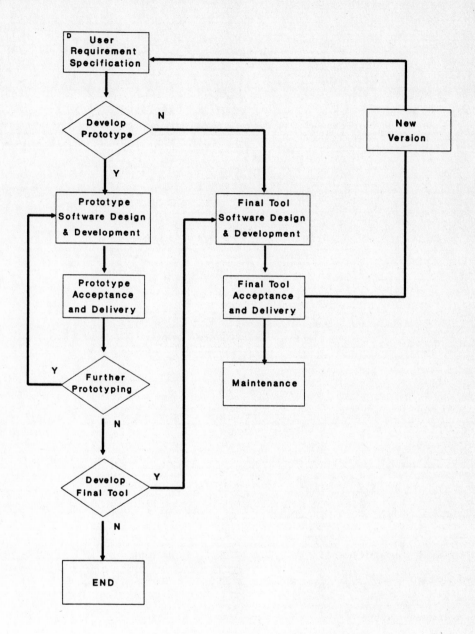

Fig 1   Goal- oriented failure analysis software lifecycle

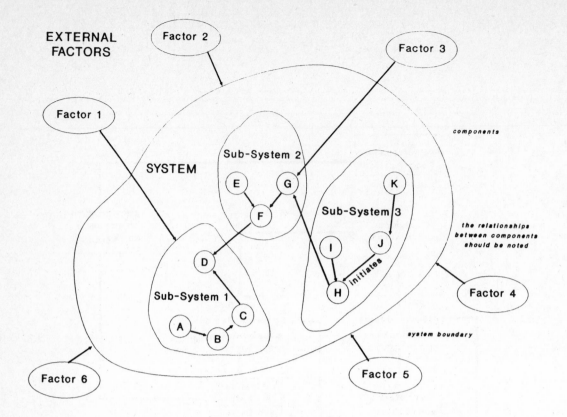

Fig 2   System diagram format

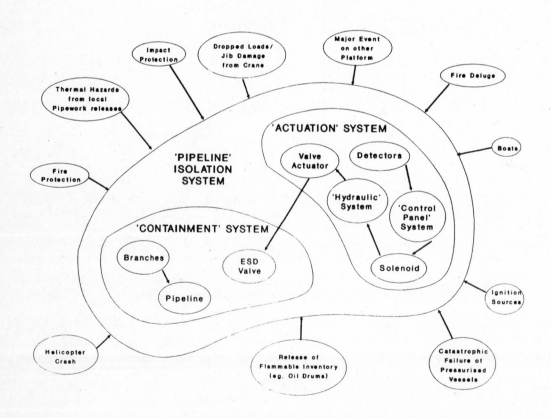

Fig 3   System diagram for an emergency shutdown system

C409/030

Experience feedback from event reports: the human contribution

E SWATON and V TOLSTYKH
International Atomic Energy Agency, Vienna, Austria

Analysis of reported events reveals that in a large number of areas human intervention contributed to the initiation and/or development of these events. Since an accident at any nuclear power plant can have a world-wide effect on public acceptance, the need for attentive and reliable human behaviour assumes an even greater significance. The identification of areas where human interaction can have an impact on safe operation is mainly relying on the analysis of events reported to the nuclear community. Any substantial compilation of safety significant operational events such as contained in the IAEA-IRS (Incident Reporting System) is bound to provide valuable and factual insights into problem areas, their origin, development, impact and some remedial actions. Thus a systematic analysis has been carried out on over 200 events where a human contribution could be identified. Some events of particular interest will be discussed and furthermore generic lessons will be presented. In addition the Assessment of Safety Significant Event Technique (ASSET) developed within IAEA which provides a structured methodology to identify not only the direct cause explaining why an individual failed but more important, insights on the root causes explaining why this latent deficiency was not detected earlier through the plant surveillance programme was applied.

1. INTRODUCTION

Since 1983, the IAEA Incident Reporting System (IRS) has been collecting, assessing and disseminating information on unusual events in nuclear power plants with safety significance. The main objectives of the IAEA-IRS activity are to prevent repetition of unfavourable events and to improve nuclear safety. At present, the IAEA-IRS file is a 'mixed set' of unusual events that have safety significance of general interest to the international nuclear community, because important lessons can be learned. The advantage of this set is that it reflects the operational experience of a variety of nuclear power plants and different conditions in the world. During 1989, 230 incident reports were received, bringing the total number of incident reports in the IAEA databank to 862.

Well defined analysis activity on an international level is one way to discover all potentials of IRS information. IAEA-IRS analysis activity consists of two main parts: the national investigation of unusual events in nuclear power plants with subsequent presentation at the international level and the analysis of unusual events and/or populations of events by international expert groups. Recently the IAEA extended the scope of the Incident Reporting System from mainly collecting reports of safety significant events to a more thorough analysis of these reports. The specific areas covered include, amongst others, evaluation of the appropriateness and completeness of corrective actions, human factors considerations and the identification of generic lessons.

Systematic analysis of nuclear power plant events demonstrates that existing latent weaknesses in personnel, equipment or procedures which were not detected and corrected on time were root causes of incidents or accidents. This idea was used as the basis of the IAEA-ASSET (Assessment of Safety Significant Events Team) procedure to analyze reported events.

The systematic ASSET approach to the analysis of events reported in the IRS revealed that a considerable number of events could be traced back to direct human intervention. Thus generic lessons were formulated, drawn from the collected insights on the human failures and their causes which initiated or contributed to these events. The remainder of this paper will be devoted to presenting these generic lessons and describing symptomatic occurrences for illustration.

2. SELECTED EVENTS AND THEIR EVALUATION

A brief description of one or more symptomatic events is followed by an analysis of the human involvement with the direct actions leading to the event underlined. Subsequently the most prominent root causes are presented and suggestions for improvement are made.

2.1 Verification of equipment operability

Three similar occurrences are described from different PWRs to illustrate the problem of insufficient vigilance. They relate to the ice condenser containment which is divided into three main compartments: the lower compartment, the ice condenser and the upper compartment. The primary circuit is located in the lower compartment of the containment. In a loss of cooling accident the steam is discharged from the small lower compartment through the ice condenser to the large upper compartment. In the ice condenser the major part of the steam condenses. Thus pressure and temperature of the containment are limited. The ice condenser is equipped with inlet doors which are closed during plant operation. In a loss of cooling accident the doors will swing open by pressure differential and allow the steam to flow into the ice condenser. During cold shutdown the inlet doors are blocked in the closed position by a blocking device to ensure that the inlet doors do not inadvertently open. Prior to restarting the door blocking devices are required to be removed.

One plant entered hot shutdown and startup testing with 23 of 24 inlet doors blocked closed (the blocking device of the remaining door had slipped out of place). This was noticed after 9 days by health physics technicians entering the ice condenser for other reasons. In a second plant all inlet doors of one half of the ice condenser had been blocked during power operation for about 2 hours when the situation was discovered. In a third plant a lot of ice had entered the flow channels between the ice baskets inside the ice condenser, thus partially blocking them. This deficiency was discovered more than half a year later.

In all three events the deficiency was due to human error. The direct cause can be traced back to work control deficiencies. In the first event the work request for unblocking the inlet doors had been issued to the staff responsible for planning on the same day the work should be done. This led to the work request being overlooked as an outstanding item for entry into hot shutdown. Therefore the work request was never issued to Mechanical Maintenance. The Maintenance Representative was under the impression, from conversation with a co-worker, that the door blocking devices had been removed and signed the appropriate procedural step. In the second event operators in the main control room discovered after the periodic inspection of the ice condenser that not all inlet doors of the ice condenser were closed. The shift supervisor asked the group that had performed the inspection to close the doors. They misunderstood the order and locked the doors in one half of the ice condenser with blocking devices. In the third event some amount of ice had been added to the ice condenser during the annual maintenance to replace the ice evaporation during operation. This obviously had been performed carelessly.

The reports themselves did not identify specific root causes for these occurrences. However, taking the subsequent corrective actions into account, some common root causes can be suggested:

-   Ineffective work verification. Since there was no independent verification of proper completion of the task a safety system could be disabled without being noticed.

-   Poor work organization. The system to monitor work progress was inadequate and did not alert the operations staff to the actual conditions.

-   Lack of motivation and communication. This includes work requests not processed, misunderstanding of work orders and careless execution of tasks.

All events involve very conventional components forming part of a passive safety system. The events highlight that such components are very sensitive to human errors. Furthermore the events point out that less attention has been paid to such safety systems compared to other active safety systems. Though no functional tests can be performed on this kind of equipment after maintenance work, it appears necessary to implement a strict verification procedure on the operability of such systems.

2.2   Procedural deficiencies

Procedures not covering all details of the relevant actions can be a starting point for further undesirable developments. The example involves two 3-loop PWRs, with unit 1 in cold shutdown and unit 2 in hot shutdown on request of the load dispatcher.

After completion of containment testing in unit 1, a larger number of valves, including the four valves isolating the residual heat removal system from the reactor coolant system, had to be reset. Following the procedures the operators had to check if the four isolation valves in the residual heat removal system were in the open position. These valves were found to be open. Instead of a verification of the proper valve position, the operators tried to perform a test on the valves. The operators closed the first of these valves from the control room but the valve failed to reopen. When the same happened to the second and the third valve the operators investigated the cause to be an erroneous high primary coolant pressure signal which had not been correctly reset following previous activities.

Since another team, not present on site at that time, was responsible for those circuits the operators decided to reopen the valves by use of the motor actuator control centers in the electrical building thus by-passing all interlocks.

When the operator subsequently went to the electrical building at 4.00 a.m. and a Sunday morning he went to the corresponding room of the wrong unit and operated the control centers for the same equipment of unit 2, which stayed in hot shutdown. After opening the first valve the operator tried to open the second isolation valve in the same line. Fortunately, he did not succeed since the protecting device of the motor actuator immediately tripped.

Due to alarms in the control room of unit 2 the control room operators of that unit realized what happened and ordered the operator in the electrical building to reclose the isolation valves immediately.

If the operator had succeeded in opening the second isolation valve in the line connecting the residual heat removal system to the reactor coolant system, reactor coolant at high pressure and temperature would have been applied to the residual heat removal system not designed for those conditions. Thus probably a loss of coolant accident via the residual heat removal system would have occurred.

The direct causes of this occurrence can be identified relatively straight-forwardly from the description of the actions performed. The root causes seem to be found in lack of adequate guidance for the specific situation and could be outlined as follows:

- As mentioned in the event report the expression 'to check the valve position' was used with a different understanding throughout the plant procedures. In the procedure followed in this event the operator should ensure that the valve was in the correct position, whereas in other procedures 'to check' implied operating the equipment concerned. This deficiency in the procedures may explain why the operators tried to close and reopen the valves in the residual heat removal system.

- Since there was obviously no need from the time schedule to complete the procedure at that time, stress by the time schedule can be excluded as a root cause. But seemingly the operators wished to complete the procedure. Perhaps they were afraid of problems that may occur if a procedure is interrupted and completed later on or they wished the unit to stay in a condition with no actions pending. Nevertheless the decision to complete the test may have implied some subconscious stress on the operators.

Again a contributing factor was some deficiency in the procedure since it did not contain sufficient information on all equipment involved. Nor did it contain sufficient information for the coordination of the different teams carrying out work at that time.

- Even if not explicitly mentioned, it can be concluded that the decision to bypass the interlocks to reopen the isolation valves in the residual heat removal system was not forbidden by the procedures with the unit in cold shutdown and the fuel in the fuel building. In fact there were no safety concerns with respect to unit 1 to do so. Thus the operators did not have the impression of taking an important decision.

- Taking the information provided into account it seems to be impossible to identify the exact root cause for the operator going to the equipment of the wrong unit. The event report points out that there is a clear labelling of the unit numbers on all rooms and equipment. However, a contributor to the operator error may be the time, 4.00 a.m. on Sunday morning.

The event also highlights the problems that may occur in 2 unit stations with one unit in cold shutdown and the second unit in operation. Actions which are of no safety concern with respect to the unit in cold shutdown may be of large safety relevance for the unit in operation. Thus, if operators are convinced that the unit they are dealing with is in cold shutdown they are likely to perform tasks without hesitation which they would not perform if they were aware of the fact that this unit was in operating condition.

2.3 Problems with multiple actions during plant outage

The attempt to minimize the length of plant outage by performing multiple tasks at the same time can result in adverse configurations leading to degradation of safety-related systems, as presented in the following occurrences.

Relay testing of circuit breakers on the safety buses was in progress during a refuelling outage. The circuit breakers under test were in the power supplies to the two safety buses from the station transformer. This transformer was de-energized for the tests.

In addition, a number of other maintenance activities were in progress on the electrical distribution system, including the replacement of a transformer in the off-site power supply to one of the safety buses, cell replacement on the battery of one d.c. bus and modifications to the battery on a second d.c. bus. The two emergency diesel generators were tagged out to prevent auto start during the breaker relay testing. The sole source of power to the system was the off-site supply to the second safety bus.

Due to the number of on-going modifications, the distribution system line-up was in a significantly altered configuration.

When the relay test procedure required the opening of the circuit breaker in the supply from the station transformer, the circuit breaker in the off-site supply was erroneously opened (both circuit breakers are on the same safety bus). This resulted in the loss of supply to both safety buses, all 480V essential buses, one of the three d.c. buses (but all three battery changers) and two a.c. instrument buses.

The loss of these power supplies had an impact on the following station equipment:

- loss of shutdown cooling, compressed air, turbine plant cooling water.

- loss of control room indications.

- initiation of safety signals to the pressurizer low pressure, safety injection actuation, containment actuation and ventilation isolation actuation.

Since the control power to the breaker that was inadvertently opened, came from the de-energized d.c. bus, the power to the safety bus could not be immediately restored. However prompt action by operations personnel, through manual switching of control power to its emergency source, provided power to all buses and restored the shutdown cooling, turbine plant cooling water and compressed air systems.

The human error, that occurred at a time when a number of maintenance activities with safety implications were being carried out on various components in the electrical distribution system, led to loss of important power supplies. This resulted in a short-time degradation of safety-related systems and of system required to control temperature and pressure.

It should however be noted that plant communications, fire protection, plant lighting and security systems were maintained during the period while the electrical distribution system was degraded.

In reviewing the event and the activities in progress at the time, one might question the necessity for so many jobs to be scheduled during the same period and the resulting requirement for an unusual configuration of the electrical distribution system.

Overall, it appears that the work planning and scheduling, with due regard to maintaining the integrity of essential support systems was not adequate.

Thus some root causes which should trigger corrective actions can be identified:

- Improvement of work organization taking into account the necessity to perform certain tests at a given time and considering the potential problems which might occur.

- The error committed by the technician during the relay tests was probably due to lack of vigilance (under pressure to get the work finished?). For a more detailed analysis of the event it would be necessary to explore if there was an error of communication or if the two relay cubicles were poorly identified and insufficient separation between them. Such an in-depth analysis could also help to prevent recurrence.

3. ADDITIONAL INSIGHTS FROM EVENT ANALYSES

The areas presented in the previous section as being major contributors to occurrences where human intervention is involved are certainly not exhaustive. But it was felt that illustrating some areas with concrete examples of human actions would be of interest to the nuclear community. The in-depth review of over 200 reported events naturally also revealed additional areas of problematic conditions for the operating staff.

One of them refers to latent weaknesses in the design which later can manifest themselves in an adverse manner, thus leading to occurrences unforeseen by the designers or operating organizations. In some cases these events involve multiple random or common cause failures which can result in unsuspected events. Other events, each in principle covered by the design, occur more often than originally expected. Surveillance programs have in some cases revealed deficiencies in materials or construction which were not foreseen. These design deficiencies can lead to unanticipated complications for the operator. Particularly, proper diagnosis can become more difficult but also actions required for systems alignment, identification of plant conditions and monitoring of technical specifications, amongst others, can be jeopardised by unexpected deficiencies. They might occur in all modes of operation, but will be especially noticeable in startup and during shutdown when due to the multitude of actions and decisions to be carried out simultaneously the functioning of the system in its complexity is needed.

Another area which could be identified were overall shortcomings in plant organization and management. For quite a number of events the root causes could be traced back to insufficient support by plant management and organizational procedures. Specifically these deficiencies include insufficient feedback of operational experience, partly within the plant but more often regarding international sharing of experiences and extended in-depth education about consequences of various actions pertaining to safety related equipment. In addition quality assurance programmes were found to be deficient in making adequate provisions for the maintenance and updating of procedures. Furthermore, when implementing corrective actions these were mainly done based on the direct causes identified and rarely went so far as to systematically address the problems in more depth to prevent recurrence. Here it is interesting to note that, in the event reports, deficiencies in plant organization and management are seldom referred to as potential causes for an event.

4. CONCLUDING REMARKS

Timely detection of latent weaknesses and effective restoration are the ultimate means to prevent and reduce the occurrence of unfavourable events in NPPs.

The detection programme should aim at thoroughly assessing proficiency of personnel, usability of procedures and operability of equipment if it is capable of identifying latent weaknesses which might lead to personnel, equipment or procedural deficiencies under adverse circumstances.

The restoration process should aim at eliminating the latent weaknesses detected in order to recover fully operability of the functions 'man', 'machine', and 'interface of man-machine' and at preventing any recurrence of such weaknesses:

- Either by eliminating the deficiencies found in the programme for quality assurance of the various preparatory activities involved in quality of personnel (recruiting, training, motivating and licensing), of equipment (designing, manufacturing, storing, installing, maintaining and qualifying), and of procedures (writing and validating).

- or by eliminating the deficiencies of the programme for surveillance of quality of these elements in the course of operation.

However, one should be aware of the problems associated with making all errors free of consequences because that goal can never be completely accomplished. On the contrary, this could create the feeling that no attention has to be paid to operating the plant in a cautious and responsible manner. Therefore trying to eliminate all consequences of failures and errors could

very well head in a completely wrong direction, i.e. the over-complacent operating staff. As long as an error leads to consequences which are minor and thus tolerable and also manageable there is no need to reduce these consequences to zero. Such an approach should assure that the operating staff remains alert and retains a certain responsibility for their actions.

To assist staff in their responsible execution of duties more information should be collected on regular behaviour of humans. One important area appears to be a more thorough understanding of the functions of the brain. Taking the Three Mile Island and Chernobyl accidents, one can point out that both of these accidents occurred at midnight to early in the morning, when human consciousness begins to drop or the error potential begins to increase. Thus the alertness at critical hours should be monitored and supported.

The IAEA-IRS is now developing into a system for the information exchange on policies to prevent unfavourable events occurring in nuclear power plants. The first step in this direction is the application of the ASSET systematic approach for thorough analysis of events. In addition, a methodology for meaningful analysis of the human contribution is being developed. Furthermore, Probabilistic Safety Assessment (PSA) techniques and insights will be incorporated. The recently established International Nuclear Event Scale (INES) is designed to categorise the severity of nuclear events internationally in a uniform way to improve communication with the media and the public.